IMAGES
of America

OLD FORT

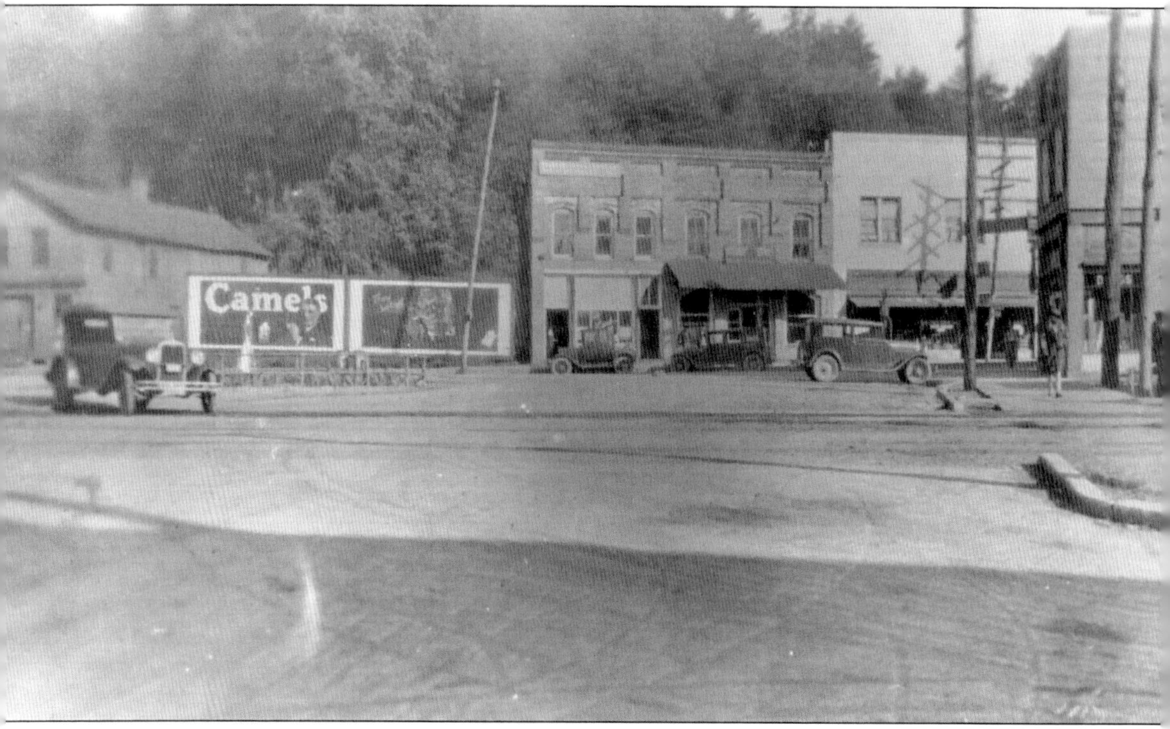

Pictured here in 1928 is Old Fort's town square, with the Bank of Old Fort, located in the Mashburn Building, straight ahead. Calvin Coolidge was the president of the United States, Amelia Earhart had recently begun her attempt to become the first woman to cross the Atlantic Ocean in an airplane, the first Mickey Mouse cartoon had just appeared, and the stock market crash was a year away. (Courtesy of Peggy Silvers.)

On the Cover: Old Fort's arrowhead monument was unveiled in the town square on July 27, 1930, to commemorate Davidson's Fort, the original fort from which the town received its name. Over 6,000 people attended the dedication ceremonies. Built in the late 1700s, Davidson's Fort had stood less than 100 yards to the south of the marker's location. (Courtesy of Mountain Gateway Museum.)

IMAGES
of America

OLD FORT

Kim Clark

ARCADIA
PUBLISHING

ISBN 978-1-4671-2333-4

Published by Arcadia Publishing
Charleston, South Carolina

Printed in the United States of America

Library of Congress Control Number: 2014952497

For all general information, please contact Arcadia Publishing:
Telephone 843-853-2070
Fax 843-853-0044
E-mail sales@arcadiapublishing.com
For customer service and orders:
Toll-Free 1-888-313-2665

Visit us on the Internet at www.arcadiapublishing.com

Contents

Acknowledgments

Assembling the photographs for this collection was an exciting and rewarding experience. I followed a trail of historical clues through McDowell County's public archives at the McDowell County Public Libraries, the Historic Carson House, and Mountain Gateway Museum; through North Carolina's historical archives in Asheville, Raleigh, and Chapel Hill; and through a half-dozen welcoming Old Fort homes. Along the way, historians both professional and amateur offered insight and understanding that allowed me to assemble these images in a meaningful way.

I thank the following for their kind and generous assistance: Peggy Silvers, Bill Nichols, Anne Swann, Terrell Finley, Matt Provancha of Mountain Gateway Museum, Dee Daughtridge of the Old Fort library, Jim Burgin, Patti Holda of the Marion library, Carly Kauffman of the Historic Carson House, Ann King and Pastor Todd Hinson of Mount Hebron Wesleyan Church, Barbara Meilhammer, Rebecca Knupp, Richard Sandlin Fullerton, and Stuart Adams Robinson.

Nada Carroll was particularly helpful in providing images in her possession and helping me to track down others. Nada's meticulously assembled scrapbooks of Old Fort history were my go-to source for historical details. Even though she has not published a book of her own about Old Fort, she has already put together the ultimate history of the town in those volumes.

The work of James Haney, author of Images of America: *McDowell County North Carolina 1843–1943*, provided a firm foundation from which to build this collection. Stephen Little's *Tunnels, Nitro and Convicts* and *Andrews Geyser: Star of the Mountain Railroad* were indispensable sources of information about the building of the railroad from Old Fort to Ridgecrest. In addition, Anne Swann's beautifully written *The Other Side of the River* helped me to better understand McDowell County's pre-Revolution history.

Finally, thanks to Anne Allison and Old Fort Historic Site, Inc., for asking me to take on this project for the benefit of Mountain Gateway Museum. I had a blast!

Introduction

Artifacts, historical documents, and handed-down recollections tell us that what is now Old Fort was Cherokee territory when Spanish explorers came through on expeditions in the 1500s. The Catawba tribe lived here at one time but migrated south after being decimated by war and disease. When the first European settlers began to arrive in the mid-1700s, they found Cherokee hunting camps, sacred sites, and villages. There was an uneasy alliance between native and newcomer at first, but it was soon shattered by the American Revolution and the settlers' seemingly insatiable appetite for land.

After a series of violent attacks by the Cherokee against the settlers, Gen. Griffith Rutherford launched his retaliatory campaign, "Rutherford Trace," from the fort that would later give the town of Old Fort its name. In one month, Rutherford's men left dozens of Cherokee villages in ruins with hundreds of acres of crops destroyed and livestock killed or seized.

There is an old adage that "history is written by the victors," and it is as true for the history of Old Fort as anywhere else. There are no doubt countless stories of Cherokee accomplishments and courage that have gone unwritten and will be unrepresented in this volume, lamentably so. Just as history books are written by people, people are also authors of the everyday decisions and actions that combine to weave the fabric of the history of any town. Old Fort has been fortunate—or perhaps destined—to have been home to several extraordinary authors who significantly shaped its story.

There was Maj. James W. Wilson of the Western North Carolina Railroad, who took stock of "the railroad that couldn't be built" and figured out how to build it. In less than four years after tackling the impossible, he was able to wire former North Carolina governor Zebulon Vance: "Daylight entered Buncombe County today through the Swannanoa Tunnel. Grade and centers meet exactly."

George Sandlin, who became mayor of Old Fort on his 21st birthday, gave a large share of his life force to the railroad but also found time to help those less fortunate. His undisclosed acts of generosity were such that persons unknown to his family openly wept at his funeral. After Sandlin had retired from the railroad, he provided legal council for the African American children and parents who were seeking to integrate Old Fort School in the 1950s.

Col. Daniel W. Adams came to Old Fort from Louisiana in 1911 to survey the Curtis Creek tract for the US Forest Service, which set the stage for the creation of the Pisgah National Forest. He moved his family here and set about improving life for everyone in town by building a municipal water system, constructing a dam on the Catawba River to generate the town's first electric power, and providing numerous other civic improvements. Old Fort residents used to say that they loved it when Colonel Adams went away and made money from his mining or oil interests because they knew that when he returned, he would do something for the town with his financial gain.

Albert Joyner of the Catawba View community was getting dressed for work one August morning in 1955 when he realized that a group of African American children that were supposed to be escorted to Old Fort School in a desegregation effort had been abandoned when their escorts got cold feet. Joyner led the children himself, and he was ostracized and harassed for years as a result. In later interviews, he said, "You just got to have that gettin' up spirit."

Old Fort police chief Frankie Poteat was the first female police chief in the state of North Carolina. In a television news feature that made much of the historic nature of her accomplishment, she is seen patrolling the streets as if her achievement was no big deal. She served as chief for two decades and was a beloved and respected figure.

In the 1980s, modern life was growing further and further away from the sustainable and harmonious ways that had been practiced by Native Americans. The planet—and the human spirit—seemed to be nearing a point of no return. For many, a path to rediscovery of the old ways led through Old Fort. Here, the seeker found traditional healer, herbalist, and shaman Chief Two Trees and Woody Grant, whose Native American museum on Main Street provided a respite from the modern world.

Of course there are countless other religious leaders, mayors, businessmen, teachers, and humanitarians who helped shape Old Fort and whose influence has spread far afield. Their names may not be mentioned in this book and their deeds not recorded anywhere except in the memories of those that they touched, but their impact is felt just the same.

Now, for a proper introduction to this book, I would like to turn things over to George Sandlin:

> In 1928, when New York governor Al Smith was the Democratic candidate for the president of the United States, his train passed through Old Fort while he was on his way from New York to Asheville for a two-week vacation. Smith's train stopped in Old Fort, but it was made clear that the governor would not be emerging to deliver one of his soaring speeches. Stationmaster George Sandlin was not satisfied with that course of events, so he summoned the Old Fort band to the scene. The ragtag conglomeration of brass, reeds, and drums soon attracted a crowd around the town fountain, but Smith did not take the bait. At George's urging, the band played louder and launched into a martial tune. Finally, the rear door of the Pullman car swung open and Al Smith appeared, smiling. George called out, "Welcome, Governor Smith. You need no introduction to us, but we in turn ask leave to introduce ourselves to you. This is Old Fort, North Carolina, the front door and main entrance into the Land of the Sky!"

One

On the Edge of the Frontier

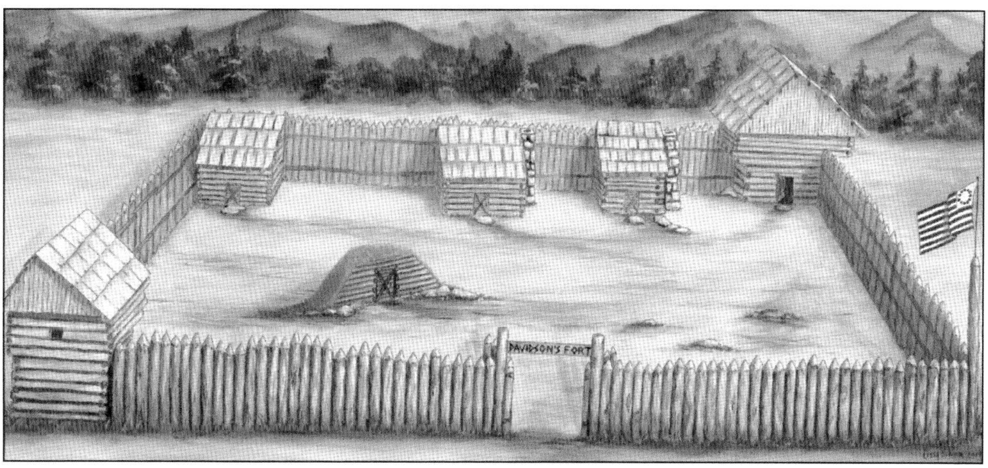

The original fort from which the town of Old Fort takes its name probably looked similar to the one in this sketch. The sides were most likely log palisades with a corner blockhouse. The presence of barracks and a magazine for storing powder and weapons are also likely. In addition, historical documents mention a trading post at the fort. (Drawing by Lissa Silver; courtesy of Davidson's Fort Historic Park.)

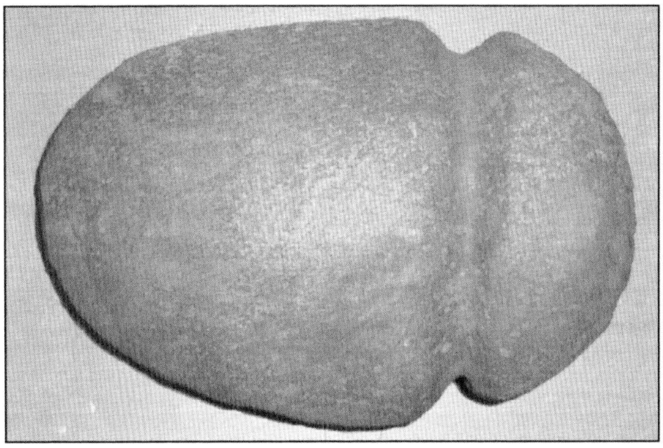

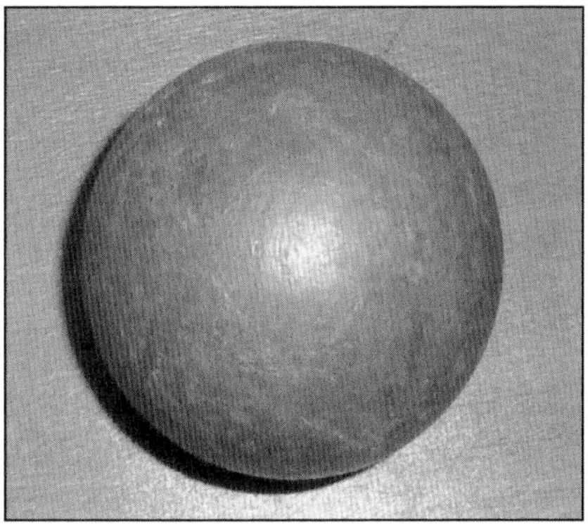

Artifacts discovered on the grounds of Mountain Gateway Museum underscore the fact that the area was a crossroads of Native American and early settler activity. The Cherokee ax head was recently uncovered during the plowing of a garden, and the cannonball was found during 1937 building construction. The cannonball could date to the time of the American Revolution. (Courtesy of Mountain Gateway Museum, Photograph by Kim Clark.)

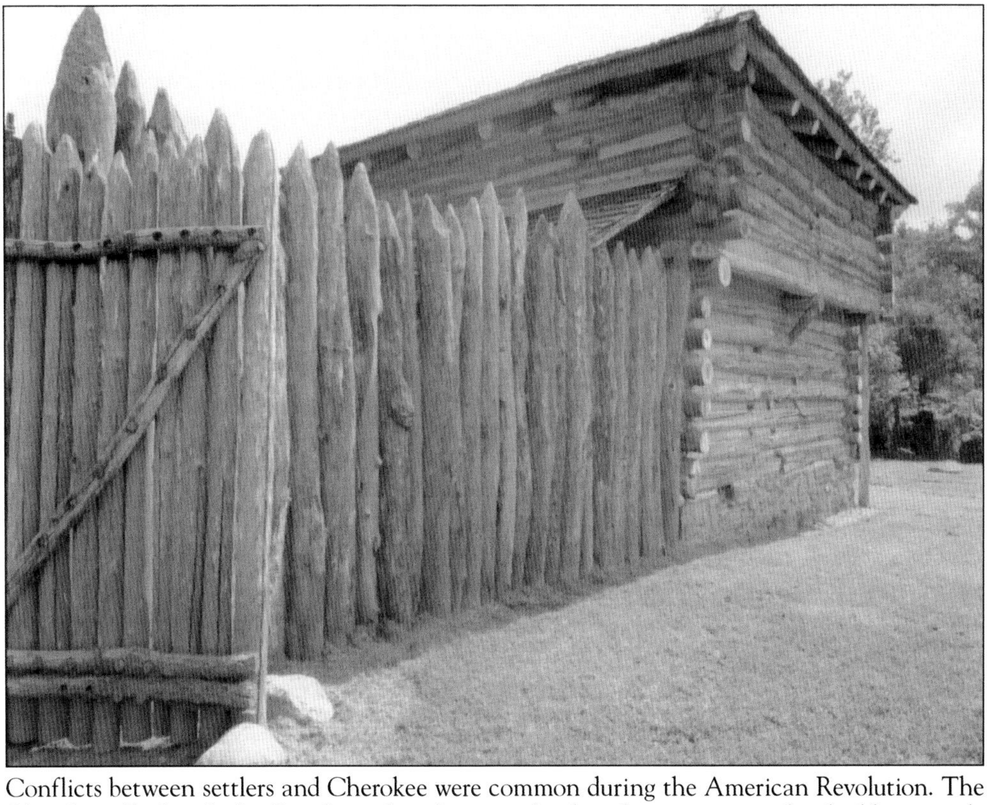

Conflicts between settlers and Cherokee were common during the American Revolution. The Cherokee allied with the British, and settlers were loath to honor a treaty that had been made between the British and the Cherokee that designated the Davidson's Fort location and points west as Cherokee territory. This replica fort now standing in Old Fort represents the original structure that was built for protection by the settlers. (Photograph by Kim Clark.)

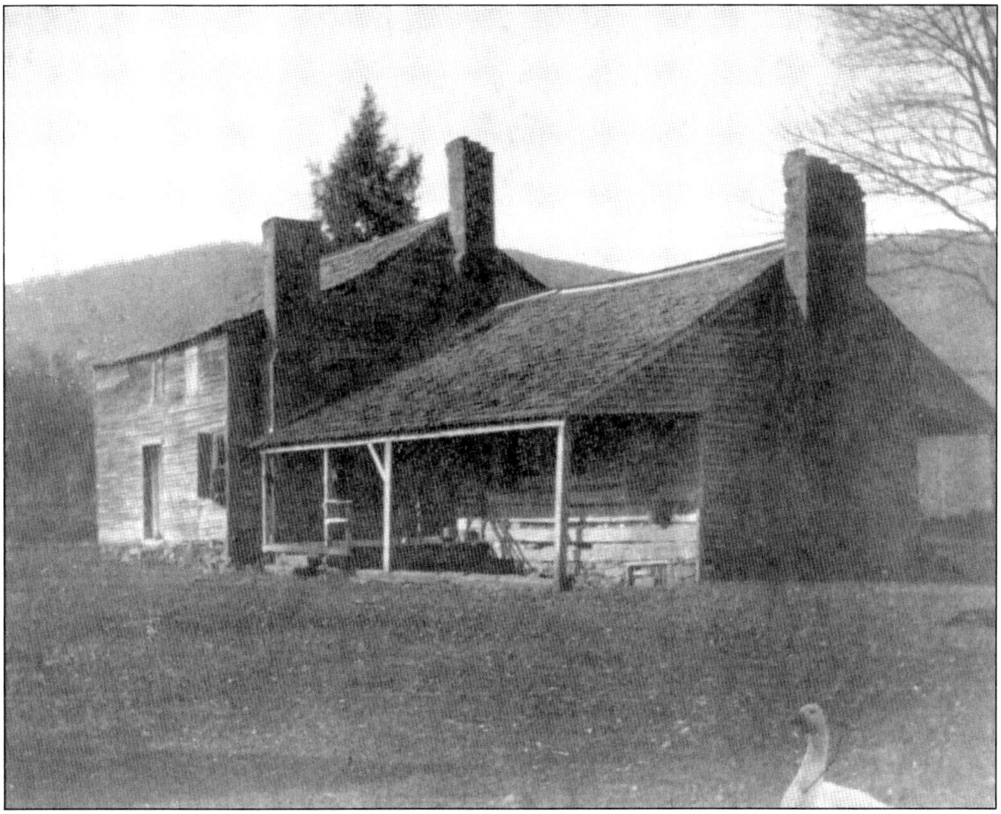

Maj. William Davidson built the log home called the Glades sometime in the 1770s. Located in what would become the Greenlee community, the house was visited by British general Patrick Ferguson in 1780 as he unsuccessfully searched for "the rebel Davidson." The house became a stagecoach stop in the early to mid-1800s. (Courtesy of Pack Memorial Library, North Carolina Collection.)

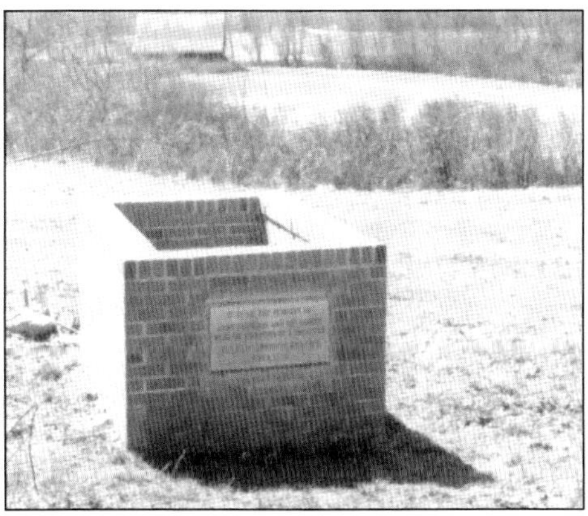

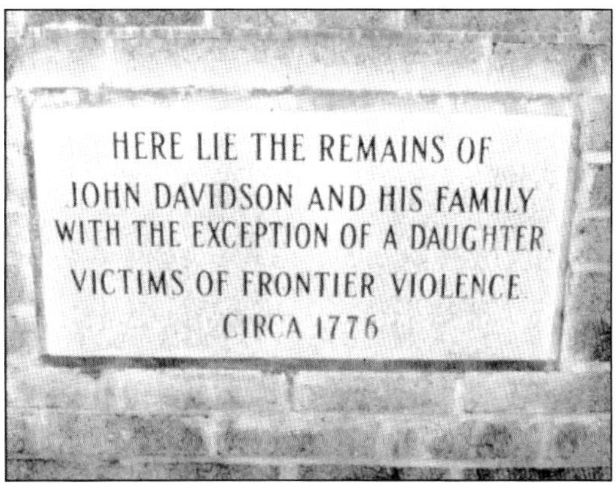

The Davidson family settled in what is now Old Fort in the 1770s, making their homes on land designated by treaty as Cherokee territory. In the summer of 1776, John Davidson and his family were massacred on their farm near Old Fort by Cherokee. Historians theorize that this event may have been the motivation for constructing Davidson's Fort. (Courtesy of Historic Carson House Library.)

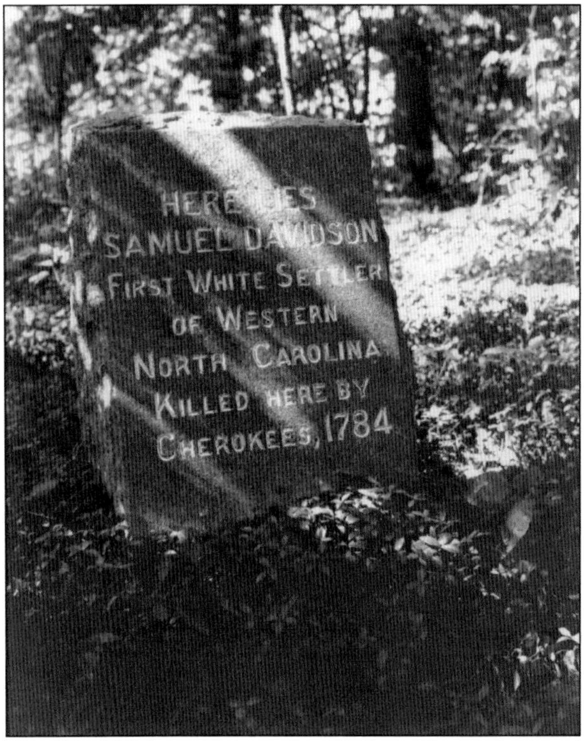

Samuel Davidson was captain of the local militia and, according to some sources, led the company of soldiers that built Davidson's Fort. He was the commander of the fort before moving his family farther into Cherokee territory, near the present-day Azalea community. There, he was ambushed and killed by Cherokees. His wife and child fled back to Davidson's Fort. (Courtesy of Pack Memorial Public Library, North Carolina Collection.)

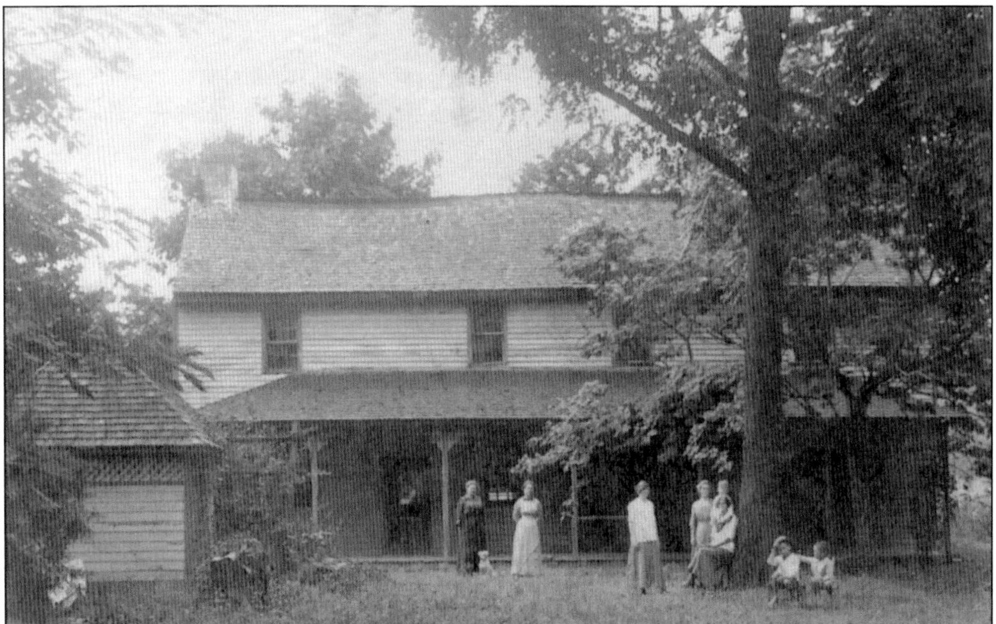

"Pioneer Ben" Burgin came to North Carolina around 1770. He was a close associate of the Davidson family and was part of a retaliatory attack on the Cherokee that had killed Samuel Davidson. Tradition holds that Burgin was also an Overmountain Man who fought at the Battle of King's Mountain. He died in 1823, and his Old Fort home (pictured) burned in 1929. (Courtesy of Peggy Silvers.)

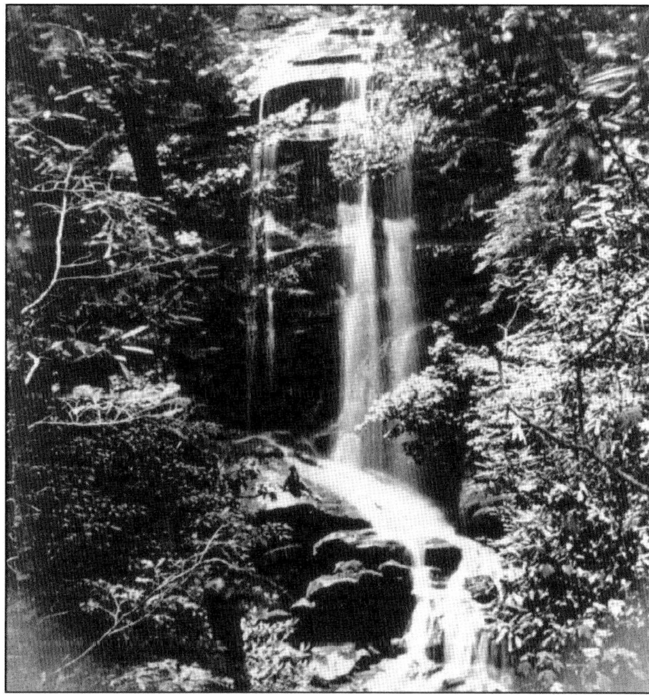

The Catawba River is named for the Native American tribe that first settled its banks. In their language, *Catawba* means "people of the river." Its 200-mile journey to the South Carolina piedmont begins 3.5 miles above Old Fort. An early trading route used by settlers paralleled the river to reach what is now Ridgecrest, North Carolina. These magnificent falls are near the river's headwaters. (Courtesy of McDowell County Public Library.)

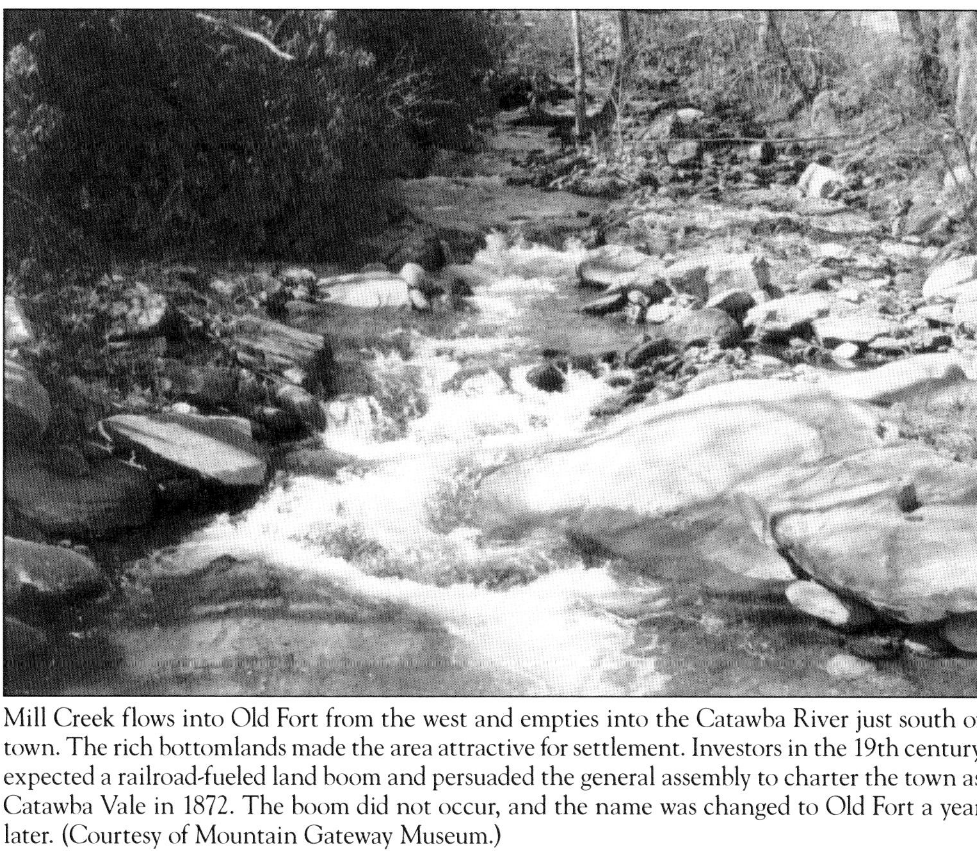

Mill Creek flows into Old Fort from the west and empties into the Catawba River just south of town. The rich bottomlands made the area attractive for settlement. Investors in the 19th century expected a railroad-fueled land boom and persuaded the general assembly to charter the town as Catawba Vale in 1872. The boom did not occur, and the name was changed to Old Fort a year later. (Courtesy of Mountain Gateway Museum.)

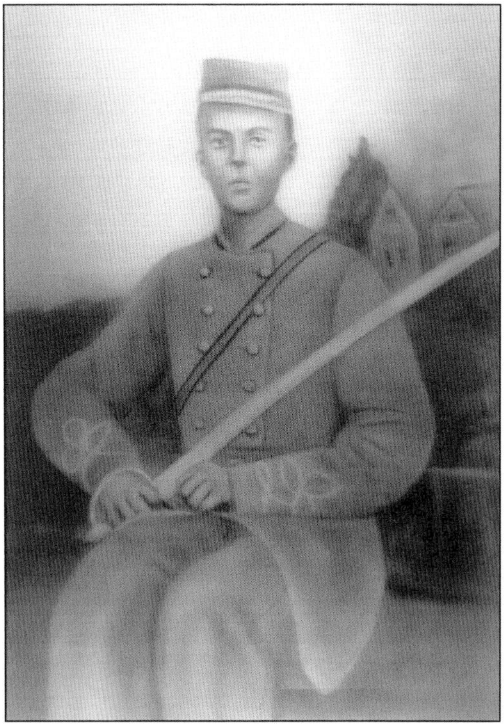

Thomas Young Lytle of the Crooked Creek community claimed to have fired the first shot of the Civil War at the Battle of Big Bethel near Newport News, Virginia, on June 10, 1861, and assisted in the capture of the war's first prisoner two days prior. Lytle had enlisted with the Buncombe Riflemen, the first Confederate troop raised in western North Carolina. (Courtesy of Barbara Meilhammer.)

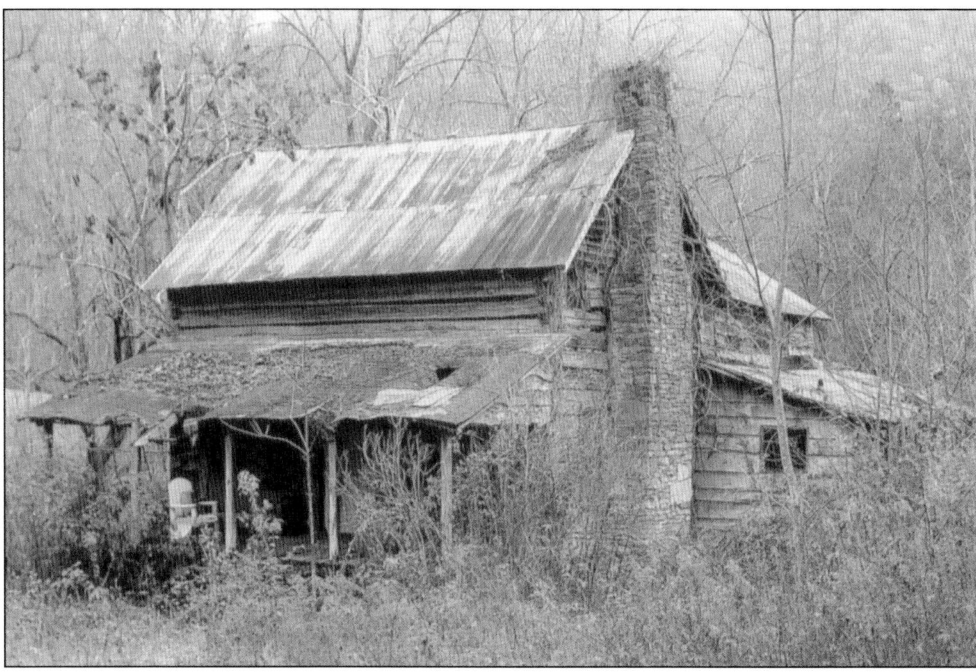

This cabin stood in the Bethlehem community off Silvers Welch Road and is typical of those built during the early-to-mid-1800s in the rural areas surrounding Old Fort. It features a dry-stacked chimney and a foundation of stacked rocks as well. Dwellers in cabins such as this one were self sufficient, raising most of their own food and making their own clothes. (Courtesy of Mountain Gateway Museum.)

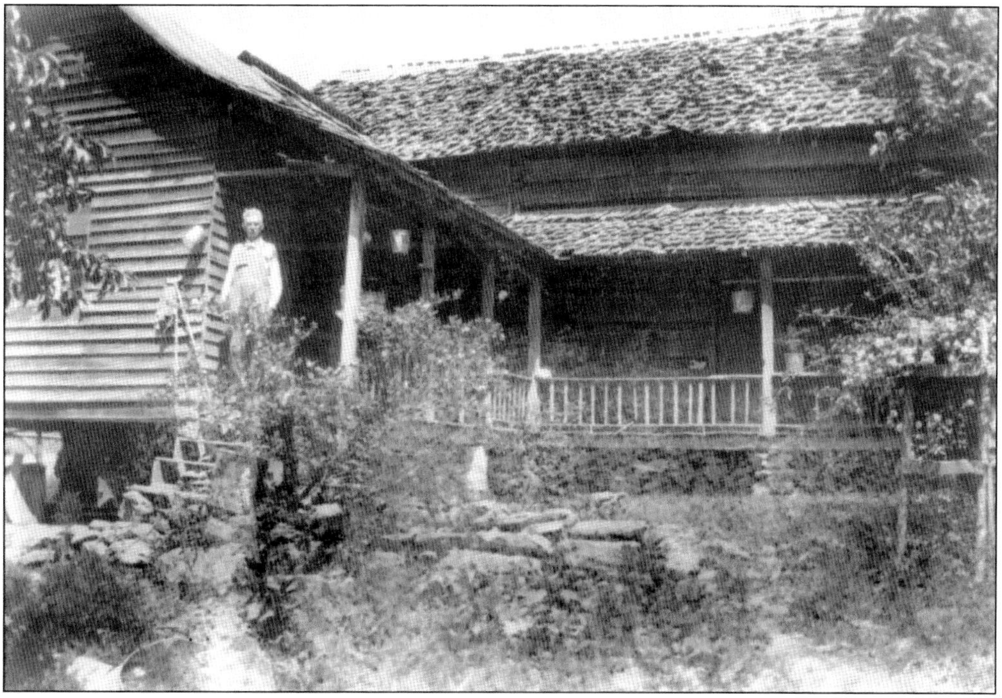

The Stepp Cabin is seen here in its original location in the Ebenezer community. It was built in the late 1860s by Confederate veteran Thomas B. Allsion, with a three-room frame wing added in the early 1900s. The original cabin was donated to Old Fort Historic Site, Inc., in 1973. It was taken apart, numbered, then rebuilt on the grounds of Mountain Gateway Museum. (Courtesy of Mountain Gateway Museum.)

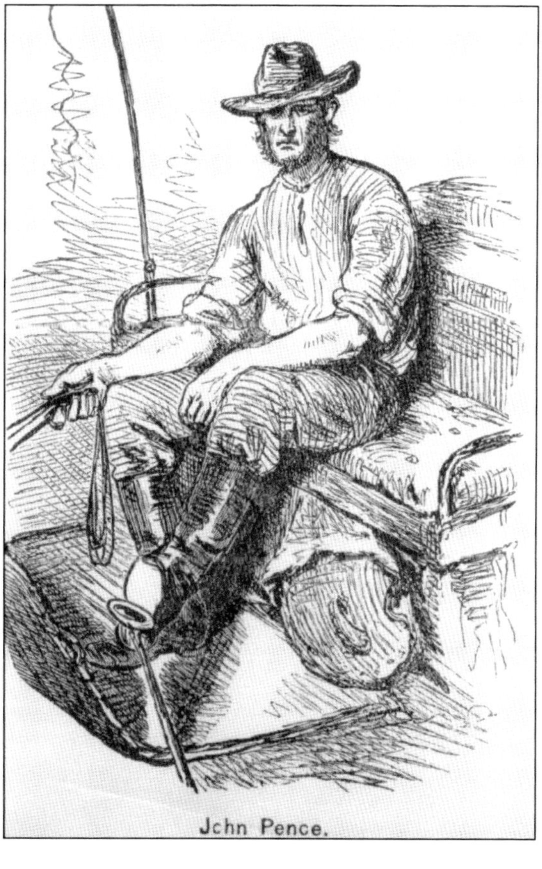

Jchn Pence.

Before the railroad was completed, John Pence drove the stagecoach "Hattie Butner" daily between Old Fort and Ridgecrest. His skill in negotiating the narrow, steep, and rocky road made him a folk hero. Author Christian Reid recalled that when one frightened passenger resolved to trust in God to see them safely to Asheville, another in the coach responded, "You can trust in John Pence, too." (Courtesy of Peggy Silvers.)

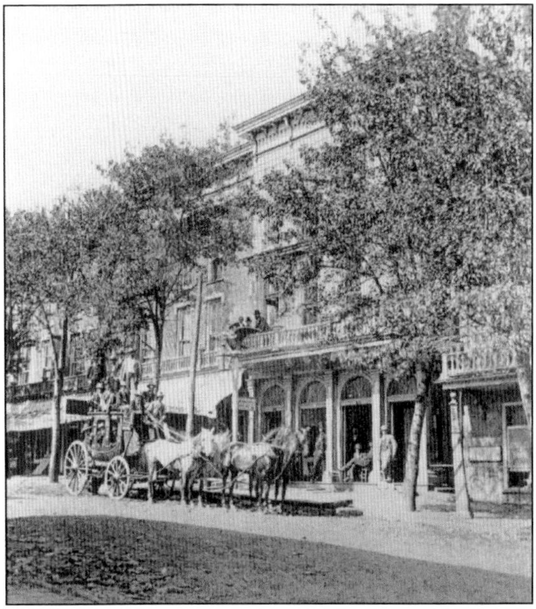

The Hattie Butner, with John Pence holding the reins, is seen at the Eagle Hotel in Asheville. The nine-passenger coach was pulled by a team of six white horses. It was owned by E.T. Clemmons of Forsyth County and named for his wife. Before the Old Fort-Asheville route, the Hattie Butner had been in service on the Salem-High Point Road. (Courtesy of Mountain Gateway Museum.)

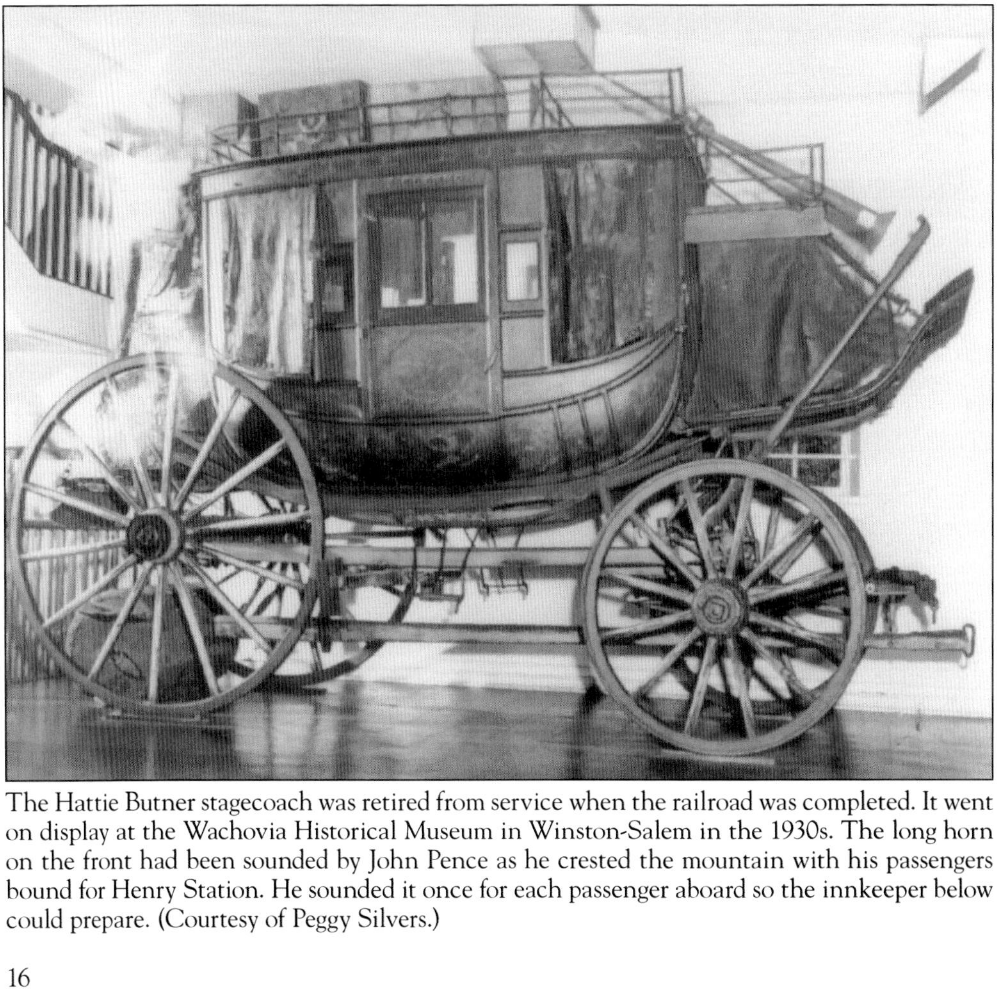

The Hattie Butner stagecoach was retired from service when the railroad was completed. It went on display at the Wachovia Historical Museum in Winston-Salem in the 1930s. The long horn on the front had been sounded by John Pence as he crested the mountain with his passengers bound for Henry Station. He sounded it once for each passenger aboard so the innkeeper below could prepare. (Courtesy of Peggy Silvers.)

Two

LAYING TRACK

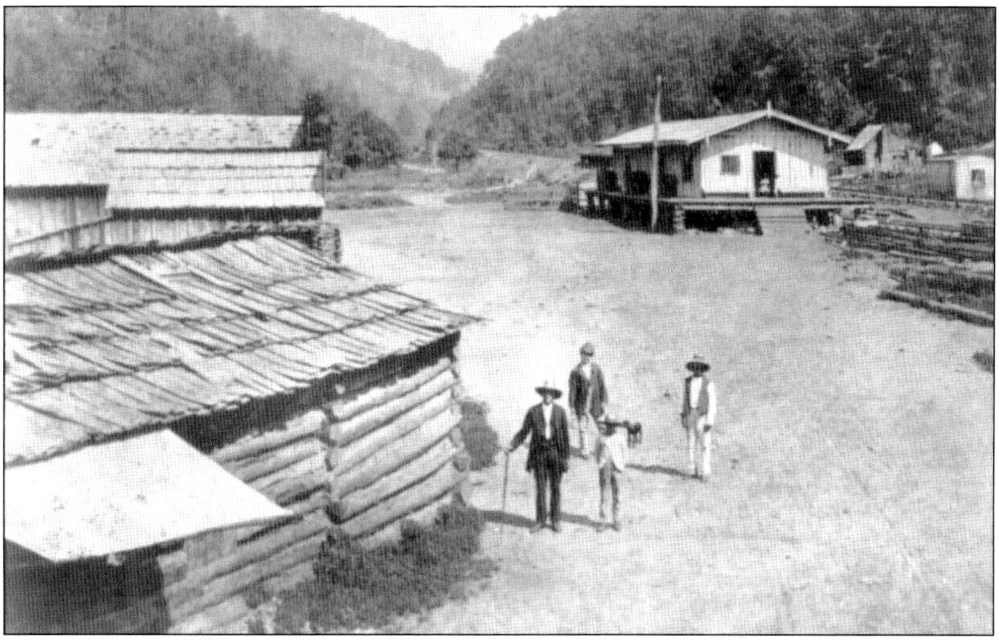

Until 1879, the railroad ended at Henry Station, located just west of Old Fort. A railroad office, supervisor's headquarters, post office, and hotel were located there. Engineer Walter Gwynn had identified a route up the steep grade to Ridgecrest in 1859, but the Civil War interrupted North Carolina's plans to complete a rail line from the Atlantic Ocean to the Tennessee border. (Courtesy of Pack Memorial Library, North Carolina Collection.)

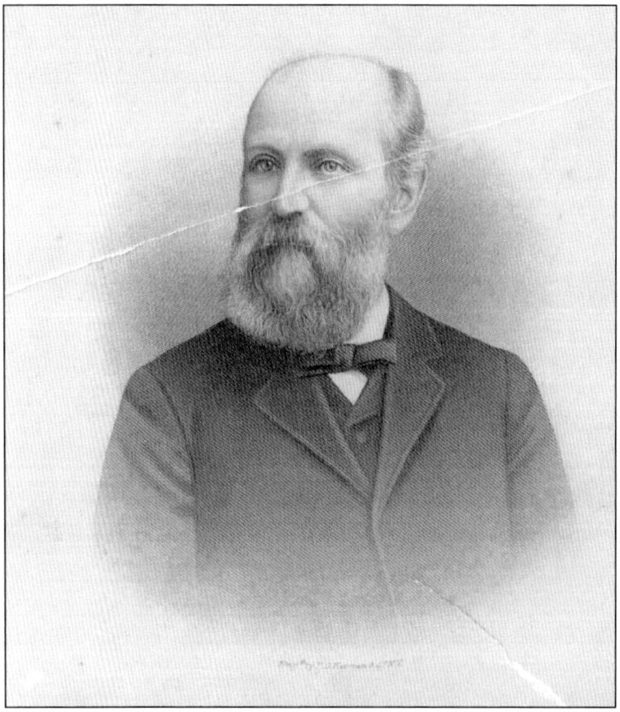

Maj. James W. Wilson was appointed superintendent and president of the Western North Carolina Railroad in 1864. The state legislature had created the railroad in 1855, with the stretch between Old Fort and Black Mountain designated as the Mountain Division. Wilson's engineering skill and logistical genius made the timely completion of the Mountain Division possible. (Courtesy of Historic Carson House Library.)

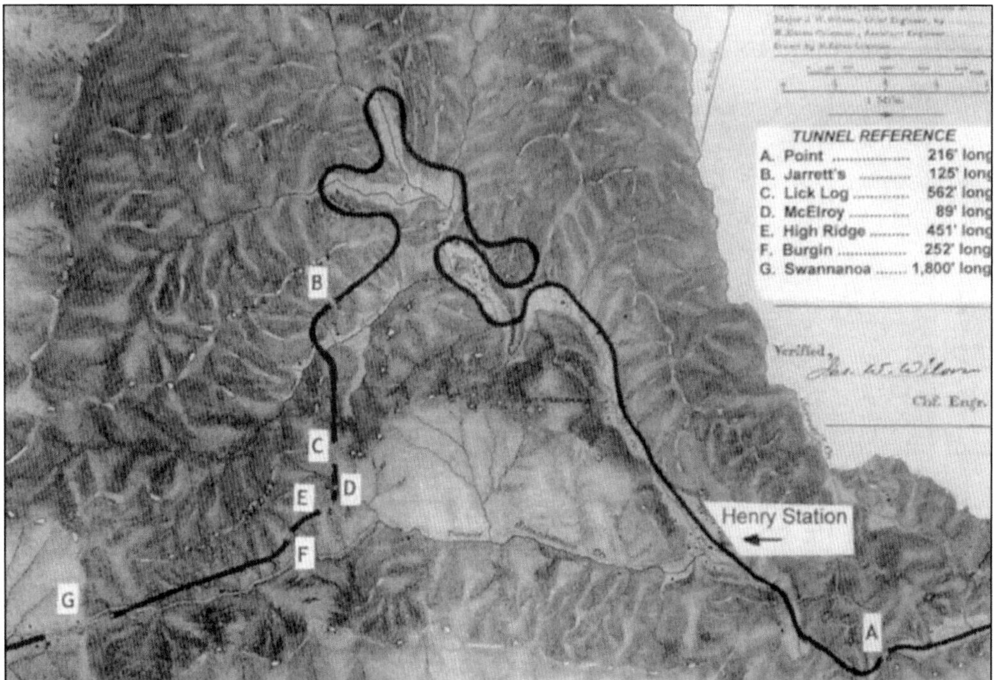

This is Maj. James Wilson's survey of the Mountain Division. The straight-line distance to be covered was only 3.5 miles, but the gain of 1,100 feet in elevation and the topographical features of the area necessitated digging six tunnels and laying more than 13 miles of track. Two large loops at Round Knob would also aid in elevation gain. (Courtesy of Mountain Gateway Museum.)

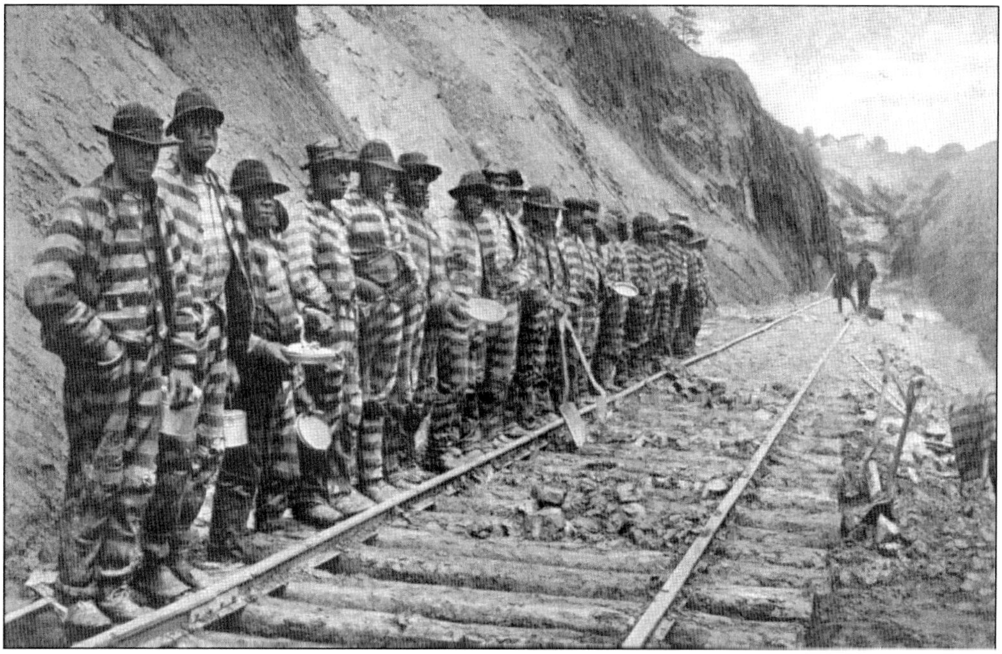

The state legislature authorized the use of convict labor in the building of the railroad from Old Fort to Ridgecrest. The number of convicts working on any one day averaged around 500. From 1876 to 1878, a total of 64 prisoners died, 8 were killed, and 66 escaped. Rations were meager, and rest was rare. The vast majority of the prisoners were African Americans. (Courtesy of Pack Memorial Public Library, North Carolina Collection.)

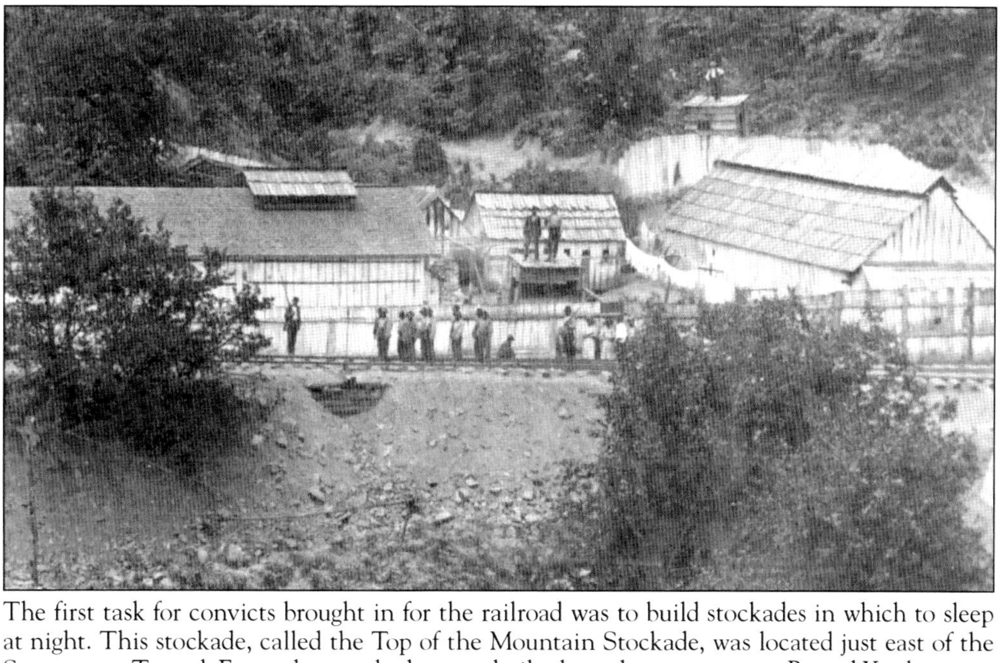

The first task for convicts brought in for the railroad was to build stockades in which to sleep at night. This stockade, called the Top of the Mountain Stockade, was located just east of the Swannanoa Tunnel. Four other stockades were built along the route: one at Round Knob, one at Lick Log, and two near the middle of the Mountain Division. (Courtesy of the North Carolina Department of Cultural Resources.)

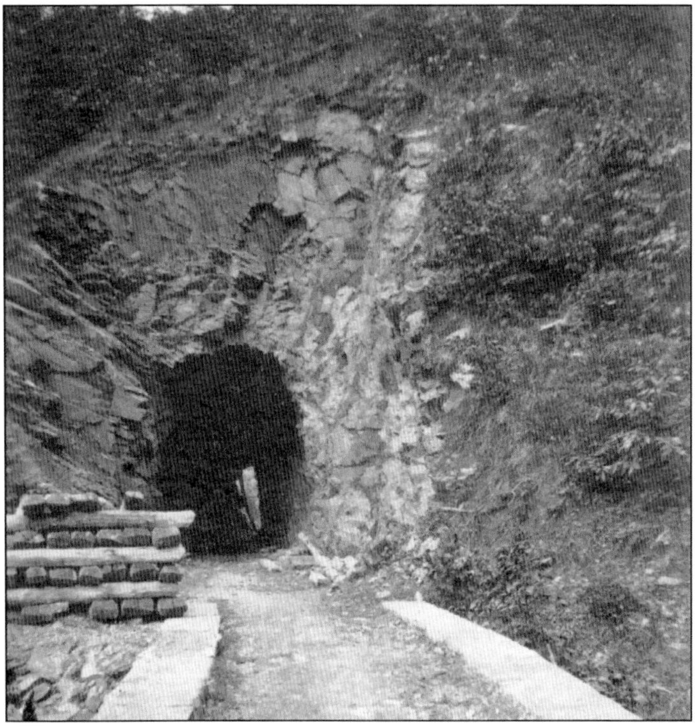

The railroad track has not yet been laid through Point Tunnel in this photograph. In preparation for the work, crossties have been stacked by the tunnel entrance. The path for the track was dug and leveled by convicts using flat rocks. (Courtesy of the University of North Carolina Library at Chapel Hill, North Carolina Collection.)

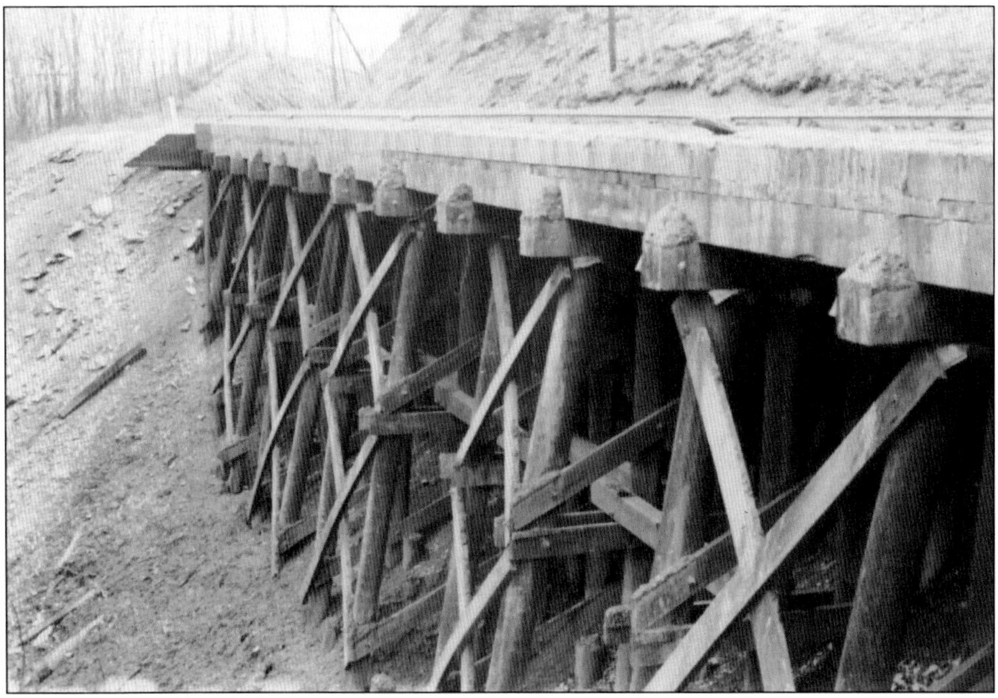

This trestle was located near Mud Cut. The convict laborers cut trees, milled the lumber, and built trestles to take sections of track over ravines or creeks. Major Wilson owned a large tract of land and a sawmill in the Round Knob area, so he was able to supply much of the wood for the many needs of the railroad building project. (Courtesy of Mountain Gateway Museum.)

Fills such as this one were constructed using dirt and rock that had been removed from tunnels and open cuts. The work of filling ravines and low areas along the railroad route was just as back-breaking as that of tunnel excavation. The 1916 flood would wash away much of the fill material, leaving tracks hanging in midair in some places. (Courtesy of Pack Memorial Public Library, North Carolina Collection.)

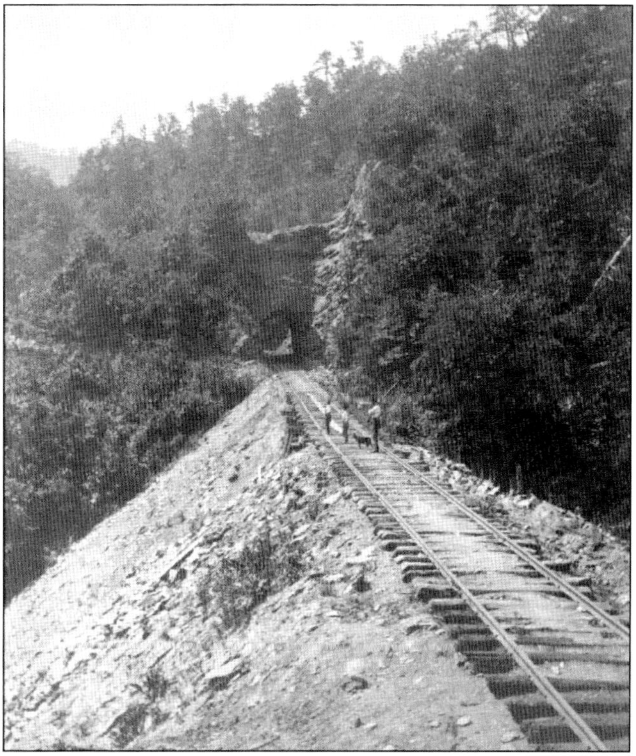

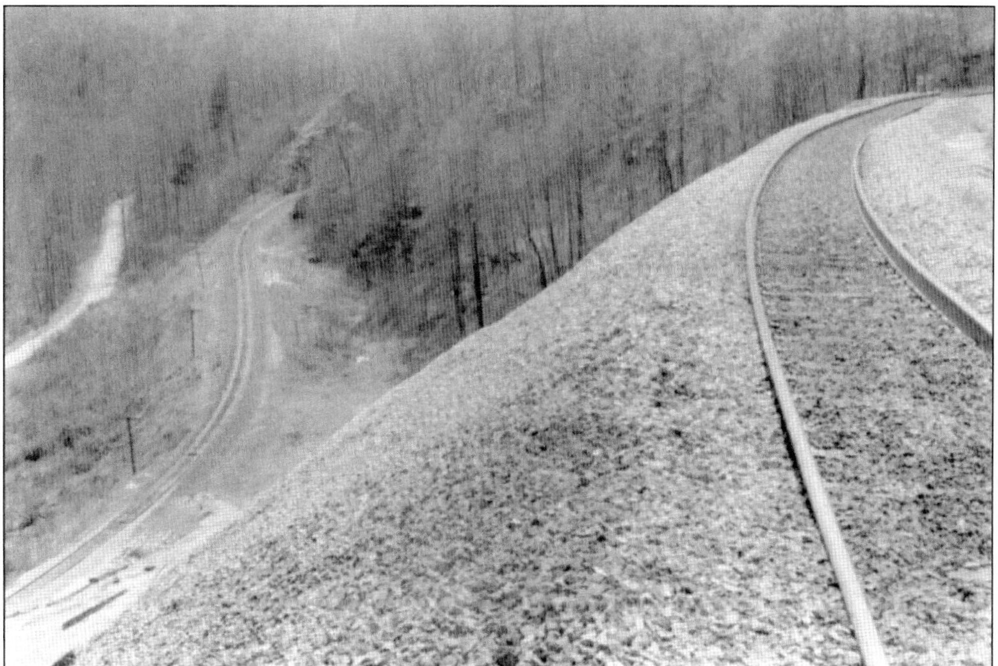

The largest loop of the Mountain Division begins and ends on the eastern side of Round Knob at a place called High Fill. The upper tracks at High Fill are 120 feet above those at the lower end of the loop, but they are separated by only 140 lateral feet. (Courtesy of Mountain Gateway Museum.)

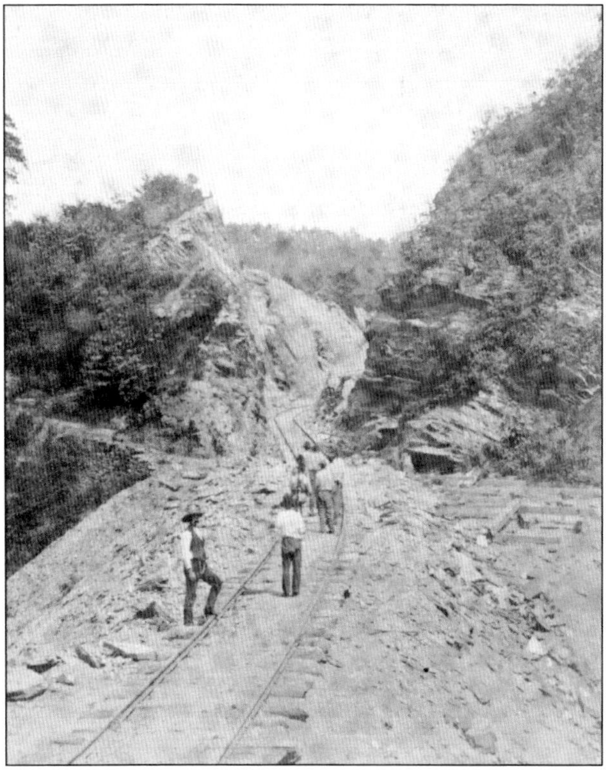

An overseer and a guard march a small group of convicts to their worksite on the Mountain Division. The prisoners endured long shifts, beginning at first light and ending after sunset. An 1879 supervisor's report related that convicts were sometimes willing to be punished harshly rather than spend another day swinging a pick or chisel inside a dark tunnel. (Courtesy of Pack Memorial Public Library, North Carolina Collection.)

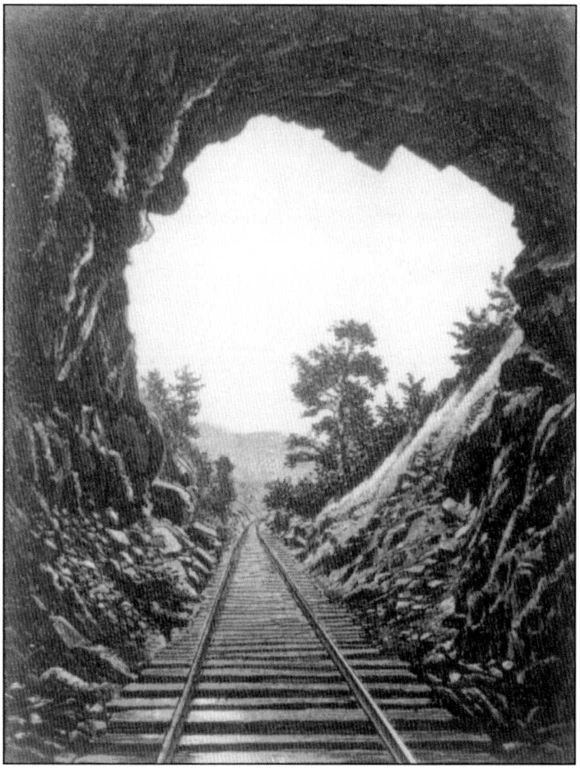

Jarrett's Tunnel was 123 feet long and the first encountered by westbound trains leaving Round Knob. Excavation of the tunnels was primarily achieved with picks and shovels. Gunpowder was occasionally used to break up stubborn sections of solid rock. Nitroglycerine was employed as well, one of the first uses of Nobel's blasting oil in the southeastern United States. (Courtesy of McDowell County Public Library.)

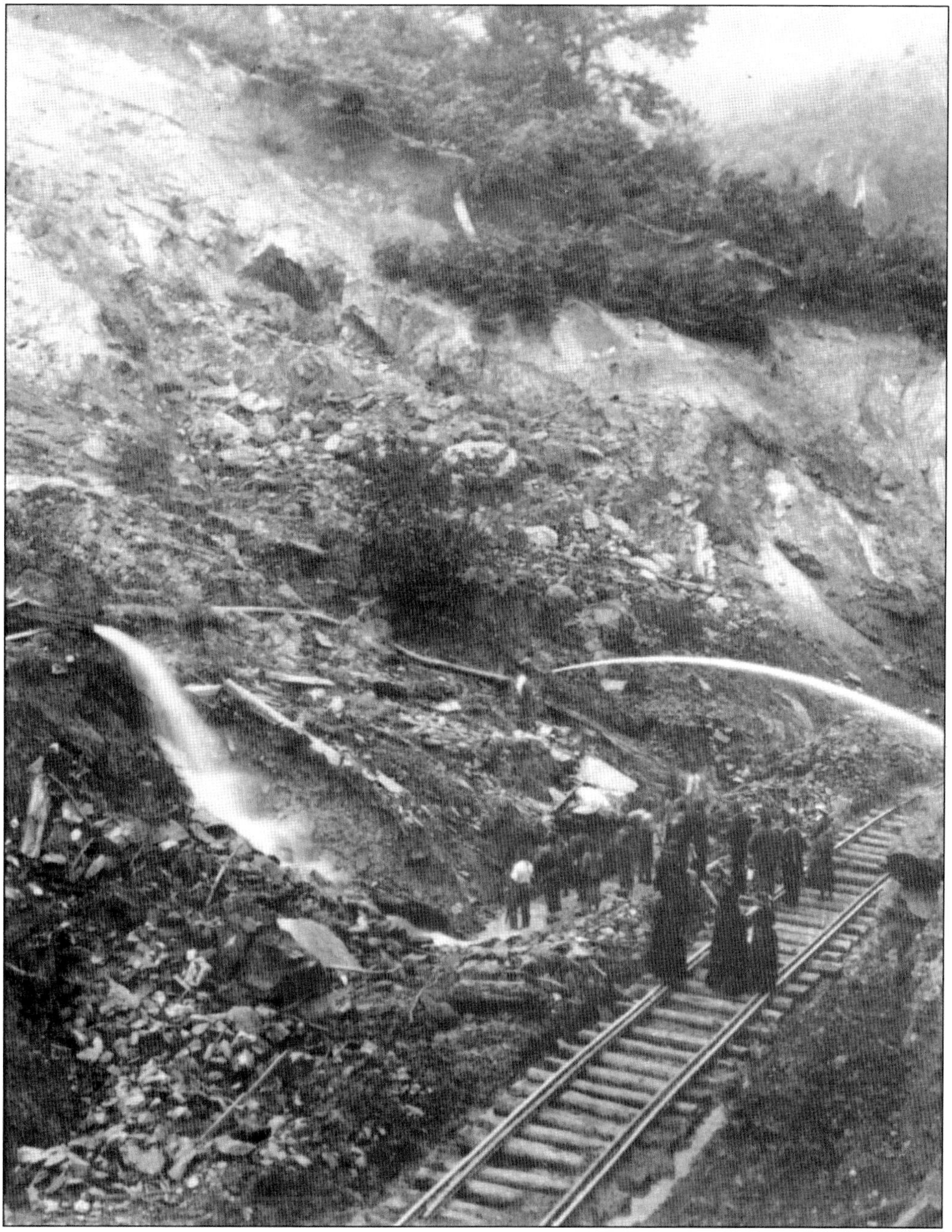

One of the most difficult areas of the Mountain Division to stabilize was Mud Cut. In this image, a mudslide is being sluiced away by water from a diverted stream. The spectators on the track may have been passengers from the Hattie Butner seeking diversion during a stop to repair the stagecoach on its route between Old Fort and Asheville. (Courtesy of Pack Memorial Public Library, North Carolina Collection.)

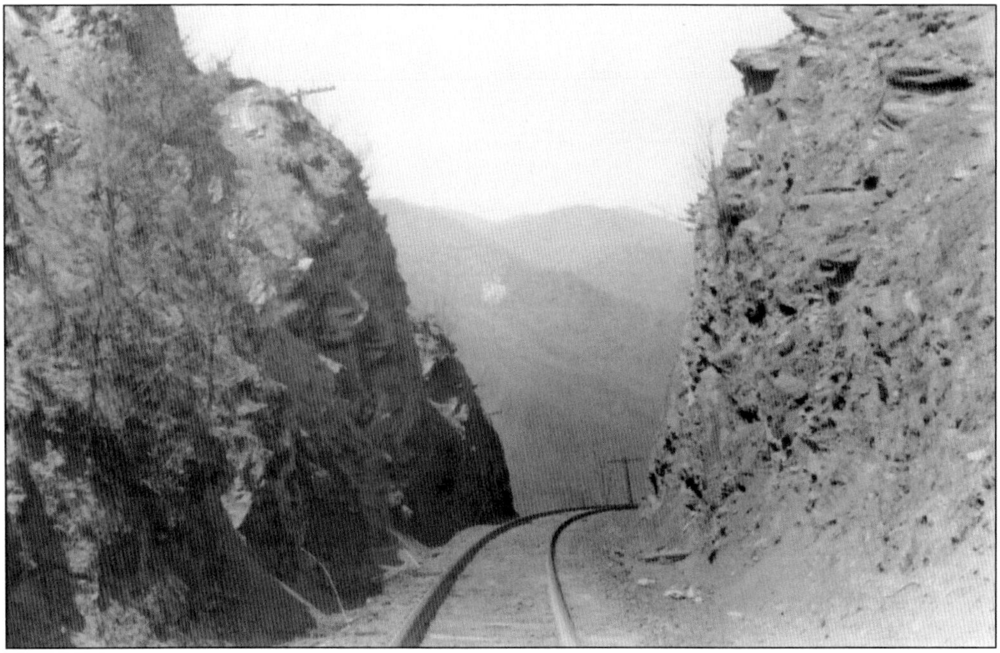

This open cut is located near Round Knob. To help break up rock in areas not tall enough to require a tunnel, large fires were sometimes built under the rock to superheat it. Barrels of cold water were then dumped on the area. The sudden and extreme change in temperature would cause the rock to crack, making it easier to break up and remove. (Courtesy of Mountain Gateway Museum.)

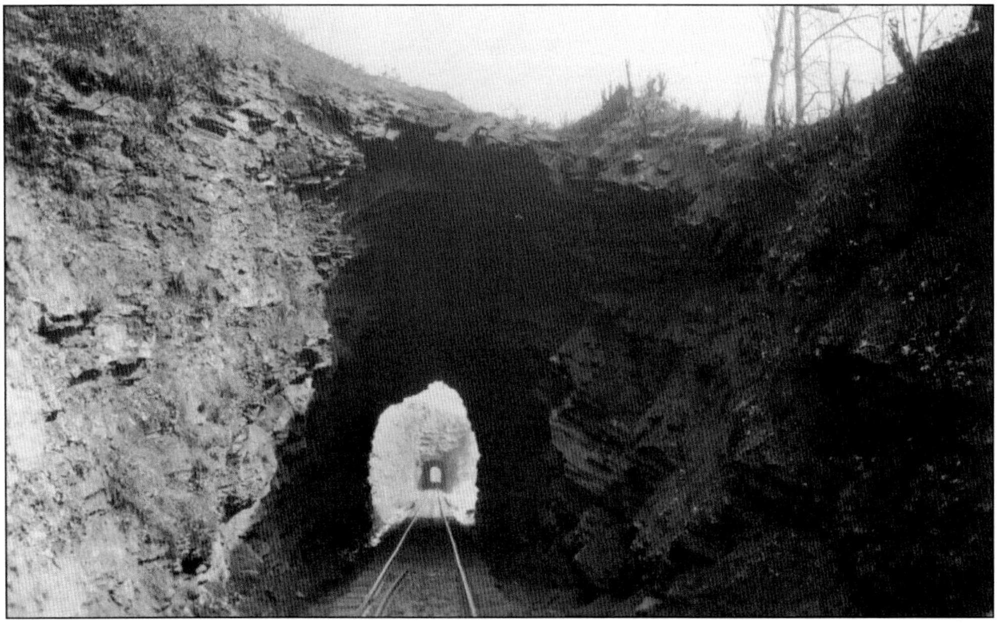

The McElroy and Lick Log Tunnels are the closest together of the Western North Carolina Railroad's Mountain Division. The 89-foot-long McElroy Tunnel, seen in the foreground of this photograph, is the shortest tunnel in the division. During construction, the dislodged rock was collected and carried out in wheelbarrows and wooden carts by the convict laborers. (Courtesy of Mountain Gateway Museum.)

A man surveys the Burgin Tunnel shortly after the completion of the Mountain Division of the Western North Carolina Railroad. The Burgin Tunnel was 252 feet long and, travelling east to west, was next to last in the series of seven tunnels. Each tunnel had to be at least 15 feet high to accommodate the smokestacks on the wood-burning engines. (Courtesy of Pack Memorial Public Library, North Carolina Collection.)

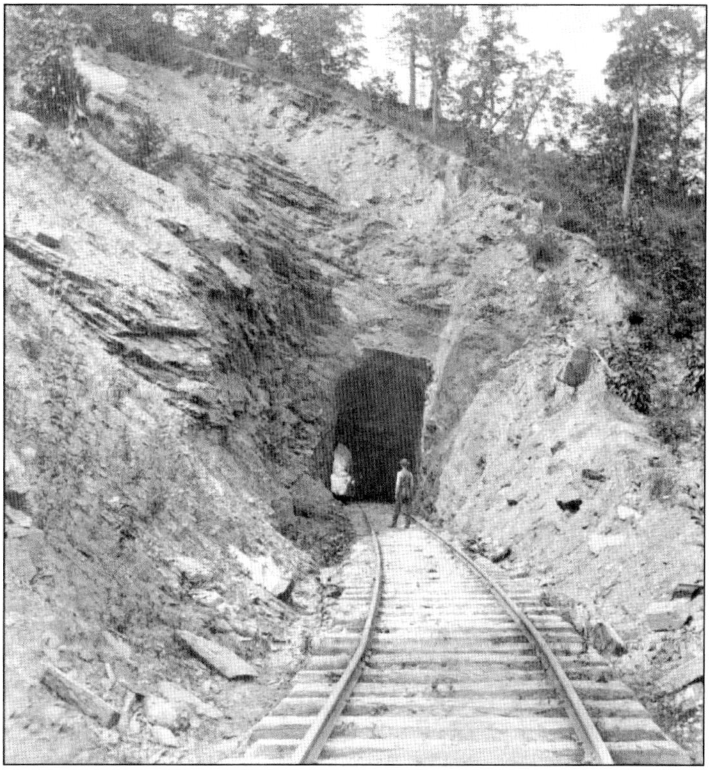

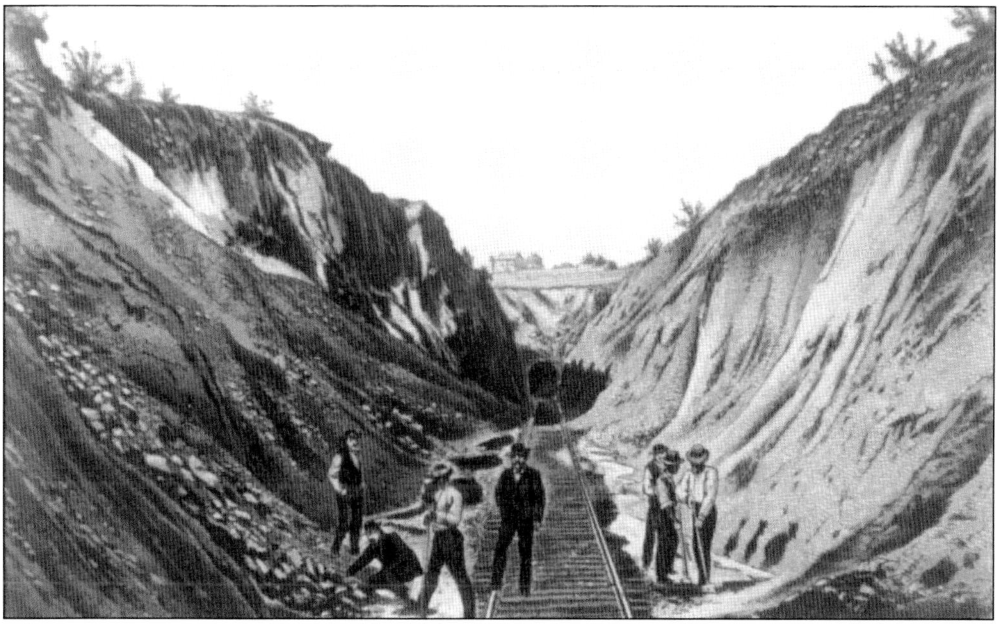

The 1,800-foot Swannanoa Tunnel is the longest of the series between Old Fort and Ridgecrest. Its construction was the final phase of the Mountain Division construction. Two work crews were needed to complete it on time, with one crew digging from the west and one from the east. The teams met in the middle—with grades and centers matching exactly—on March 11, 1879. (Courtesy of Mountain Gateway Museum.)

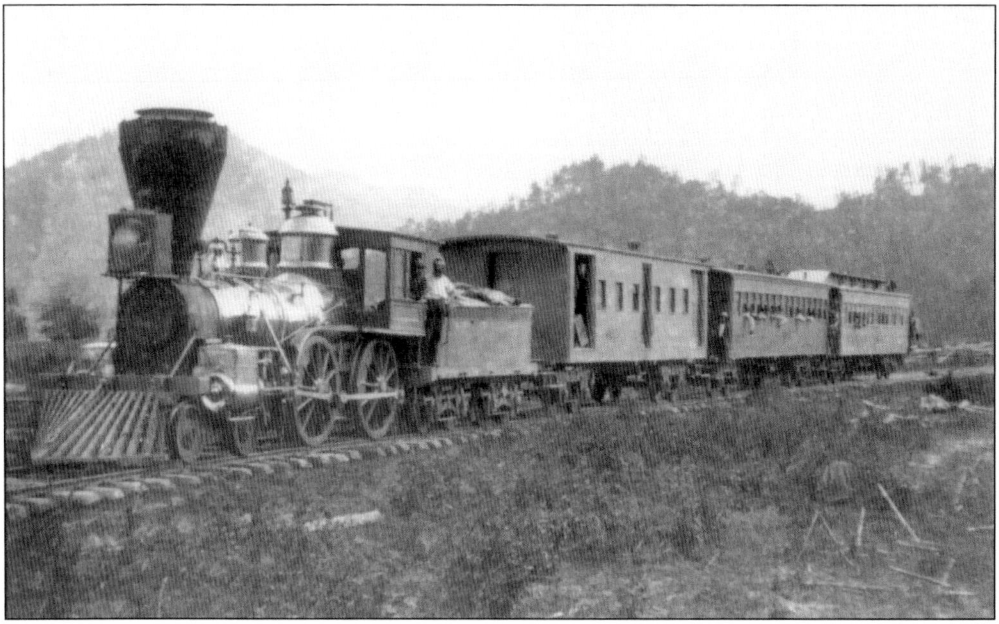

The *Salisbury* pauses with freight and passengers just outside Old Fort. To speed up the removal of debris during the last phase of the building of the Mountain Division, the *Salisbury* was lifted off the tracks at Henry Station by convict laborers, placed on temporary rails, and pushed overland by men, oxen, and mules up to the western end of the Swannanoa Tunnel. (Courtesy of McDowell County Public Library.)

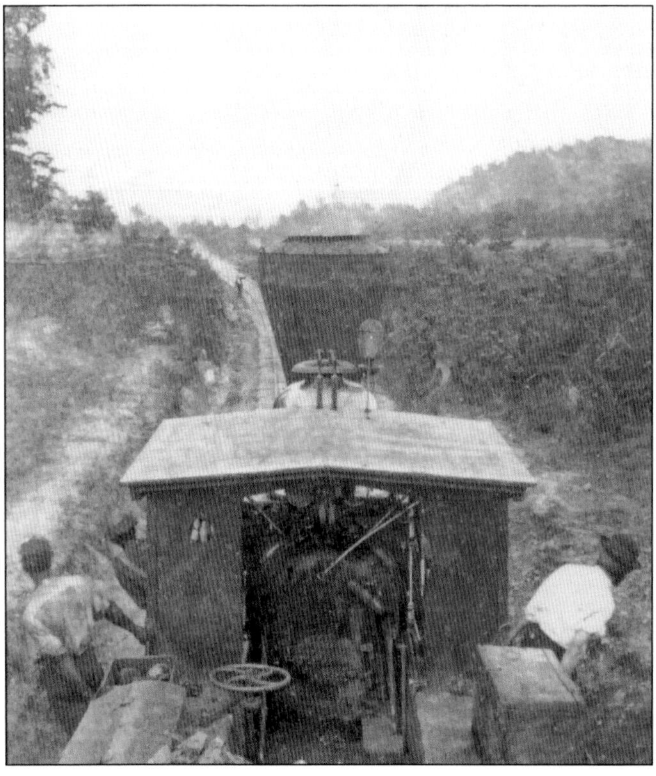

Photographer Rufus Morgan captured this unique image from his position atop the wood tender behind the engine. The crew on this Western North Carolina Railroad train are braking as a man near the track signals for them to stop. Debris or animals on the track could cause an accident, and warnings from locals about such situations were invaluable. (Courtesy of the University of North Carolina at Chapel Hill, North Carolina Collection.)

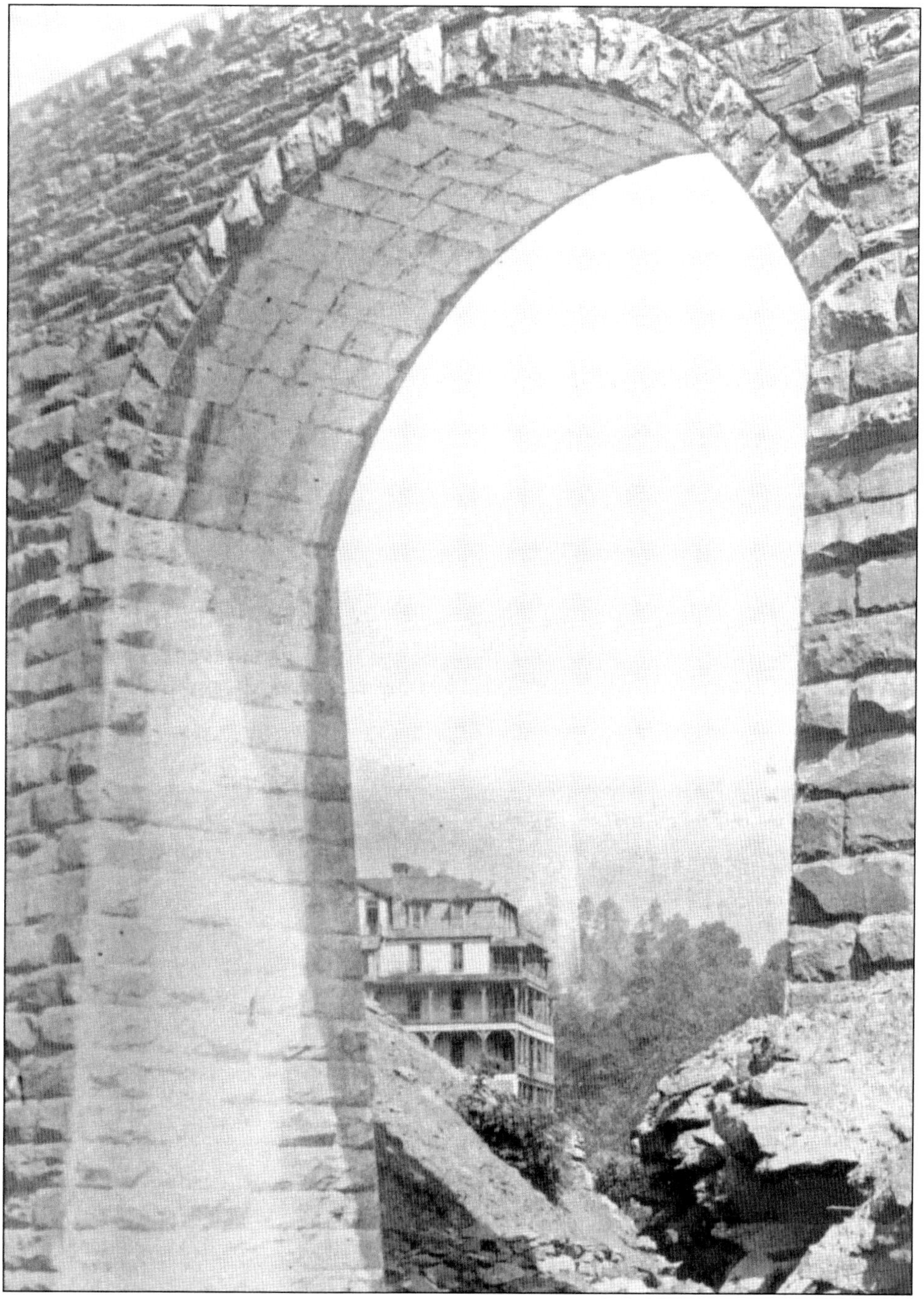

Round Knob Hotel is seen through the Mill Creek viaduct arch in this image from around 1882. Once the construction of the Mountain Division was in full swing, Maj. James Wilson had a small lodge built on land that he owned at Round Knob. The small structure was replaced in 1885 by the magnificent five-story Round Knob Hotel, which was built to compete with resort hotels in Asheville. The railroad track passed so near the hotel that when passengers disembarked from the train, they were just a few steps away from the entrance. (Courtesy of Mountain Gateway Museum.)

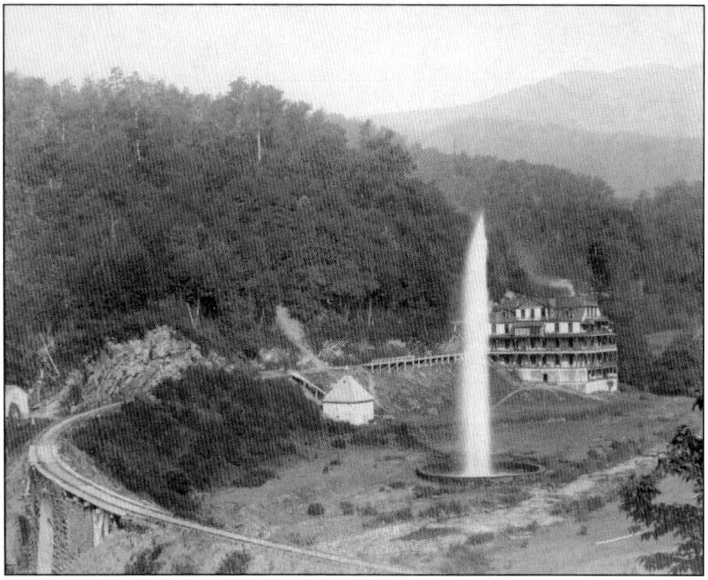

In order to promote their luxurious establishment and attract guests who might otherwise stay in Asheville, the owners of Round Knob Hotel constructed this fountain. The water was brought down through an underground pipe from a dam built on Long Branch. The drop in elevation sent the water high in the air, creating the appearance of a geyser. (Courtesy of Pack Memorial Public Library, North Carolina Collection.)

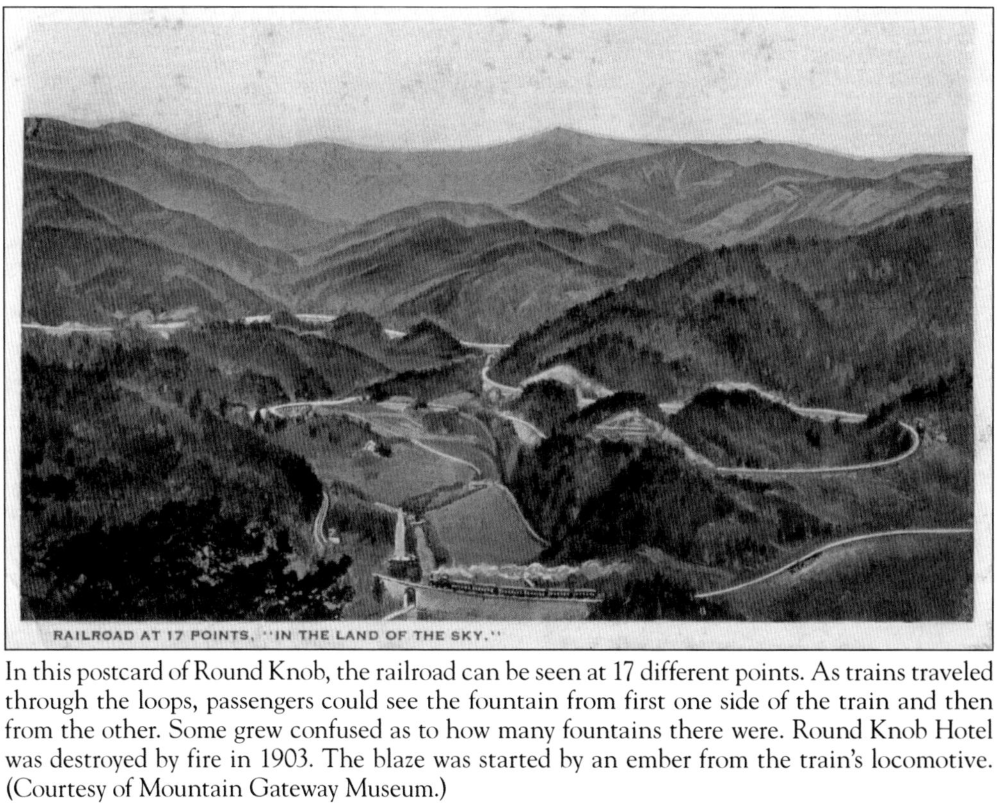

In this postcard of Round Knob, the railroad can be seen at 17 different points. As trains traveled through the loops, passengers could see the fountain from first one side of the train and then from the other. Some grew confused as to how many fountains there were. Round Knob Hotel was destroyed by fire in 1903. The blaze was started by an ember from the train's locomotive. (Courtesy of Mountain Gateway Museum.)

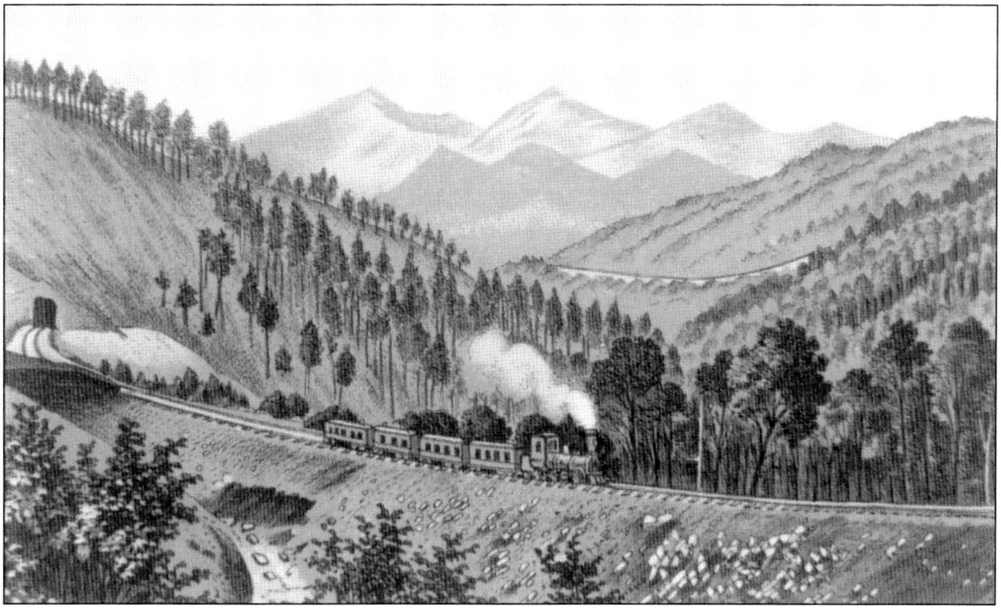

Once the Mountain Division was open to travel, it became the object of much interest. This early postcard depicts a train that has just passed through High Ridge Tunnel. At 494 feet long, it is the third longest of the six tunnels in the Old Fort-Round Knob area. High Ridge Tunnel is unique because it curves inside the mountain. (Courtesy of McDowell County Public Library.)

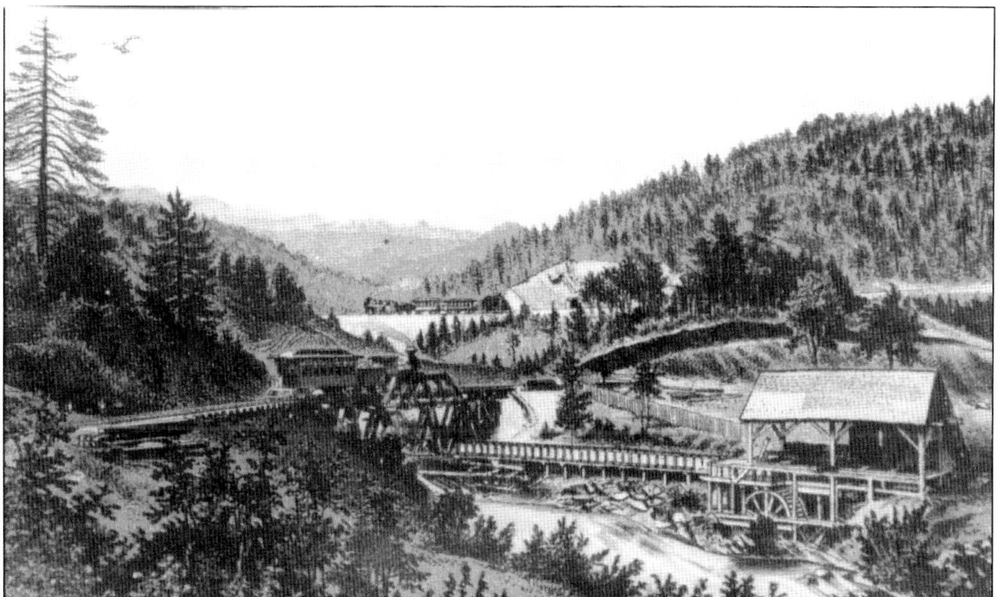

The gristmill seen in the foreground of this postcard depicting the area near Round Knob was one of many located on Mill Creek. The velocity of the stream's water flow made it ideal for such mills. (Courtesy of Mountain Gateway Museum.)

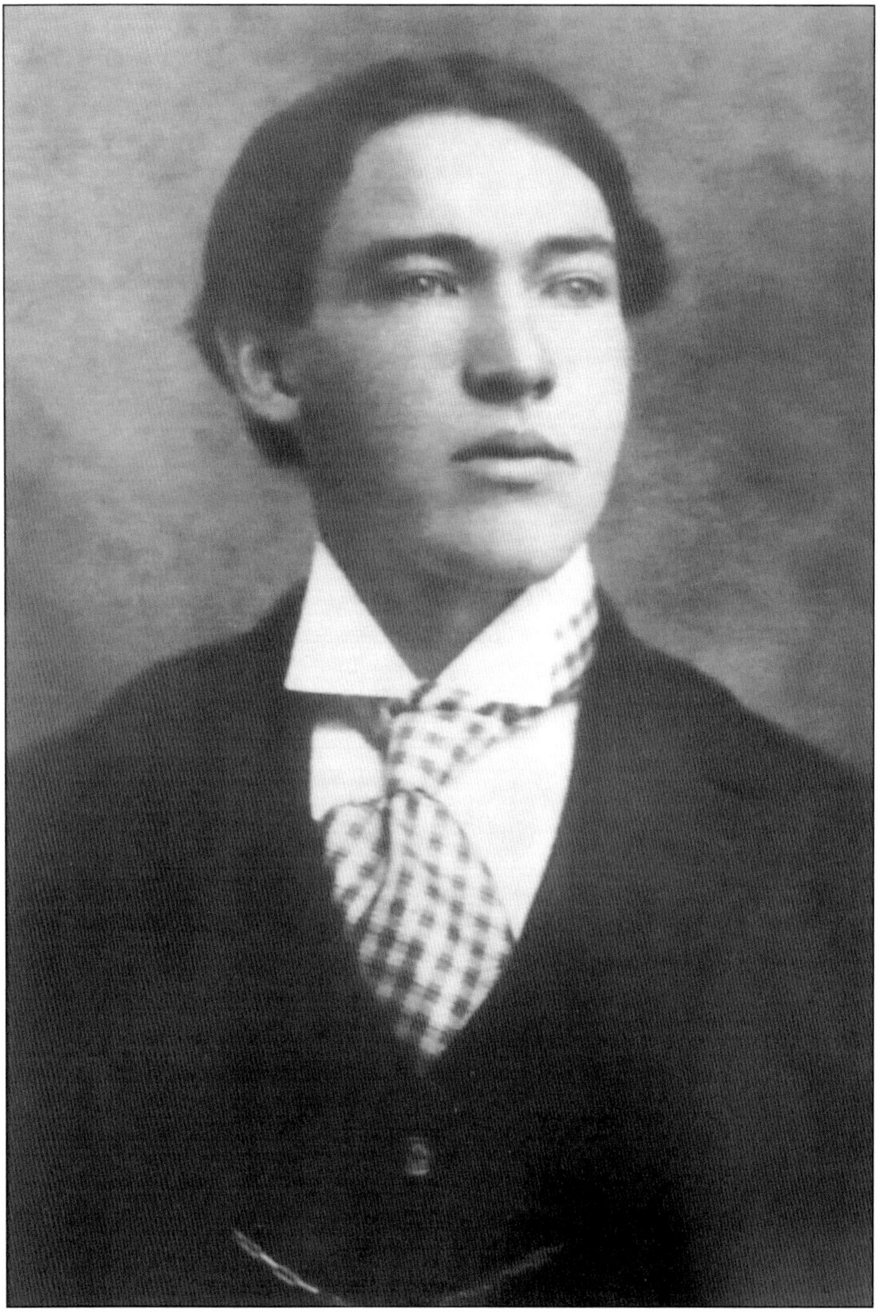

George Washington Sandlin was a railroad man for 67 years and Old Fort's youngest mayor. He was born in Old Fort in 1877 and went to work as a water boy for the Western North Carolina Railroad when he was 10 years old. At age 17, he became a night telegraph operator at Ridgecrest for the Southern Railway. He was elected mayor of Old Fort on his 21st birthday. He later became a dispatcher on the Murphy Division and after 13 years came home to Old Fort to be station agent. As his time with the railroad was winding down, he earned a law degree and was admitted to the Bar of the Supreme Court of the United States in 1944, at the age of 67. He ended his railroad career in Marion at the age of 77. (Courtesy of Richard Sandlin Fullerton.)

Three

PUTTING DOWN ROOTS

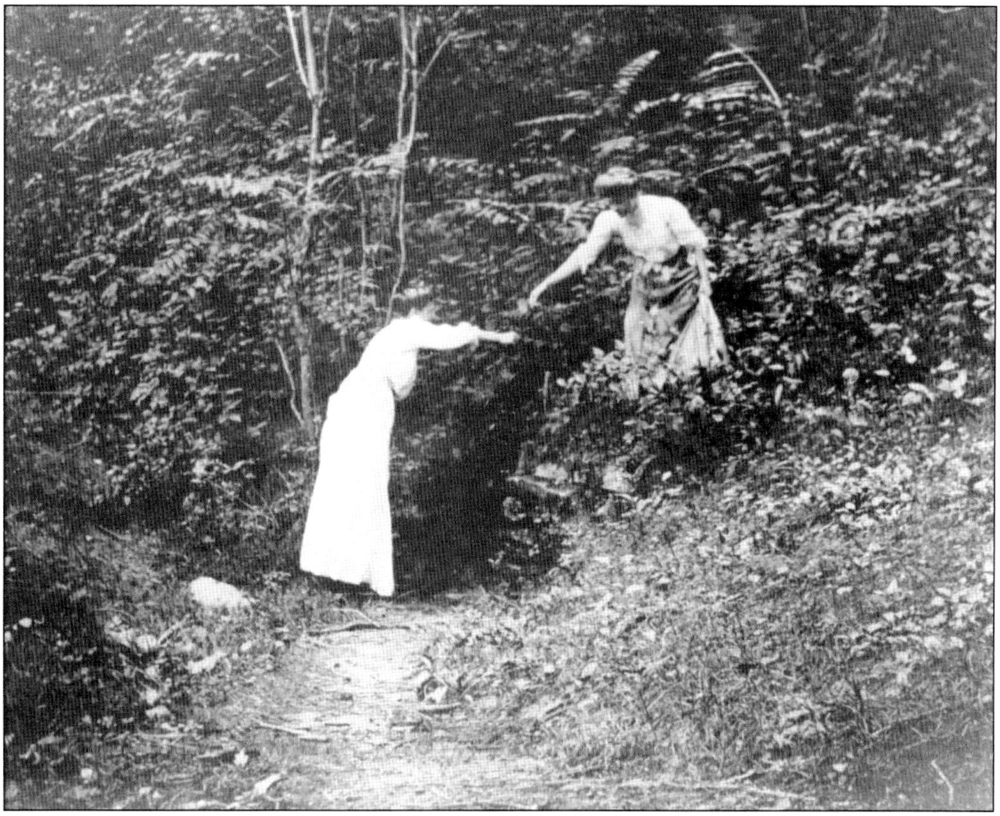

This spring, located on Spring Street in central Old Fort, was the sole source of water for many families prior to the building of a town reservoir in 1916. One story handed down through the years relates that a small boy fell into the large spring box and had to be revived by rescuers. The identity of the two women pictured is unknown. (Courtesy of Peggy Silvers.)

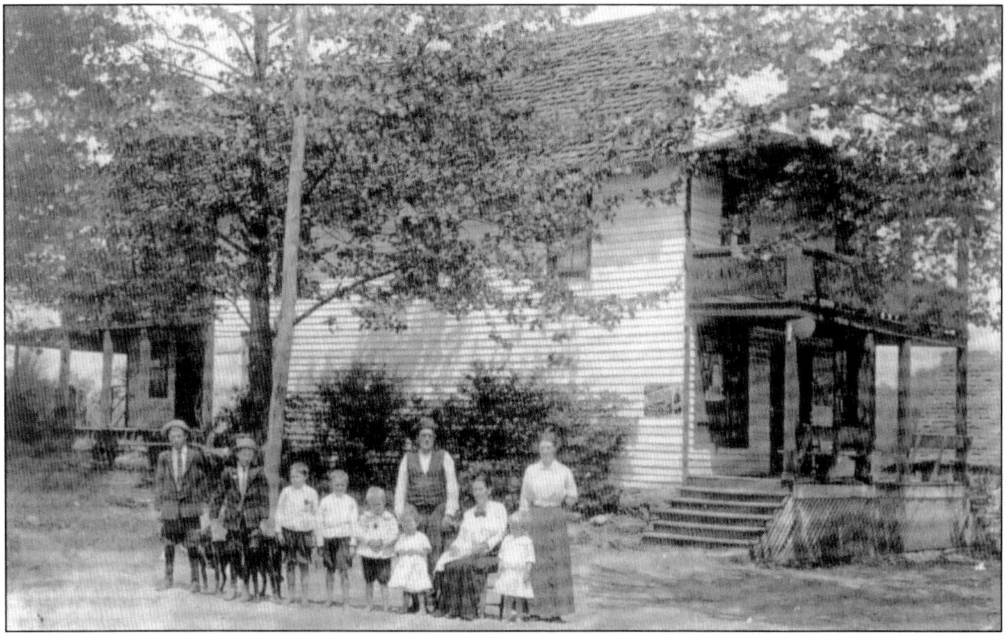

The "Heep" Greene Store was in business in Old Fort in the very early 1900s. It stood near the intersection of Main Street and Catawba Avenue. The family in the photograph is mostly likely the Greene family, whose home is at the rear of the store. (Courtesy of McDowell County Public Library.)

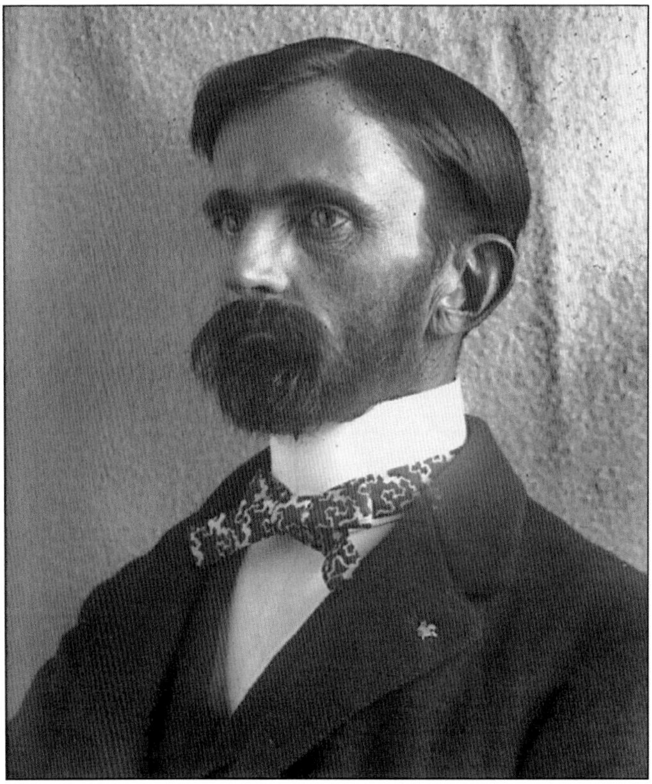

Robert Lee Greenlee (1863–1952) of the Greenlee community was an engineer for the Southern Railway. He also had a keen interest in photography and captured some of the earliest photographic images taken in McDowell County. He is buried at Ebenezer United Methodist Church along with many other members of the Greenlee family. (Courtesy of Historic Carson House.)

Located in Mashburn Building on the square, the Bank of Old Fort was first registered as a corporation in 1904. In 1921, the bank reported deposits from 750 patrons totaling over $130,000. J.S. Bradley was president, and P.H. Mashburn was vice president. (Courtesy of Mountain Gateway Museum.)

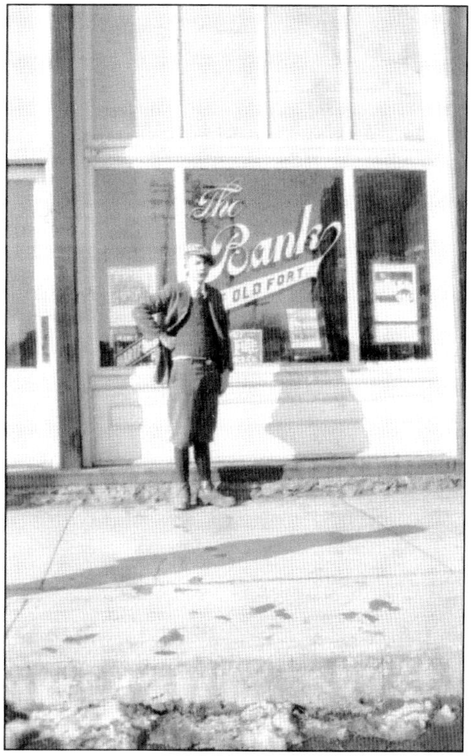

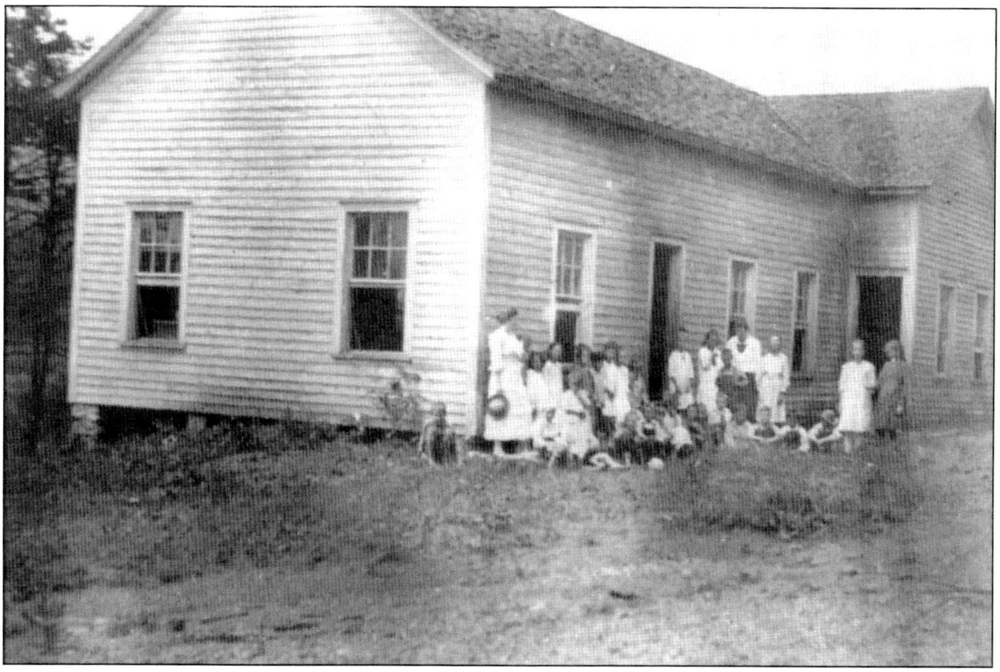

Seen here in 1916, Siloam School was typical of the rural schools scattered throughout McDowell County prior to consolidation in the 1930s. The school year was five months long, and all grades were taught in the same room by the same teacher. Instructors were often quite young, sometimes with only an eighth grade education themselves. (Courtesy of Historic Carson House Library.)

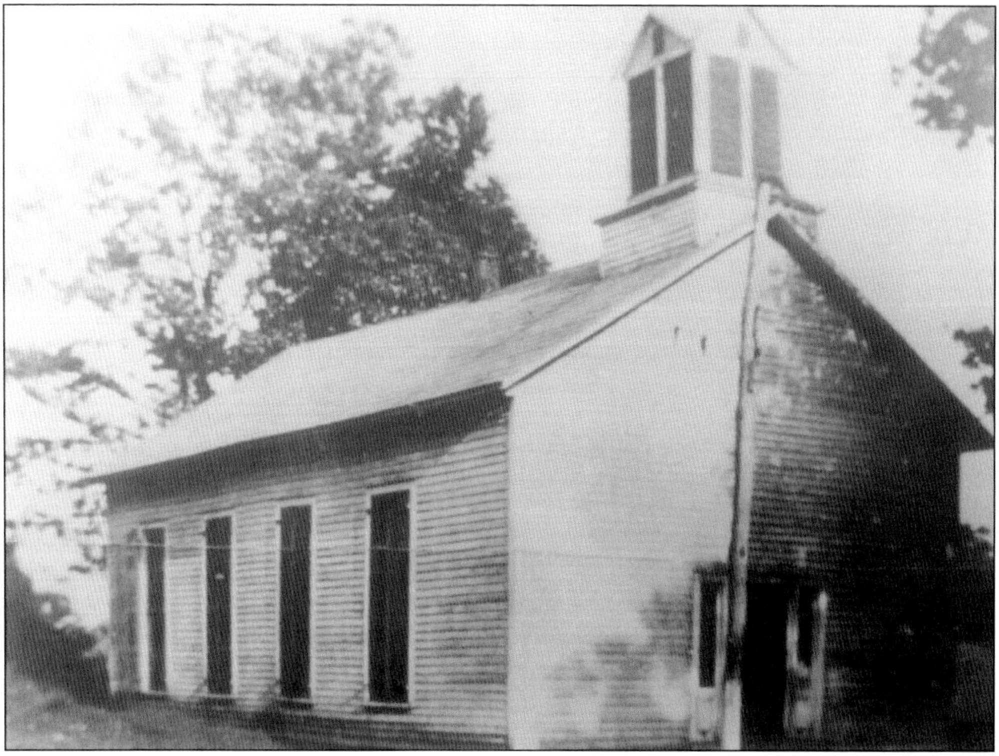

Railroad engineer W.P. Terrell organized a Baptist Sunday school at his home in Old Fort in 1882, and the congregation met there until this church building could be completed almost two years later. The frame structure was in use until 1928, and the first pastor was G.W. Harmon. (Courtesy of Historic Carson House Library.)

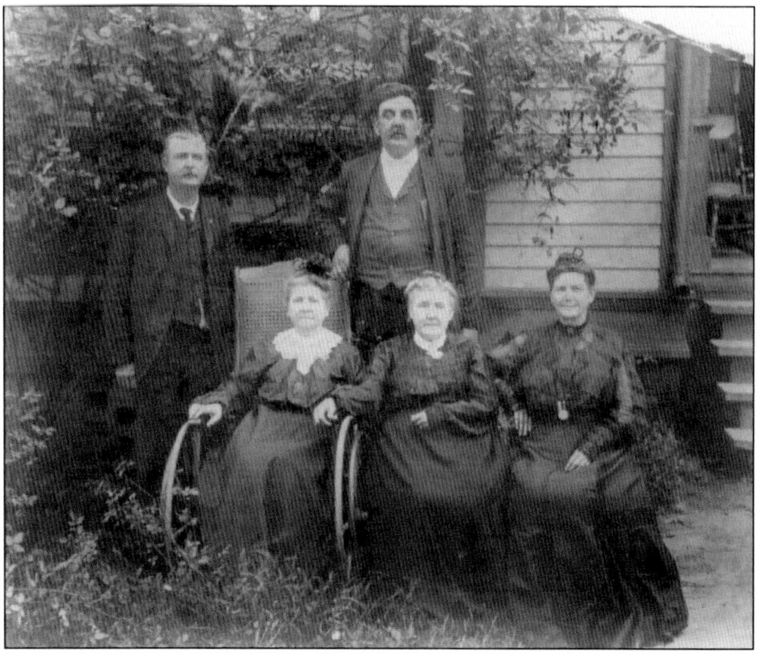

Columbus Straley Burgin stands to the left of his sisters, who are, from left to right, Eliza, Jane, and Caldonia or "Callie" at the Burgin home in Old Fort. Thomas Lytle, Eliza's husband, is to the right of his wife's chair. The Burgin siblings were the children of Benjamin Logan Burgin and Jane Dysart Burgin. (Courtesy of Rebecca Knupp.)

Henry Kyle (1820–1908) and Fanny York (1831–?) are seen on their wedding day in 1884, a year after the death of Kyle's first wife, Jemima. Kyle was a Confederate veteran who lost a leg in the war. The Kyles are buried in the old Ebenezer cemetery in Old Fort. The man behind the couple is believed to be the minister who performed the ceremony. (Courtesy of McDowell County Public Library.)

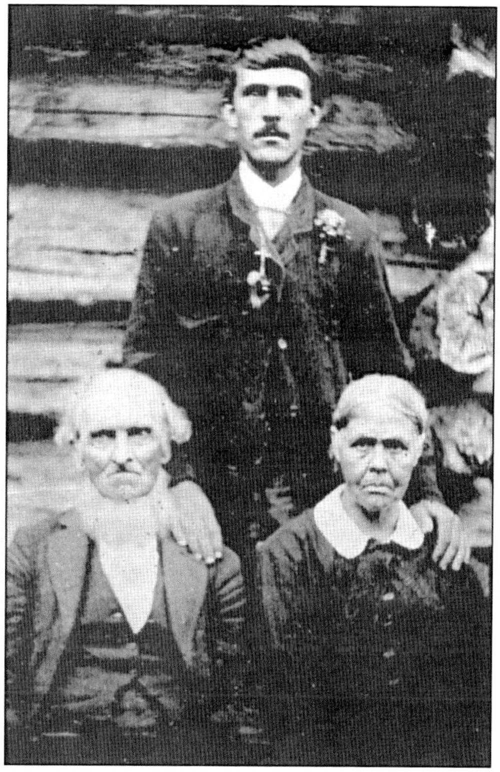

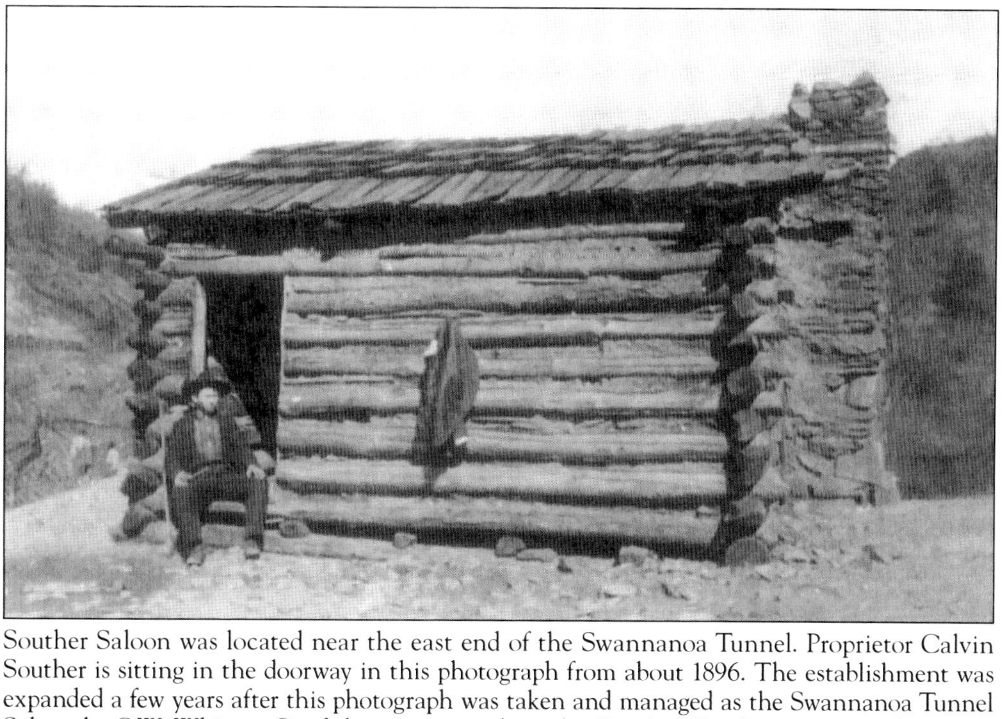

Souther Saloon was located near the east end of the Swannanoa Tunnel. Proprietor Calvin Souther is sitting in the doorway in this photograph from about 1896. The establishment was expanded a few years after this photograph was taken and managed as the Swannanoa Tunnel Saloon by C.W. White, a Confederate veteran from the Crooked Creek community. (Courtesy of Bill Nichols.)

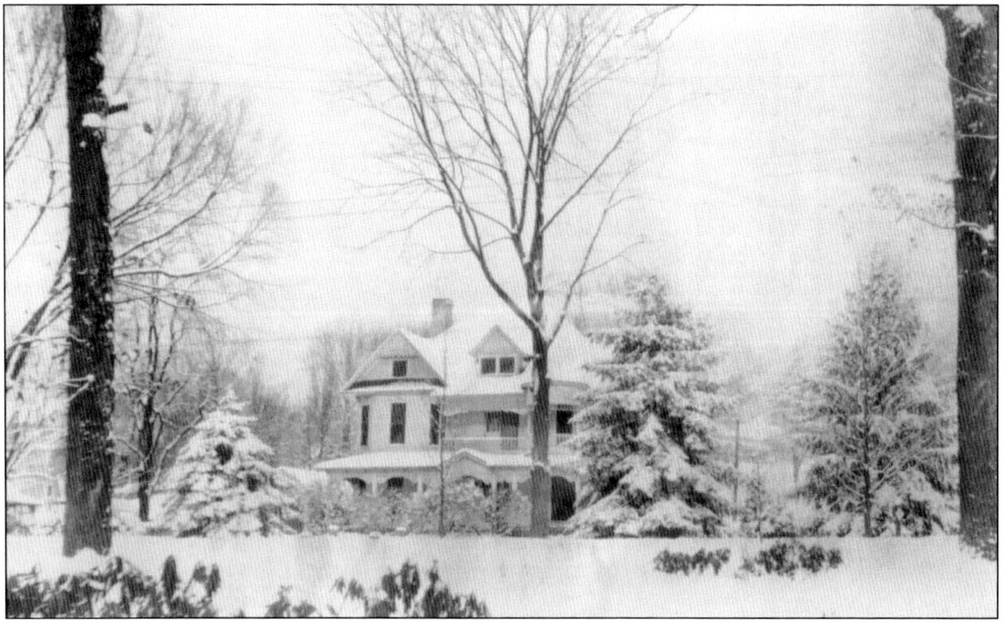

The Mashburn-Weaver house was built on Main Street in 1900 and originally owned by P.H. Mashburn. He was an Old Fort businessman and banker, McDowell County sheriff, and member of the North Carolina Legislature. Madeline Mashburn Weaver was born in the house and lived there her entire life. It was torn down in the early 1990s. (Courtesy of Nada Carroll.)

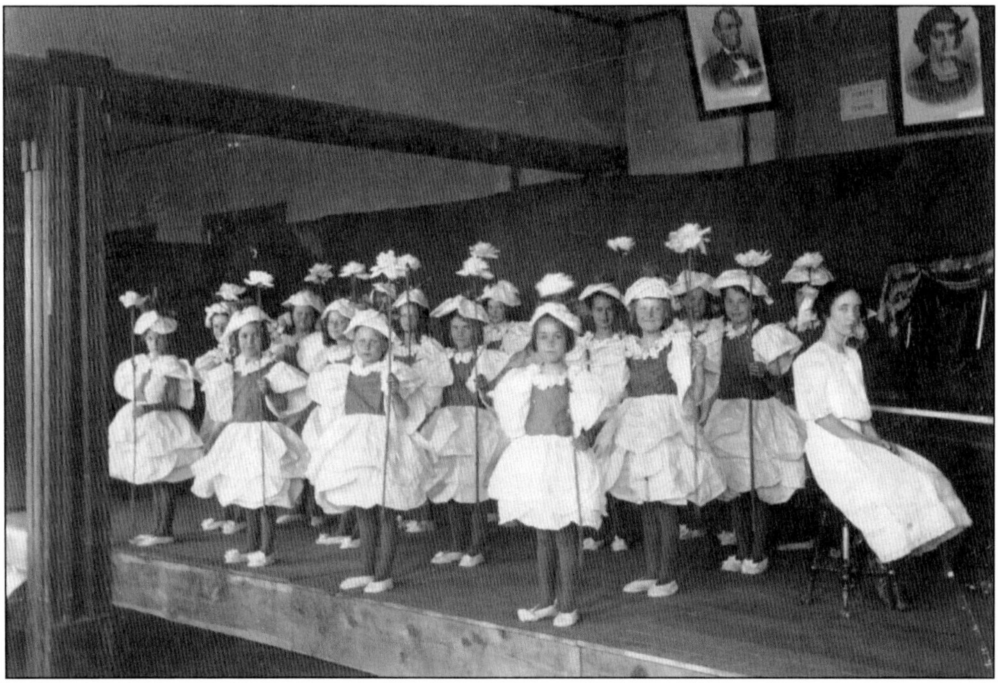

Madeline Mashburn (right) is pictured here with a group of aspiring young entertainers in the auditorium of Old Fort School. Madeline was the daughter of P.H. Mashburn, and she is remembered as a talented musician and an excellent teacher. A sign on the wall behind the girls reminds students to "obey your teacher." (Courtesy of Rebecca Knupp.)

The man at left in front of the Bank of Old Fort is Dr. D.M. McIntosh Sr., when he first started practicing in Old Fort. At center is Professor Jenkins, a teacher at Old Fort School. At right is banker and postmaster Fred Bradley. (Courtesy of McDowell County Public Library, Old Fort Branch.)

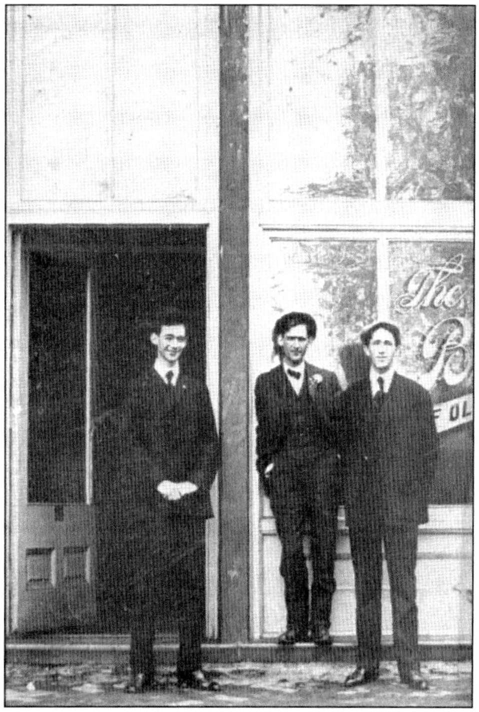

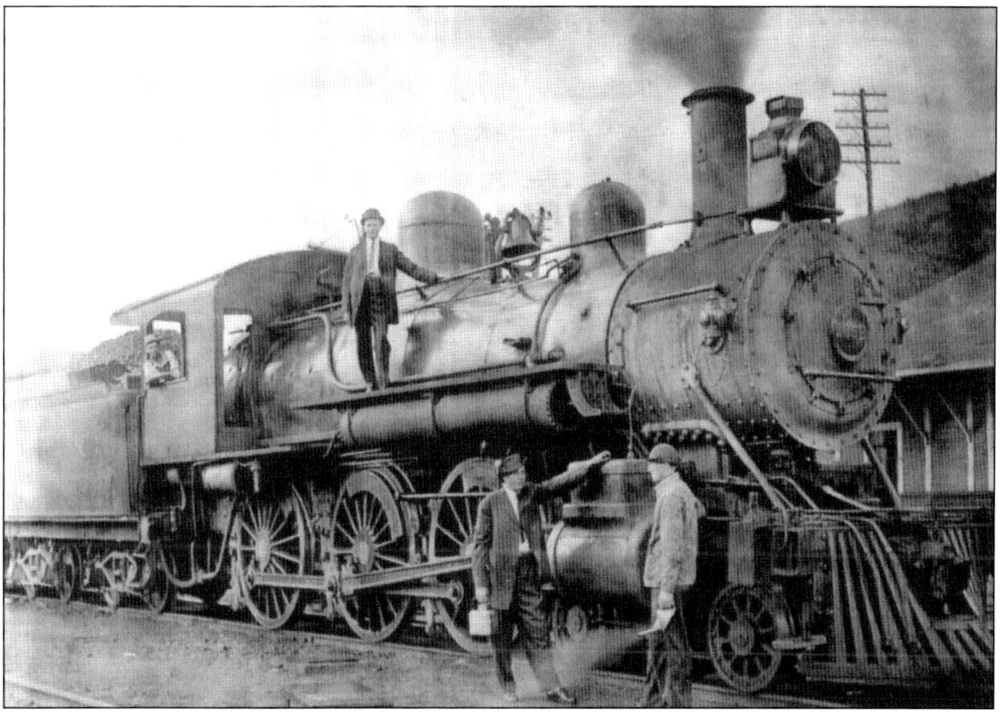

A Southern Railway steam engine pauses at the Old Fort depot on its way east from Asheville. Railroad inspector James Smith stands on the engine, and the engineer leaning out the window is R. Lee Jordan. The men on the ground are unidentified. (Courtesy of McDowell County Public Library.)

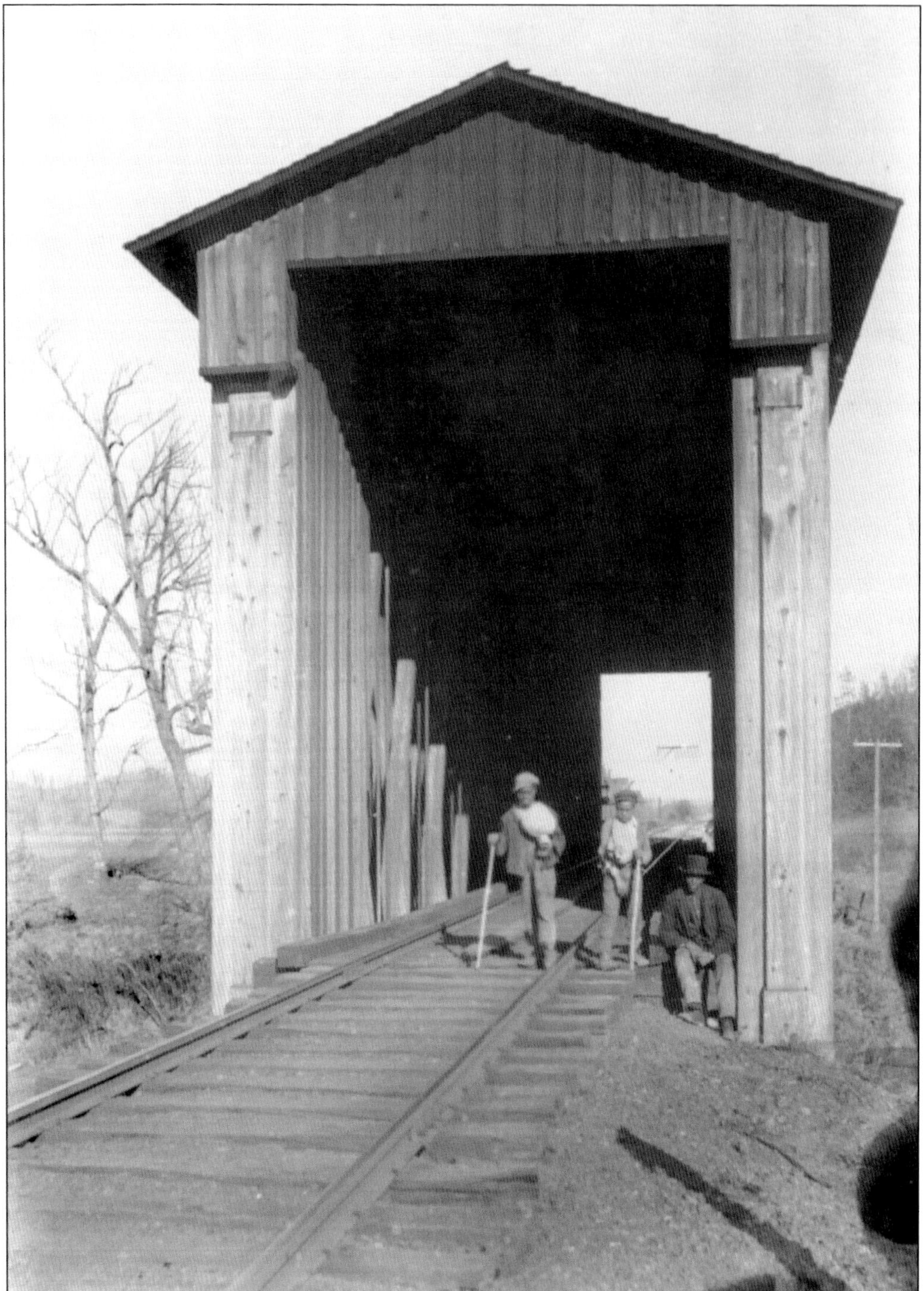

This covered bridge in Greenlee over the Catawba River was built around 1870 by the Western North Carolina Railroad, and it was the only covered railroad bridge to be constructed in McDowell County. This bridge was torn down and replaced by an iron bridge in 1910. The man sitting down is Lewis Fenister. The children are unidentified. (Courtesy of Mountain Gateway Museum.)

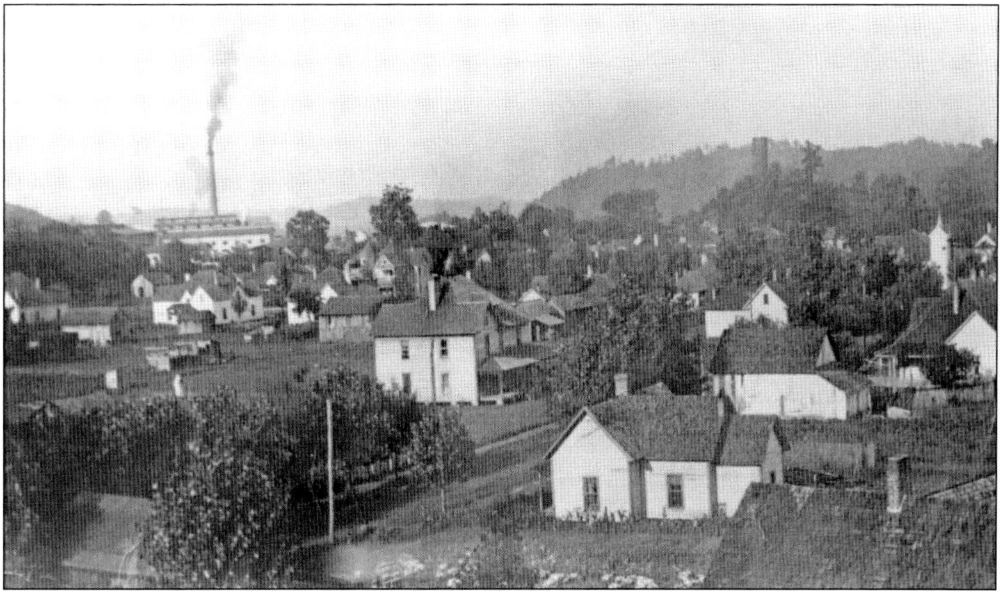

In this 1906 view of Old Fort looking south, the Union Tannery and its smokestack can be seen in the background to the left. The municipal water tower is to the right. The photographer's vantage point is approximately at the present-day location of Interstate 40, looking toward Mauney Avenue. (Courtesy of Mountain Gateway Museum.)

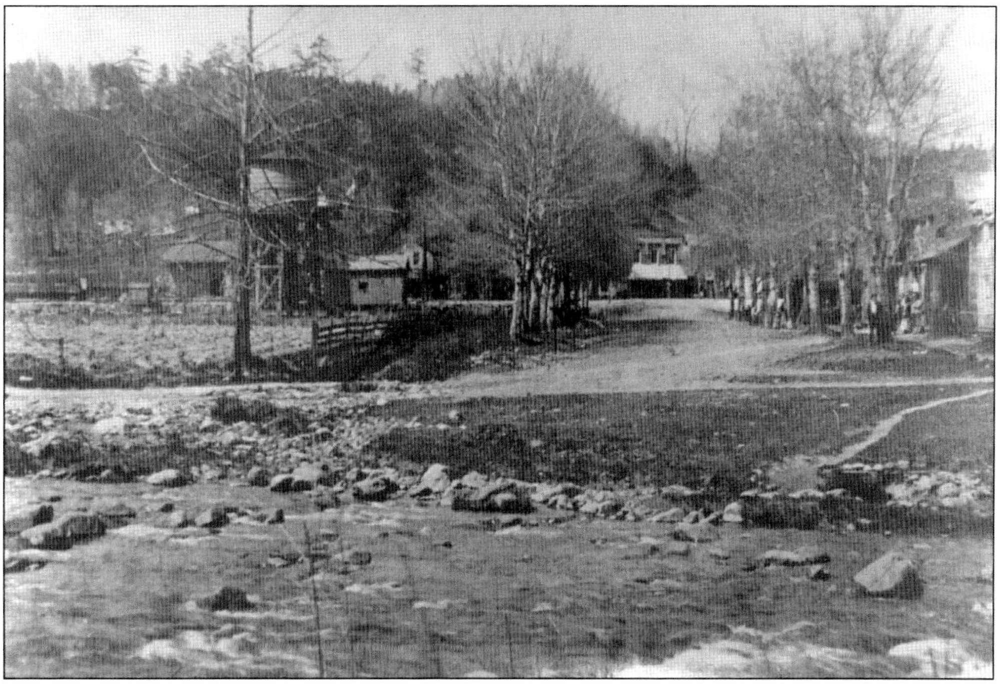

The photographer of this early-1900s image was standing on Catawba Avenue looking north, with Mill Creek in the foreground. The Mashburn Building, housing the Bank of Old Fort, is straight ahead at the end of Catawba Avenue. The water tank for the railroad steam engines is to the left. Trains had to make a water stop about every 125 miles. (Courtesy of Mountain Gateway Museum.)

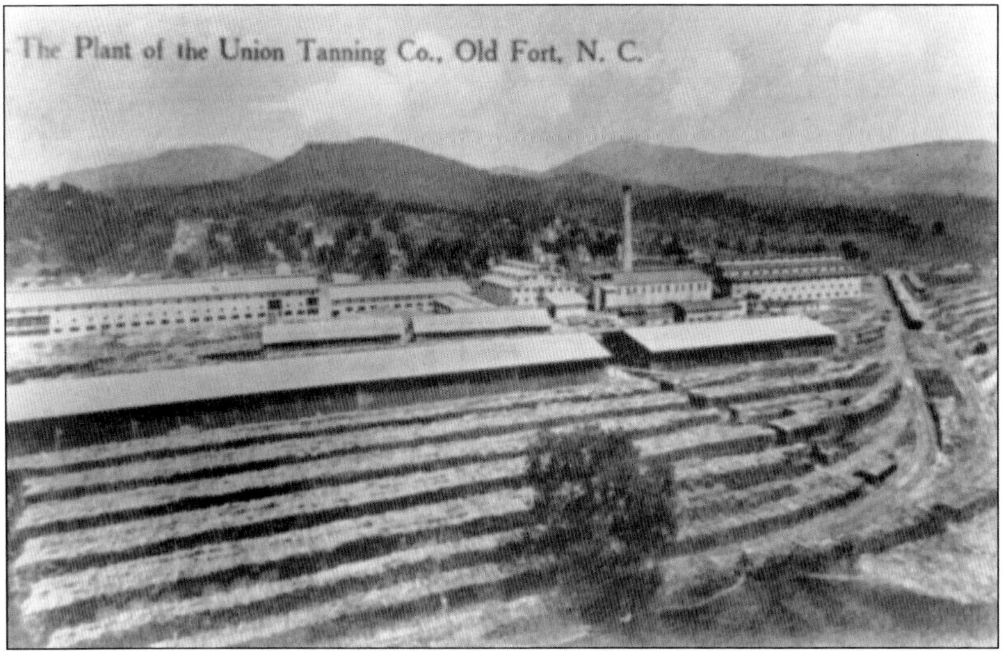

The Union Tanning Company, a branch of United Leather Company, constructed tannery and extraction plants in Old Fort in 1905. W.P Artz of Nova Scotia, Canada, was superintendent of the tannery for 23 years. At the peak of its operation, the tannery employed over 400 men and was one of the largest such operations in the world. (Courtesy of Mountain Gateway Museum.)

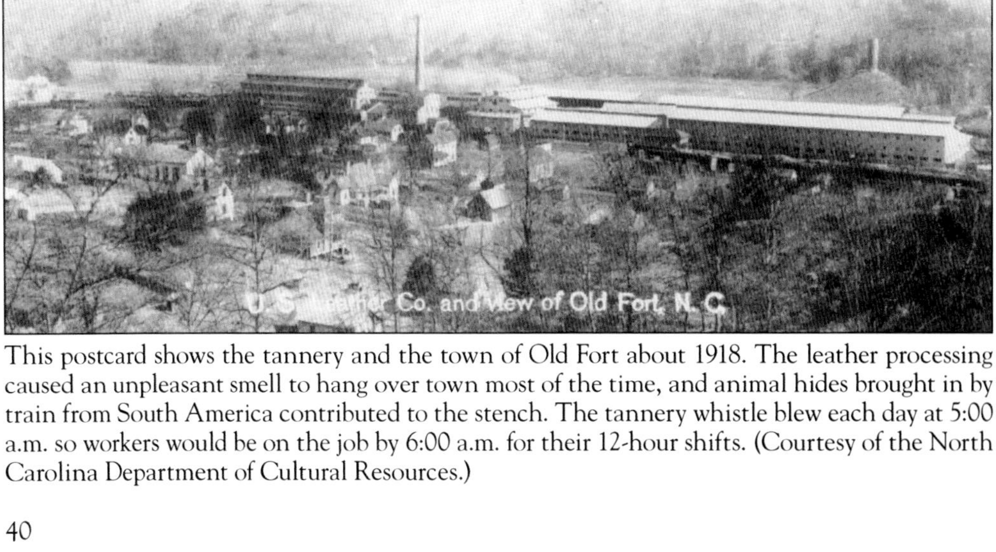

This postcard shows the tannery and the town of Old Fort about 1918. The leather processing caused an unpleasant smell to hang over town most of the time, and animal hides brought in by train from South America contributed to the stench. The tannery whistle blew each day at 5:00 a.m. so workers would be on the job by 6:00 a.m. for their 12-hour shifts. (Courtesy of the North Carolina Department of Cultural Resources.)

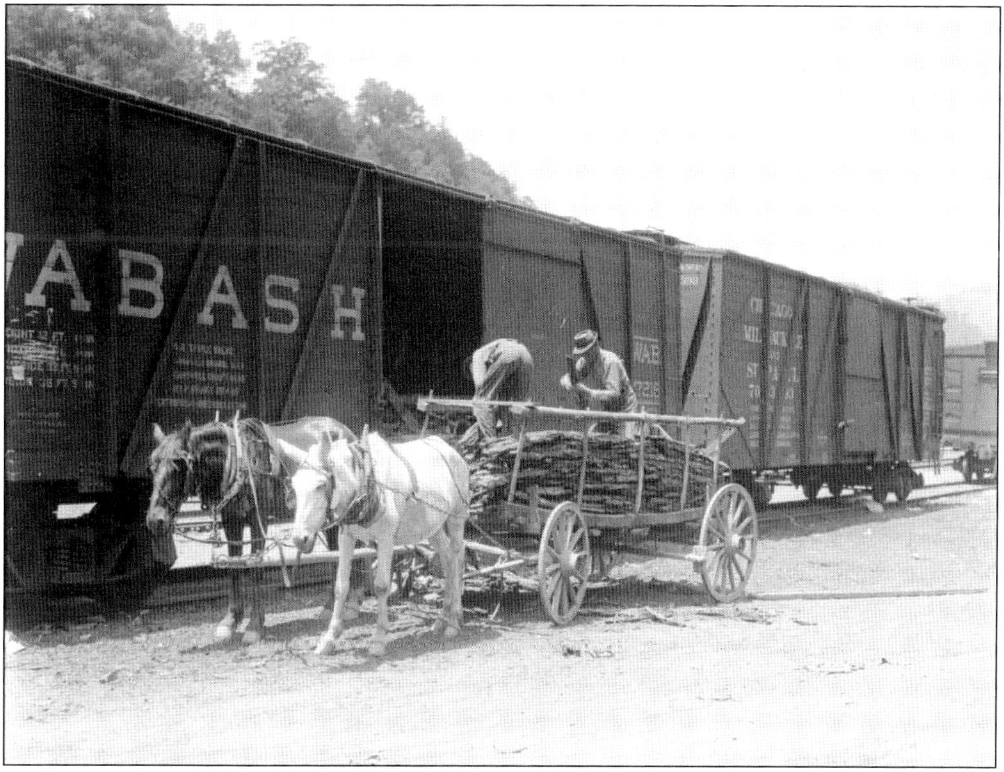

The Union Tannery also created jobs for people who were not on its payroll. These men are loading tanbark onto a train so that it can be transported and sold to the tannery. There, prepared animal hides will be soaked in the tannic acid extracted from the bark. The tannery's demand for tanbark greatly impacted forests in the Old Fort area. (Courtesy of Mountain Gateway Museum.)

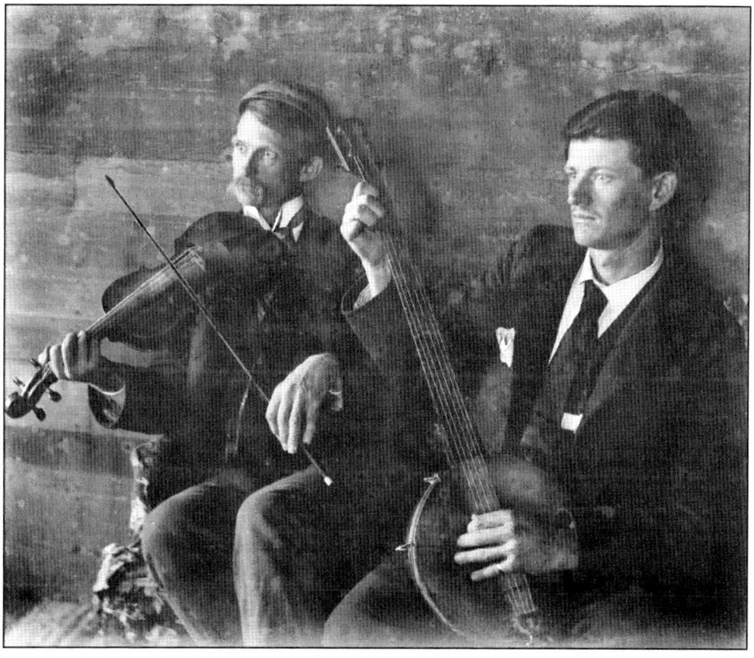

Brothers Thomas Logan Tate (left) and John Reid Tate (right) of the Greenlee community pose with fiddle and banjo around 1900. This photograph was taken by Robert Lee Greenlee and is from a series of glass-plate negatives that were handed down through the Greenlee family. (Courtesy of Historic Carson House.)

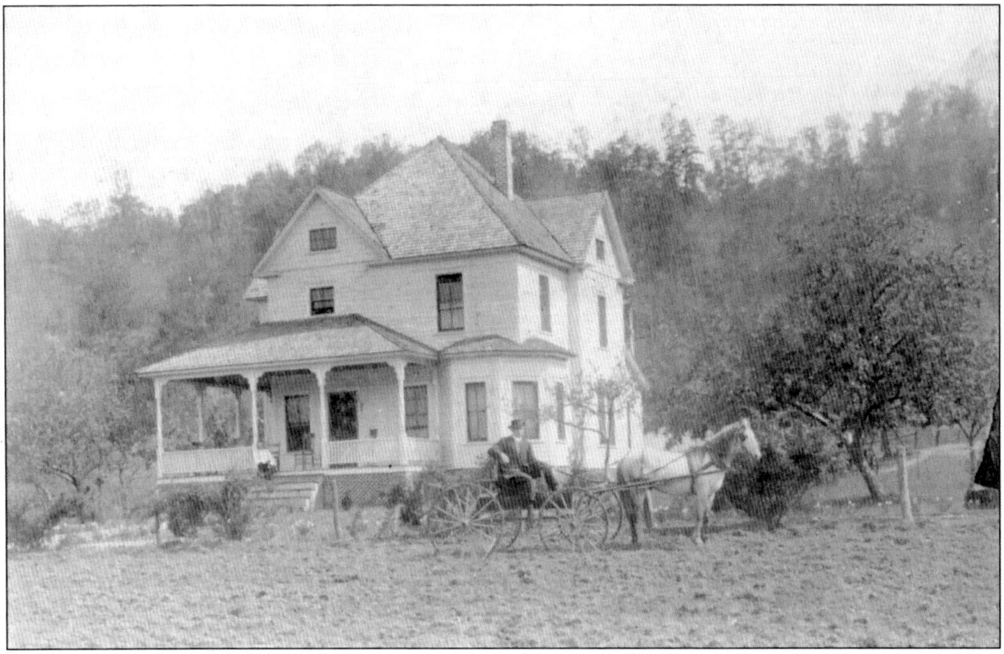

William Pitt Terrell, who was a train engineer for the Western North Carolina Railroad, built this home around 1907 on what is now Catawba River Road. His wife, Ada, helped design the farmhouse, which was built by a Mr. Harvey from Old Fort. Sadly, Ada died shortly before it was completed. Terrell and their children moved in alone. (Courtesy of Nada Carroll.)

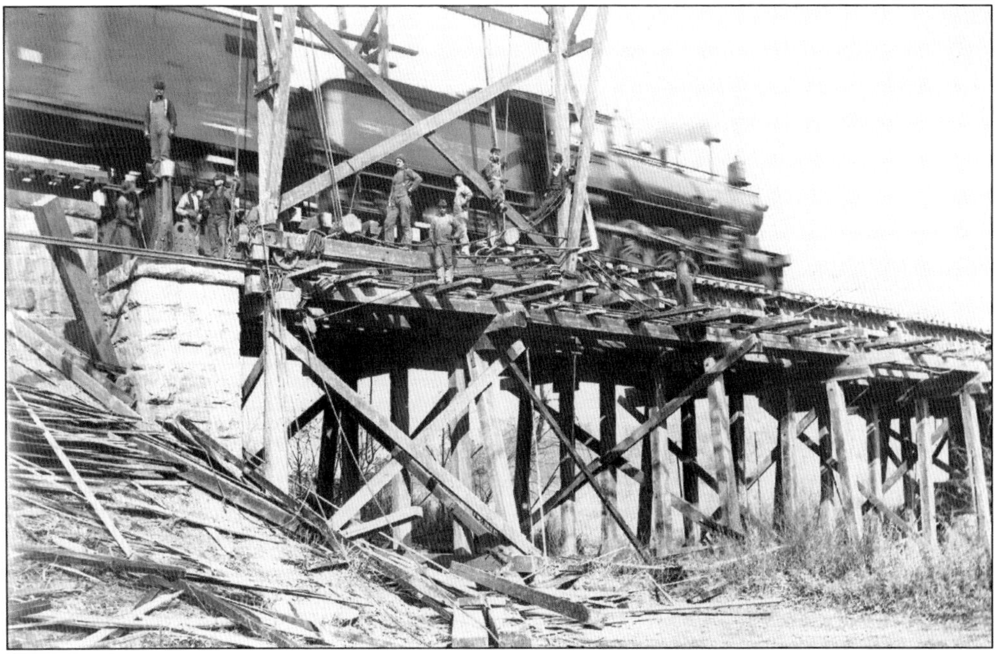

Robert Lee Greenlee took several photographs in 1910 documenting the tearing down of the old covered railroad bridge over the Catawba River in Greenlee and the construction of its iron replacement. Here, the workers pause to make way for a passing Southern Railway train. (Courtesy of Historic Carson House.)

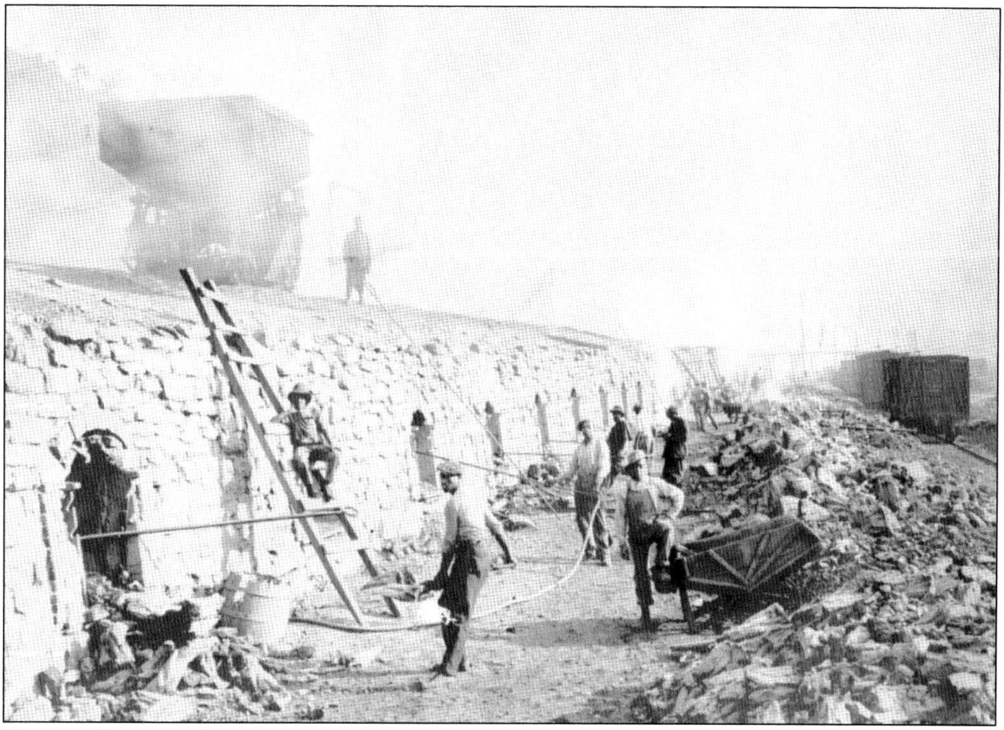

This graphite mine located above Round Knob gave the community of Graphite, or Graphiteville, its name. Graphite was extracted by hand and moved out on carts along small tracks. With the advent of the railroad, a side track was built to help move the extracted graphite. A kyanite mine also operated just above the graphite mine. (Courtesy of Mountain Gateway Museum.)

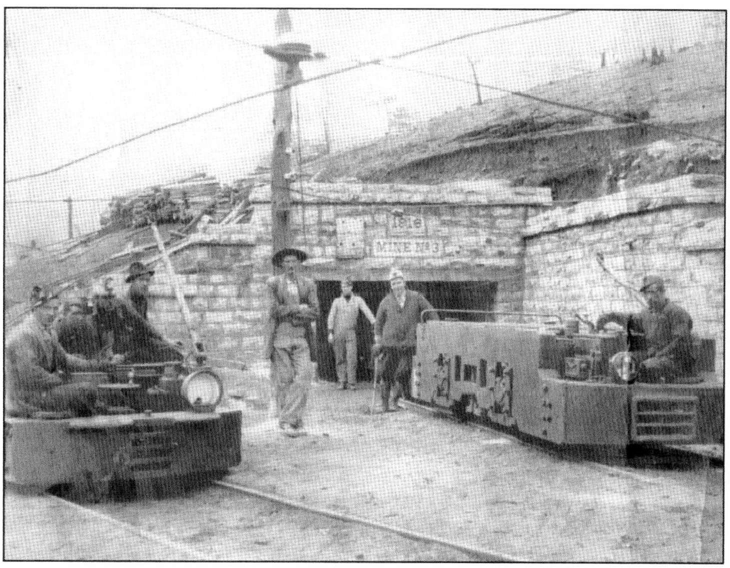

After the mine was depleted, the Graphite community continued to grow because of its location on the railroad line. Logging was also an important industry in Graphite, as is evidenced by the bare hillside in this photograph. Timber was moved down Mill Creek via a large flume. (Courtesy of Mountain Gateway Museum.)

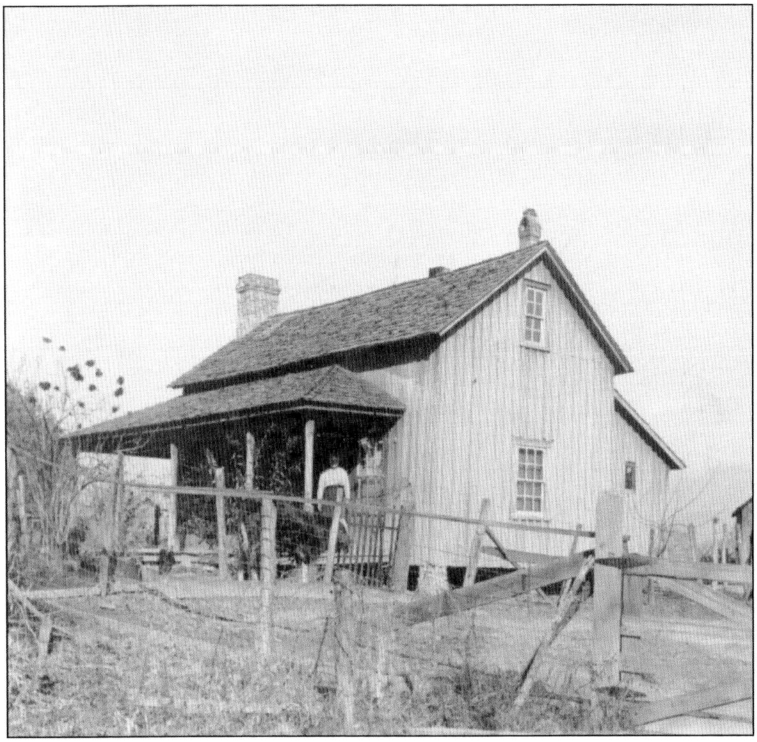

The Guthrie place was located on Moffitt Branch Road, and a Mr. Guthrie was a blacksmith. Around 1910, Bascam Lamar Lunsford and his family stayed at this house while Lunsford was teaching school. In off hours, Lunsford avidly collected traditional folk songs. He became a renowned folklorist and helped establish the Mountain Dance and Folk Festival, which has been held in Asheville since 1927. (Courtesy of Nada Carroll.)

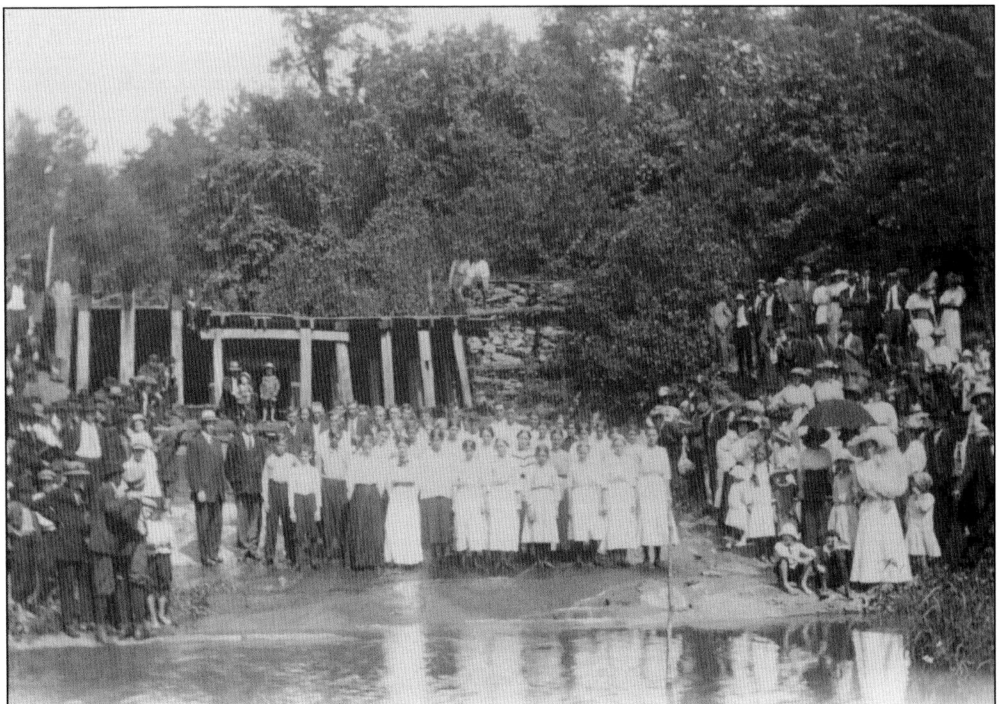

This baptism took place at the old millpond on Little Creek about 1900. Located in the Crooked Creek community, the site is near present-day Pine Cove Road. (Courtesy of Peggy Silvers.)

A familiar sight in the old days was postal employee Tyke L. Nichols (1873–1936) transporting the mail by pushcart back and forth between the Old Fort Post Office and the Southern Railway depot. Out-of-town mail was carried aboard mail cars on the train. Congress had designated all railroads as official postal routes in 1838. (Courtesy of Bill Nichols.)

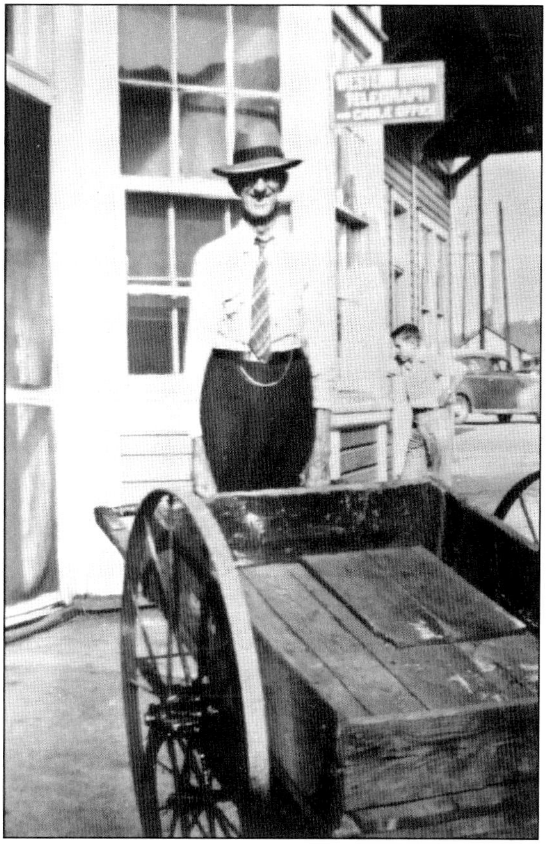

This runaway train derailed near Old Fort in 1903. Locals who came out to view the wreckage are, from left to right, Dave Arney, Maude Sides, Claude Vess, Joe Hemphill, Henry Wilson, Maggie Himes, and Fannie Hawkins. The young boys are unidentified. (Courtesy of Mountain Gateway Museum.)

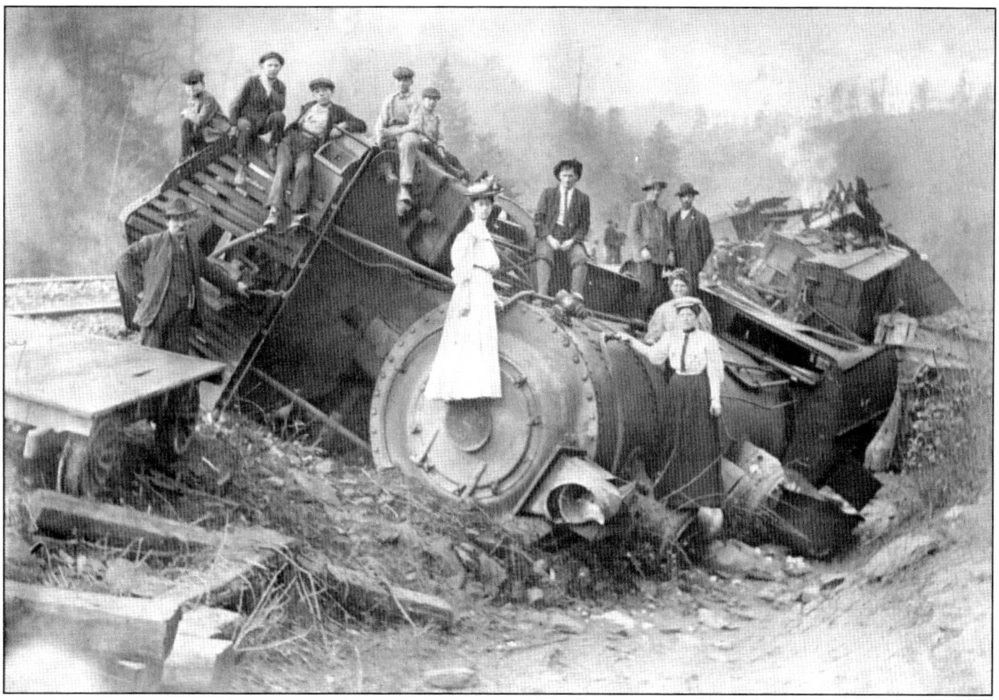

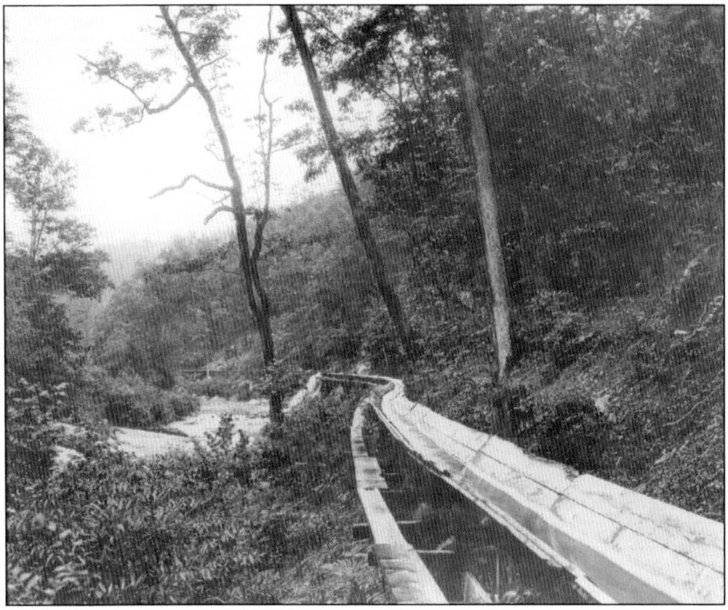

Photographed around 1912, this flume along Curtis Creek was used to float logs 11 miles downstream to the tannery in Old Fort. The planks alongside the flume were for log jammers to walk beside the flume. They monitored the flow of logs and freed any that became crossed. The flume had an average drop of eight to ten feet every 100 linear feet. (Courtesy of Mountain Gateway Museum.)

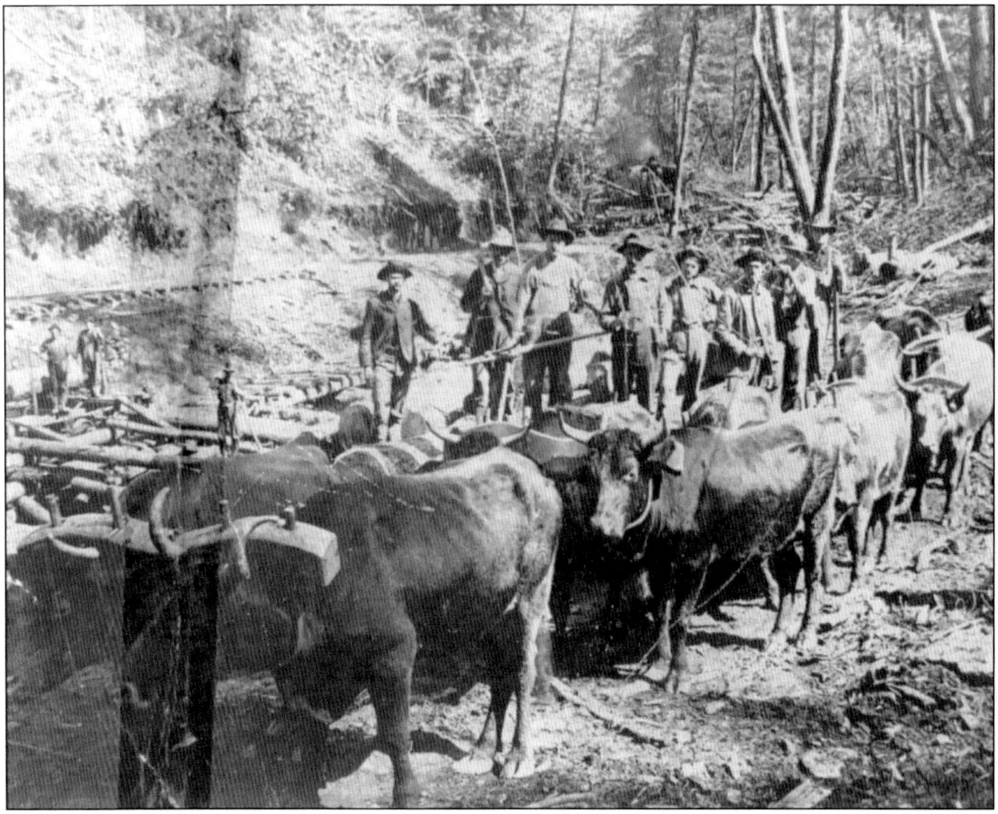

A logging crew and oxen take timber from the Curtis Creek watershed in the very early 1900s. At that time, about 70 percent of the trees in the Curtis Creek forest were chestnut, and 15 percent were oak. A few hemlocks grew along the banks of streams. Most of the virgin poplar trees had already been harvested. (Courtesy of Dee Daughtridge.)

After the introduction of machine-driven sawmills, timber harvesting became a major McDowell County industry. This steam-driven mill was in operation on Curtis Creek about 1912. In 1919, the Robert Noyes Land and Lumber Company began operations on Curtis Creek, employing 150 men and producing 80 cords of wood daily. (Courtesy of Mountain Gateway Museum.)

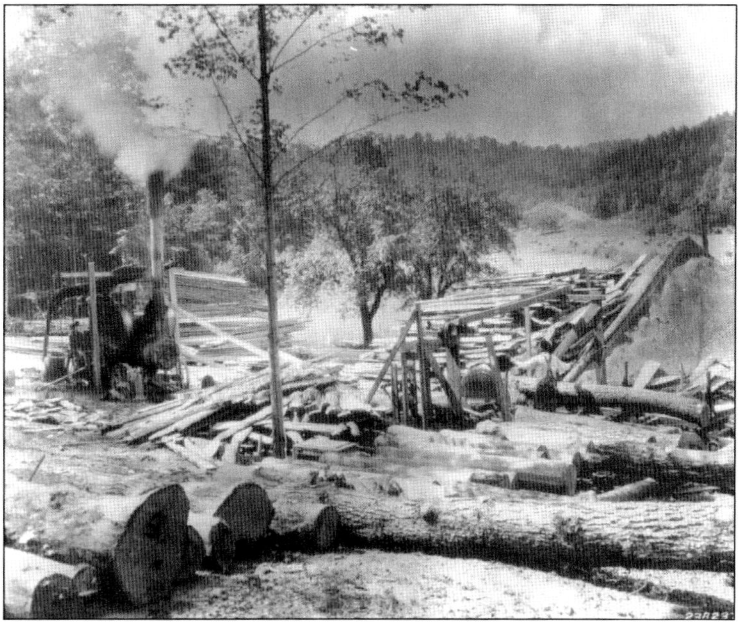

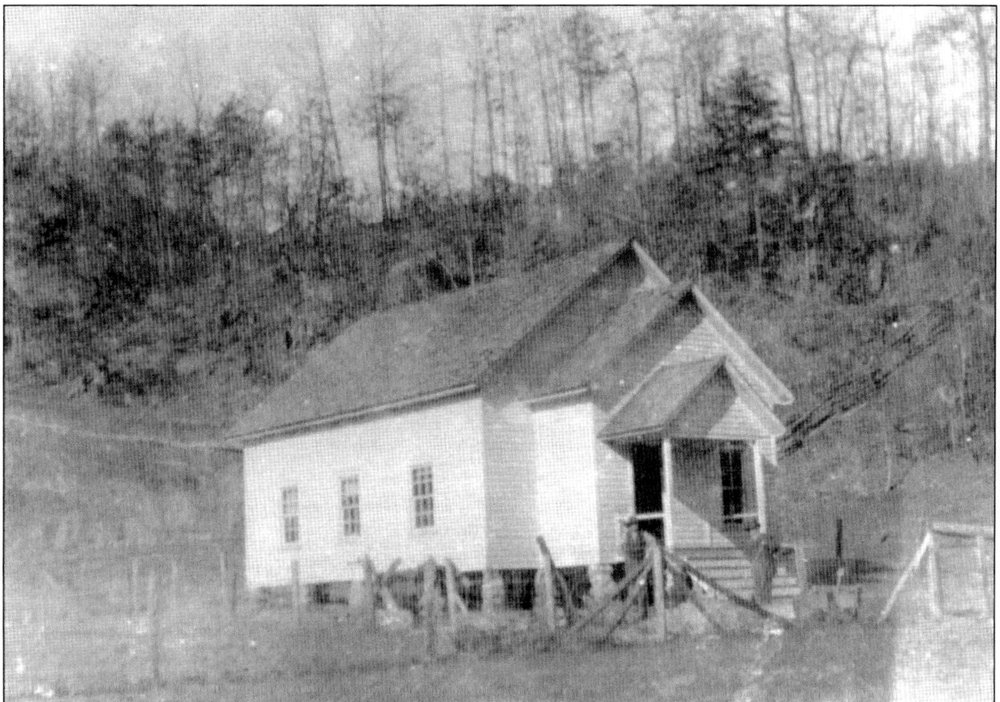

The Curtis Creek schoolhouse was built around 1910 by a Mr. Beach. Neighboring farmers provided wood for the potbellied stove, which was the building's only source of heat. Teachers included Delia Gibbs, Dora Gibbs, Anna McCall, Ada Lavender, Geneve Tisdale, Eula Pyatt, Sarah Collis Burnette, and Arwyn Steppe Allison. (Courtesy of Dee Daughtridge.)

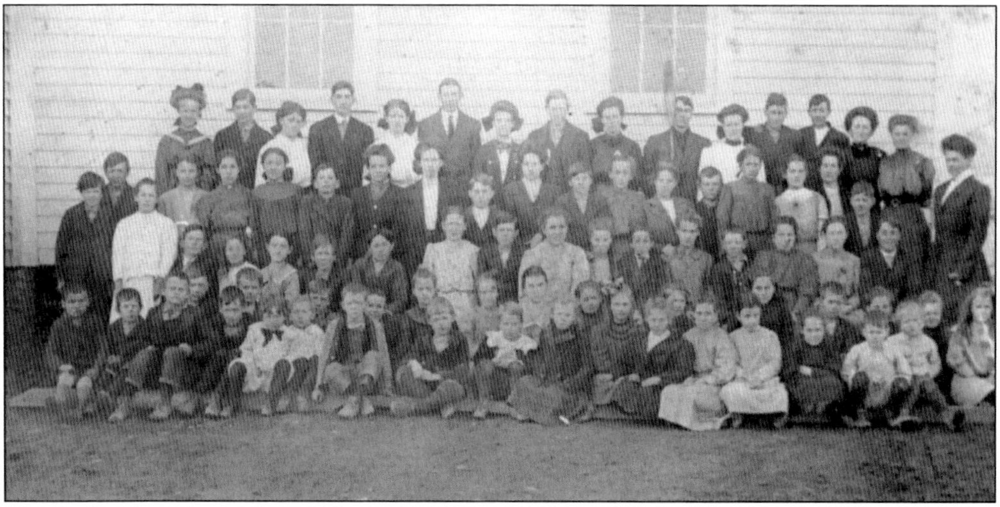

Teachers and students of Greenlee Public School are seen here in 1910. Teacher Maggie McCoy Tate is at far right. The students that have been identified are Joe Greenlee, first from left on the second row; Mabel Tate, first from left on the fourth row; Mattie Tate, seventh from left on the fourth row; and Thomas Greenlee, ninth from left on the fourth row. (Courtesy of Mountain Gateway Museum.)

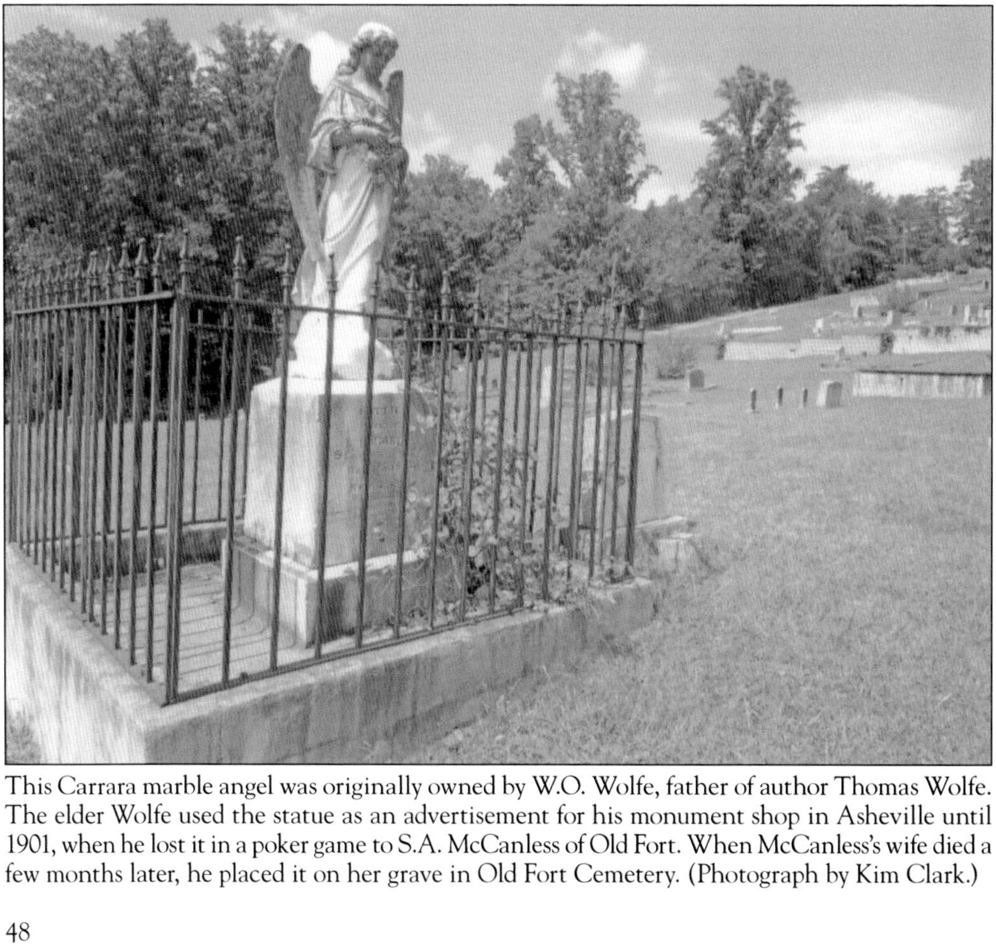

This Carrara marble angel was originally owned by W.O. Wolfe, father of author Thomas Wolfe. The elder Wolfe used the statue as an advertisement for his monument shop in Asheville until 1901, when he lost it in a poker game to S.A. McCanless of Old Fort. When McCanless's wife died a few months later, he placed it on her grave in Old Fort Cemetery. (Photograph by Kim Clark.)

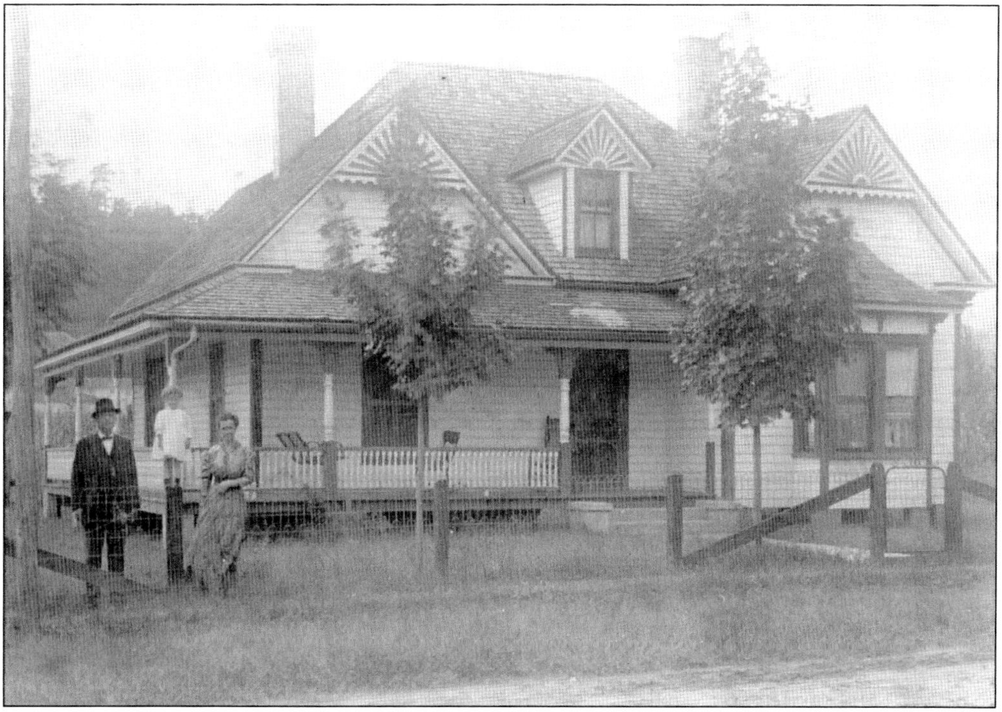

Columbus Straley Burgin, Roxie Hoyle Burgin, and their daughter Callie Jane are seen at their home on Mauney Avenue around 1914. C.S. Burgin was a conductor for the Southern Railway and was commonly known as "Cap" or "Cap'n Lum." (Courtesy of Nada Carroll.)

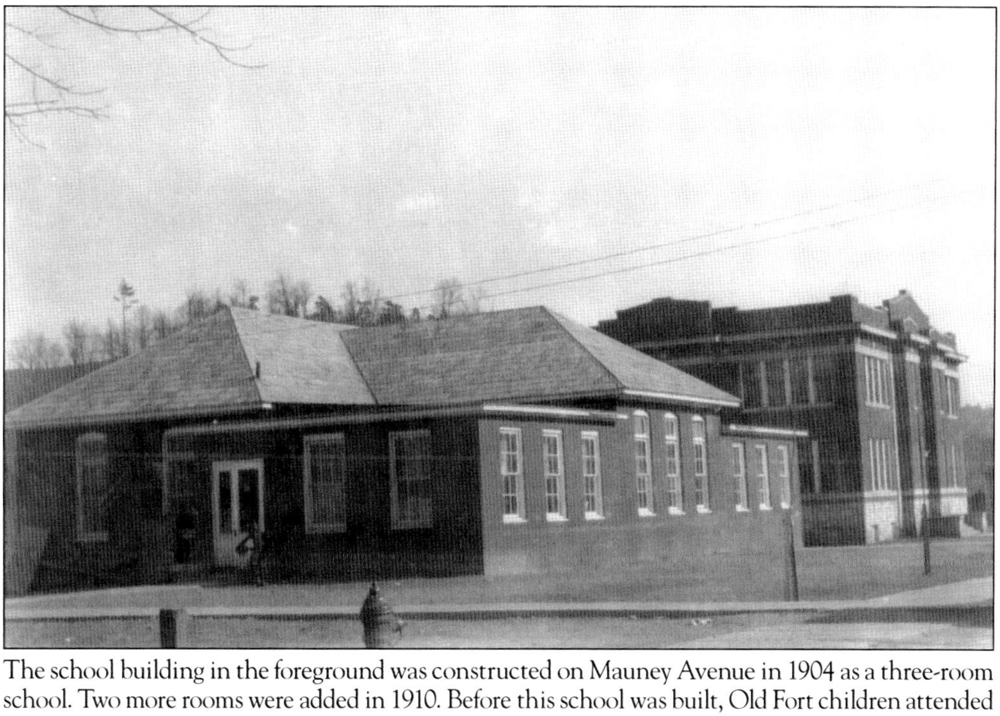

The school building in the foreground was constructed on Mauney Avenue in 1904 as a three-room school. Two more rooms were added in 1910. Before this school was built, Old Fort children attended Old Fort Academy, located on East Maple Street. (Courtesy of Mountain Gateway Museum.)

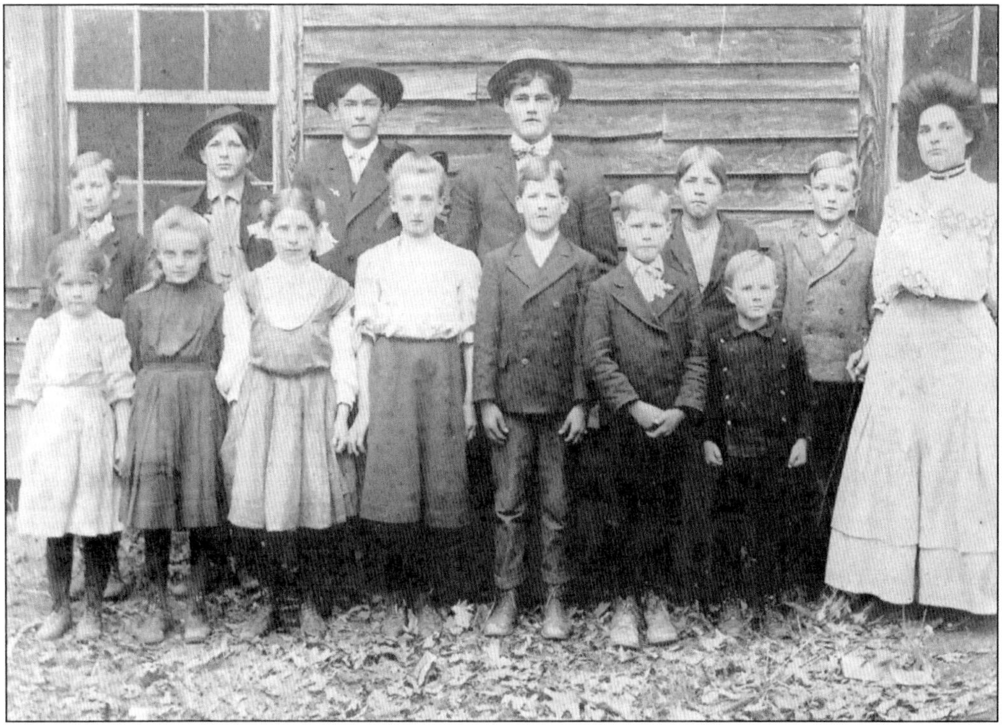

Teacher Mae Allison Porter is at right in this 1900 photograph taken at an unidentified Old Fort school. Porter later taught returning World War II veterans at Glenwood School. (Courtesy of Mountain Gateway Museum.)

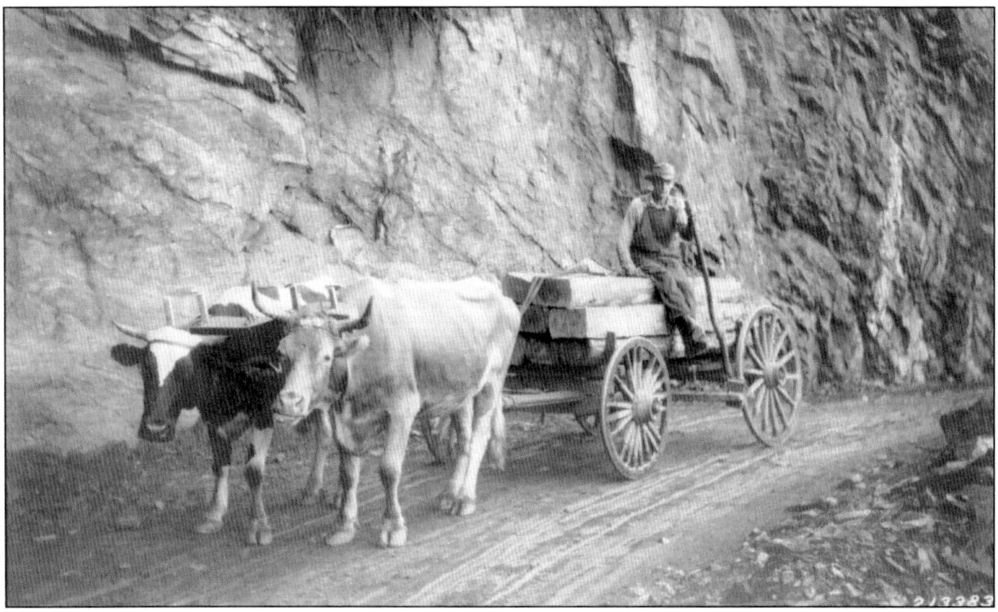

The presence of the railroad and abundant timber in the area offered opportunities for locals to earn money trading with the Southern Railway. A man who was skilled with an ax could make eight crossties in a day. It would generally take another day to haul them into town to sell to the railroad. The railroad paid 25¢ for each crosstie. (Courtesy of Mountain Gateway Museum.)

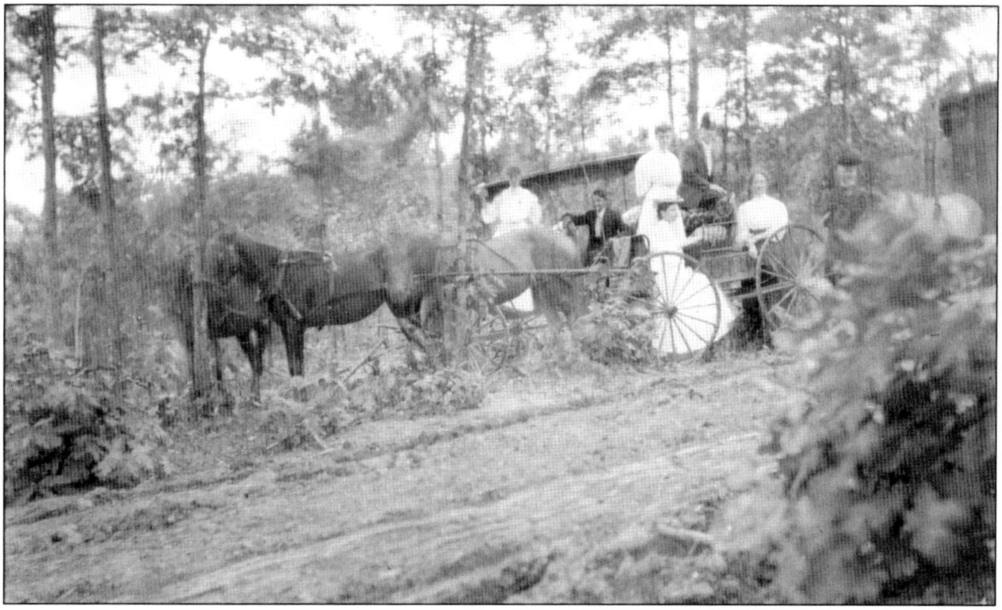

An unidentified group pauses during a Sunday outing in the Old Fort area in the early 1900s. The primitive condition of the road on which they are traveling was common for county thoroughfares at the time. (Courtesy of McDowell County Public Library.)

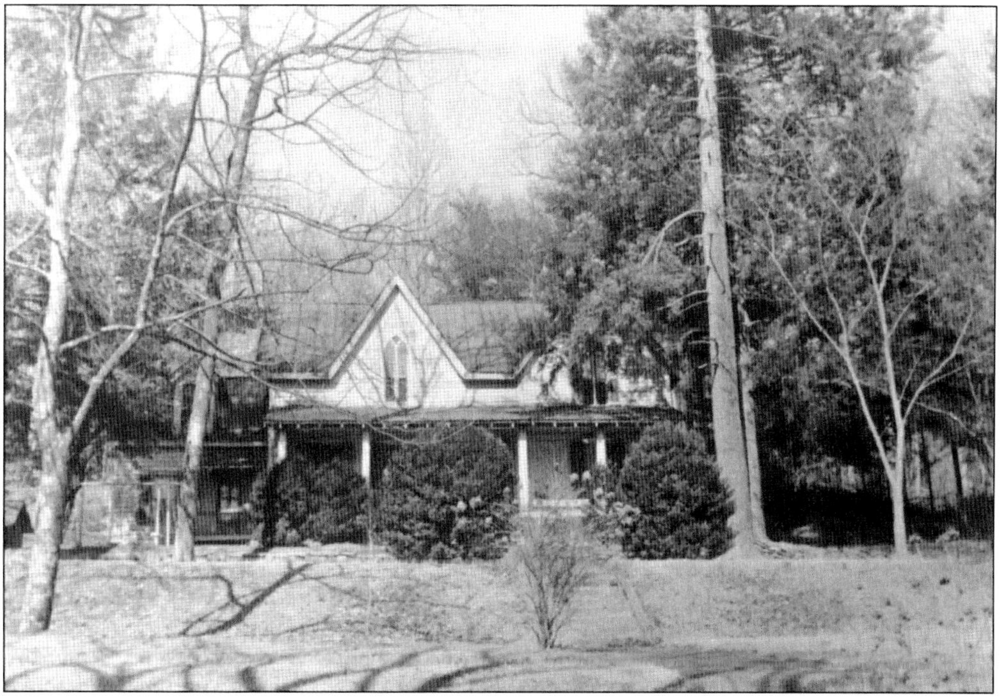

This Gothic Revival cottage became the home of Henry and Ella Dula Westerman around 1880. It stands on a hillside overlooking the railroad depot and was originally used by the Westermans as a summer retreat from the Wilmington heat. They were one of many German families that had immigrated to the North Carolina coast in the 1840s and 1850s. The Westermans eventually became full-time Old Fort residents. (Courtesy of Mountain Gateway Museum.)

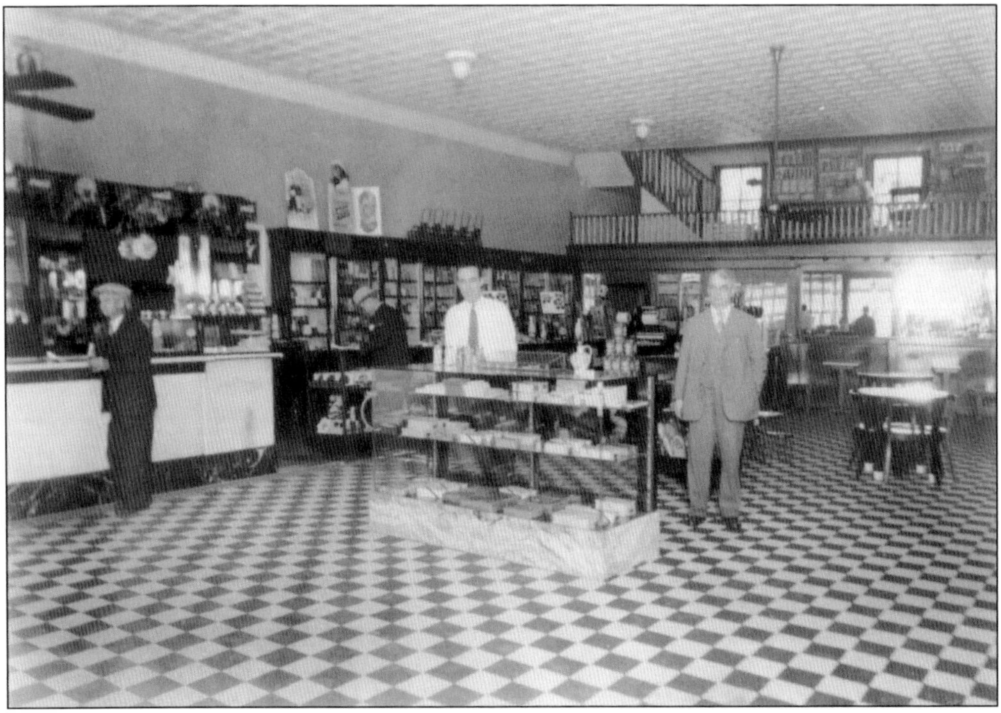

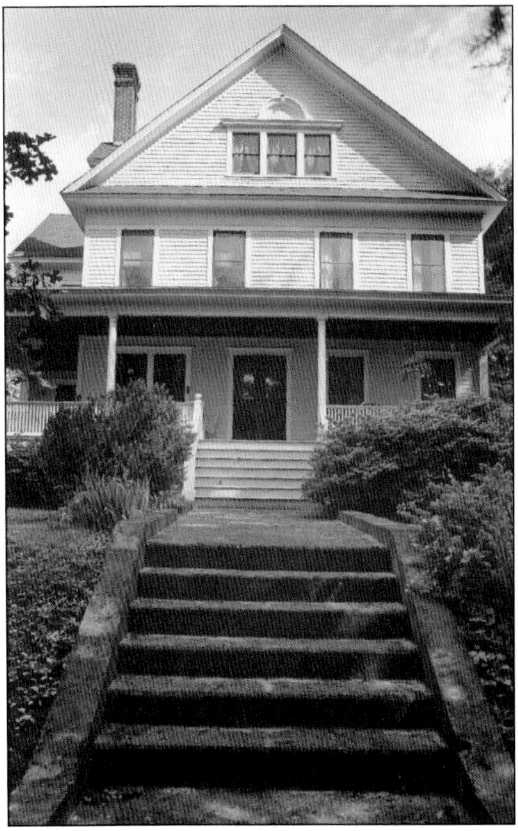

Old Fort Drug Store, located on Main Street, was operated by P.H. Mashburn. It was a popular gathering place for young people in the years after World War II. Nickel sodas, spacious booths, and permission to dance to songs from a well-stocked jukebox were prime attractions. Pictured here are, from left to right, Eddie Ragle, Doctor McIntosh, Gayden Swann, and "Doc" McMillan. (Courtesy of Bill Nichols.)

Also known as Catawba Hill, the Artz House was built around 1905 for Welsford Parker Artz, supervisor for the US Leather Company tannery located in Old Fort. It was designed by F.J. Lindsey and Son of New York and was one of the first homes in town to have running water. The Artz House is listed in the National Register of Historic Places. (Courtesy of Nada Carroll.)

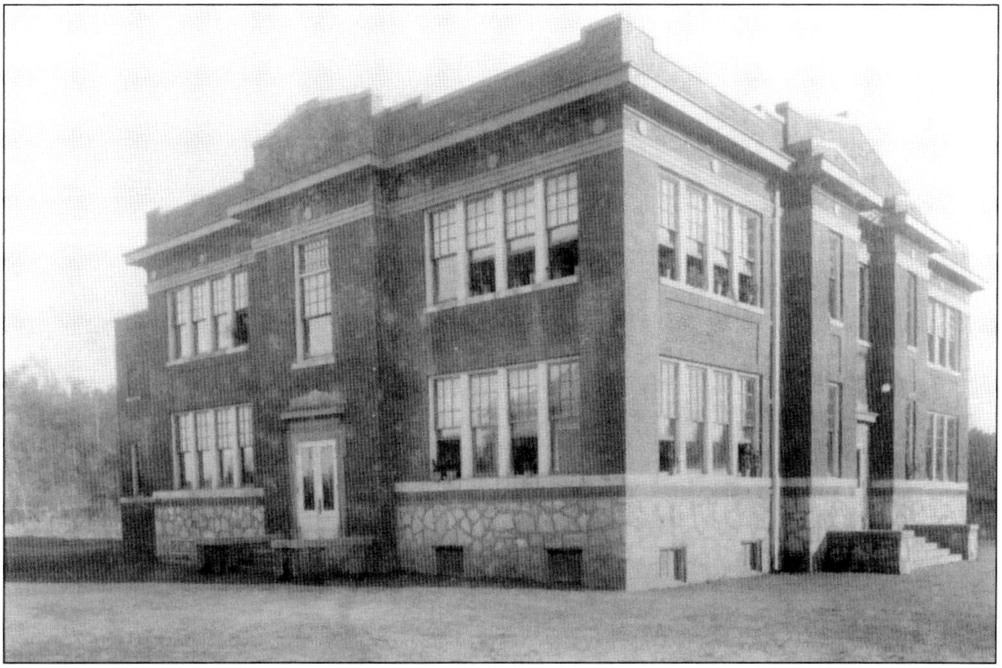

The school building seen here was constructed on Mauney Avenue in 1915. It was damaged by fire in 1923, rebuilt in 1924, and expanded in 1929. It had 20 classrooms, a library, science rooms, and an 800-seat auditorium. It became known as Old Fort Grammar School after a new high school building was constructed. This building was razed in 1991. (Courtesy of Historic Carson House Library.)

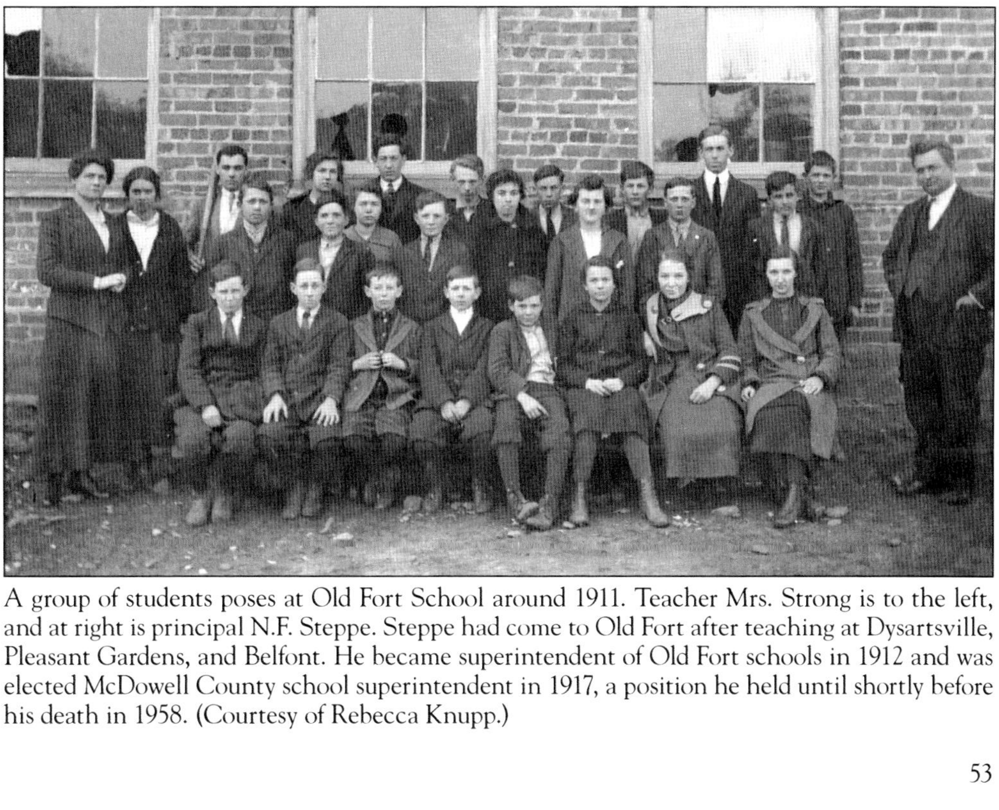

A group of students poses at Old Fort School around 1911. Teacher Mrs. Strong is to the left, and at right is principal N.F. Steppe. Steppe had come to Old Fort after teaching at Dysartsville, Pleasant Gardens, and Belfont. He became superintendent of Old Fort schools in 1912 and was elected McDowell County school superintendent in 1917, a position he held until shortly before his death in 1958. (Courtesy of Rebecca Knupp.)

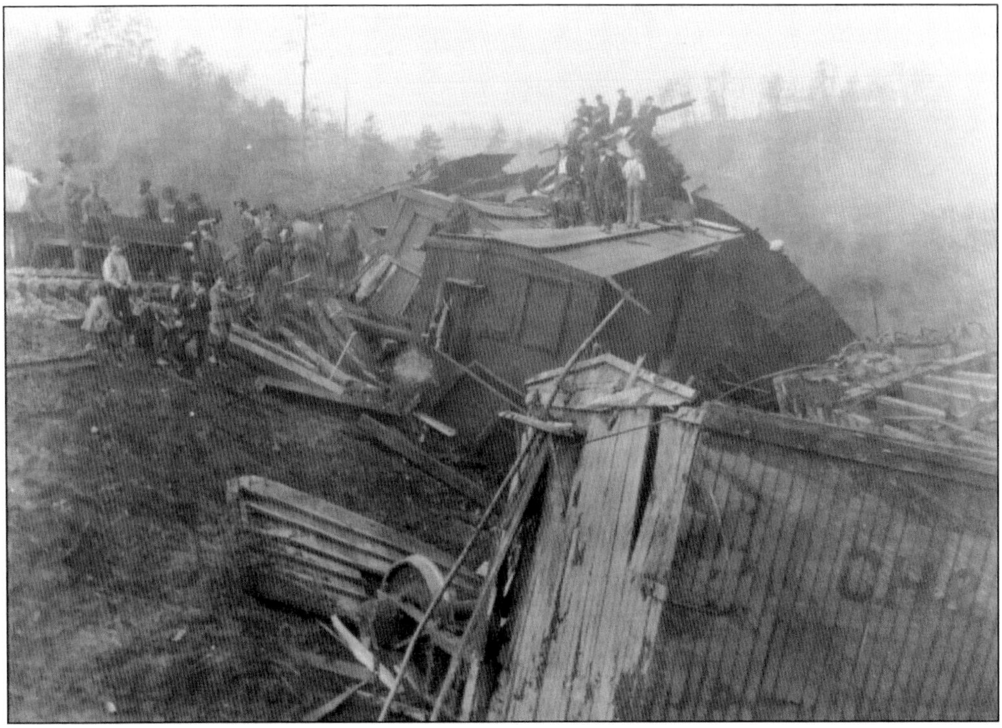

This runaway train jumped the track near Point Tunnel in 1906. Three men were killed, and 21 freight cars derailed. Later, helper engines were used to reduce the risk of runaway trains by helping to control the speed of their descent down from Ridgecrest. The helpers were also used to push westbound trains to the top of the grade. (Courtesy of Mountain Gateway Museum.)

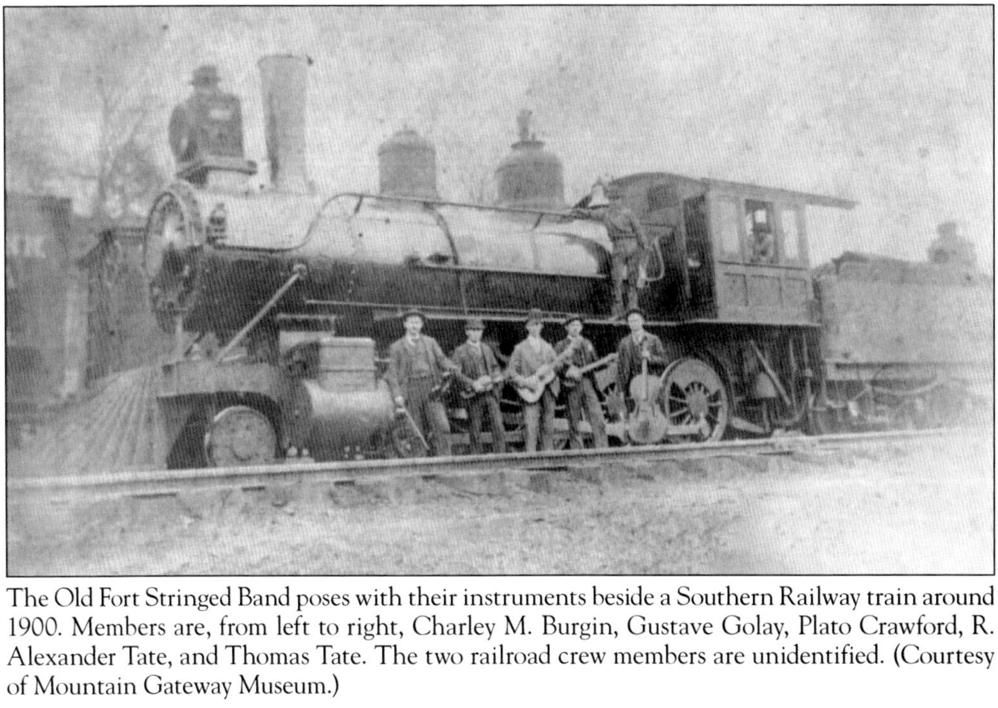

The Old Fort Stringed Band poses with their instruments beside a Southern Railway train around 1900. Members are, from left to right, Charley M. Burgin, Gustave Golay, Plato Crawford, R. Alexander Tate, and Thomas Tate. The two railroad crew members are unidentified. (Courtesy of Mountain Gateway Museum.)

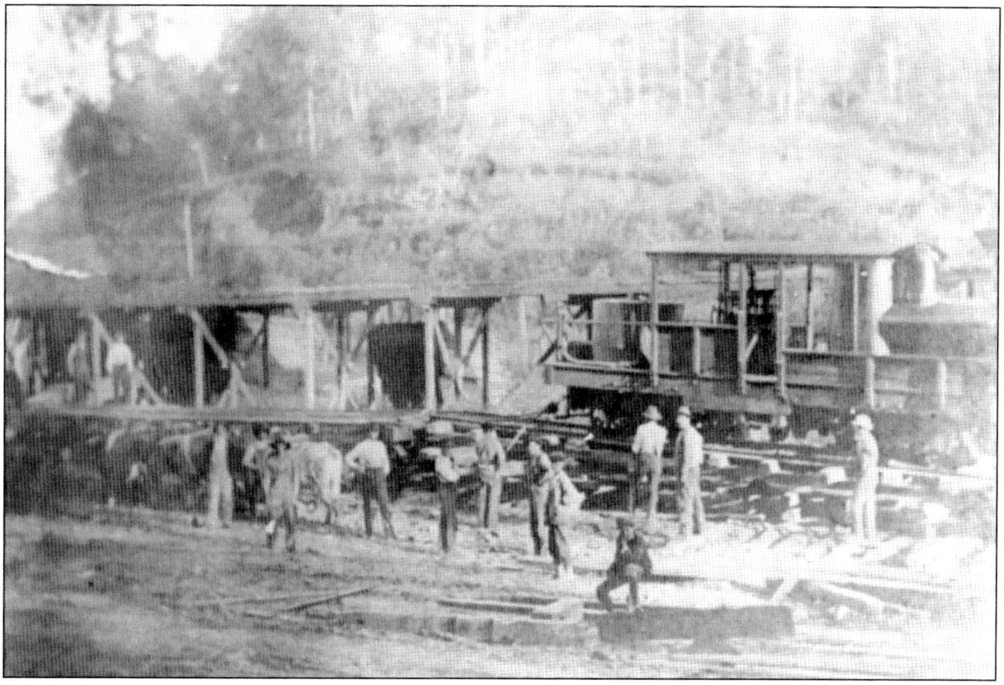

A steam engine is being unloaded from a Southern Railway car at Eberman in the Greenlee community. The engine would be used to transport logs from surrounding forests to the Eberman Lumber Company mill. (Courtesy of Mountain Gateway Museum.)

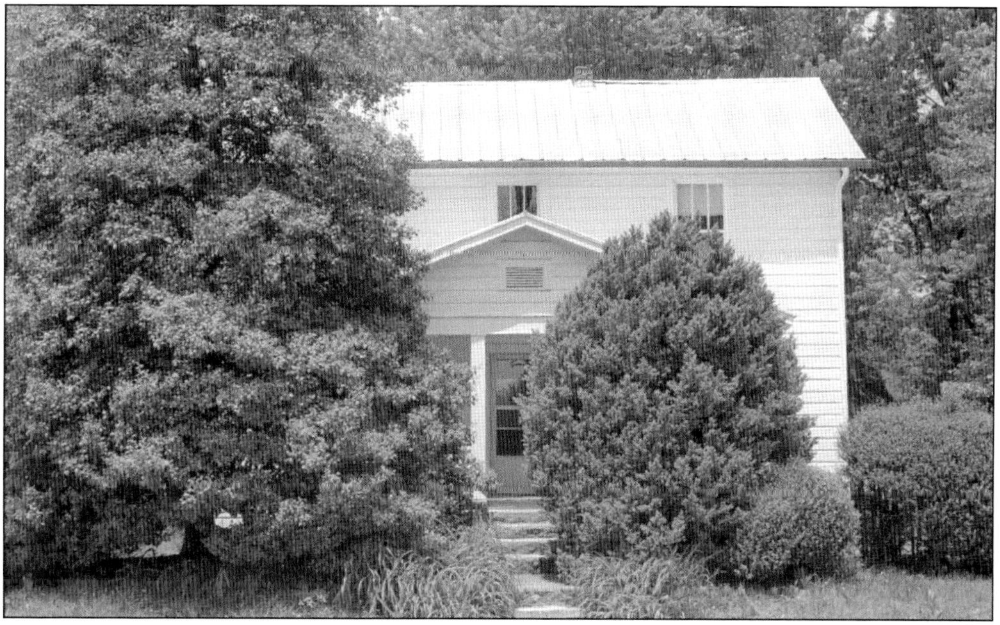

The Finch House was located on the northeast corner of Cemetery and East Main Streets and was built around 1880 by James Cabiness Finch of Cleveland County. Finch had moved to the area to take advantage of business opportunities stemming from the completion of the railroad to Asheville. The Finch House was the oldest home in town when it was razed in 1993. (Courtesy of the North Carolina Department of Cultural Resources.)

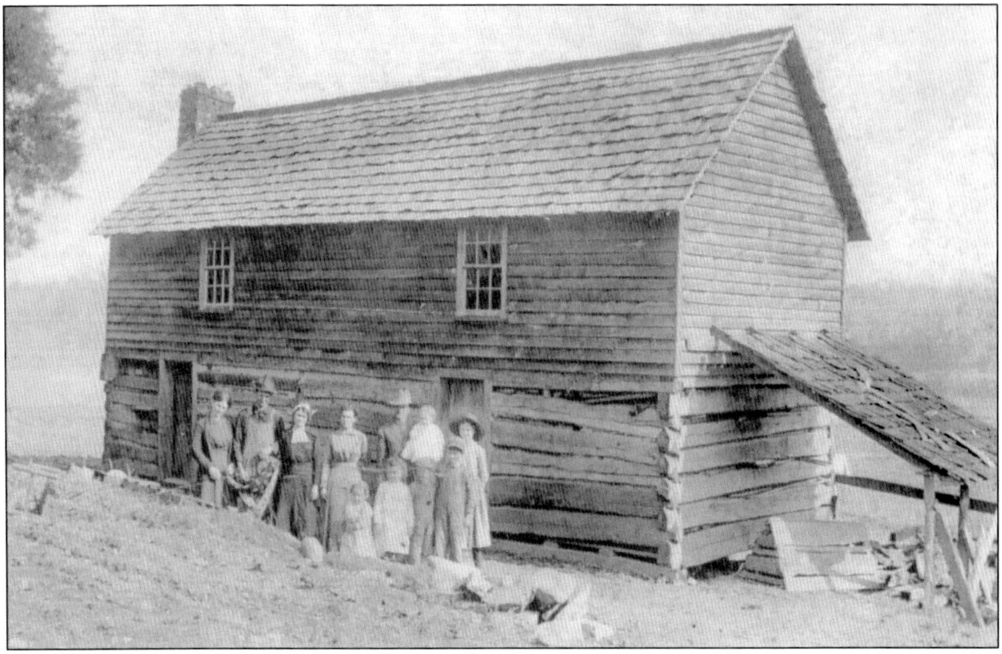

This log and frame house that stood on Oakdale Road in the Greenlee community was built by Revolutionary War veteran Capt. Thomas Hemphill. It was purchased in the late 1800s by Thomas Porter, who is pictured second from right on the second row, holding the small child. (Courtesy of McDowell County Public Library.)

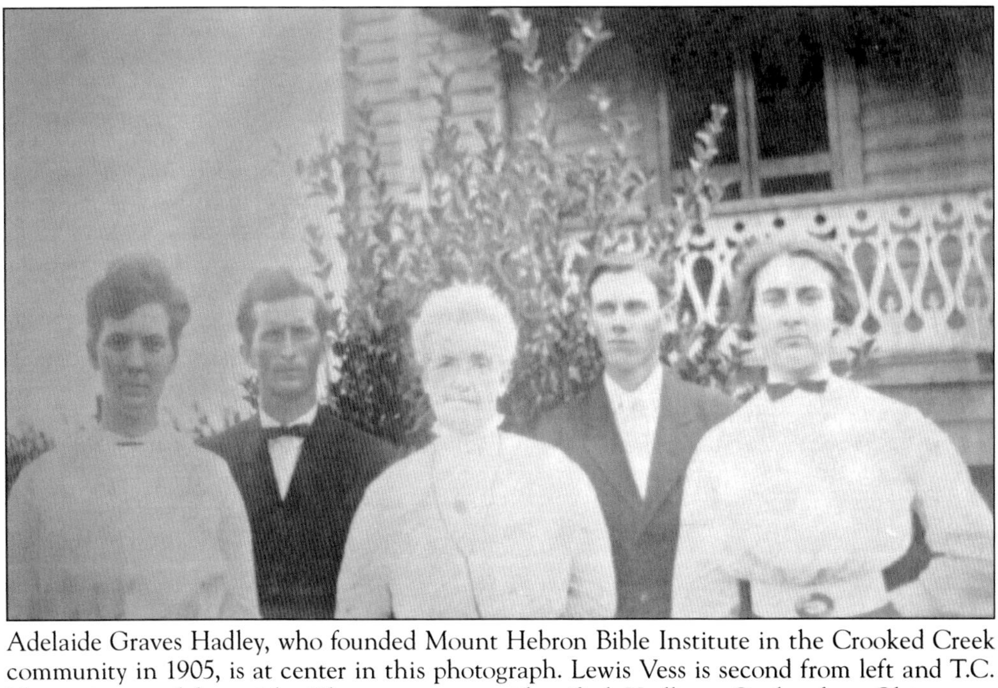

Adelaide Graves Hadley, who founded Mount Hebron Bible Institute in the Crooked Creek community in 1905, is at center in this photograph. Lewis Vess is second from left and T.C. Harvey is second from right. The women are unidentified. Hadley, a Quaker from Ohio, came here on "one of the Lord's errands" following the deaths of her husband and children. (Courtesy of Mount Hebron Wesleyan Church.)

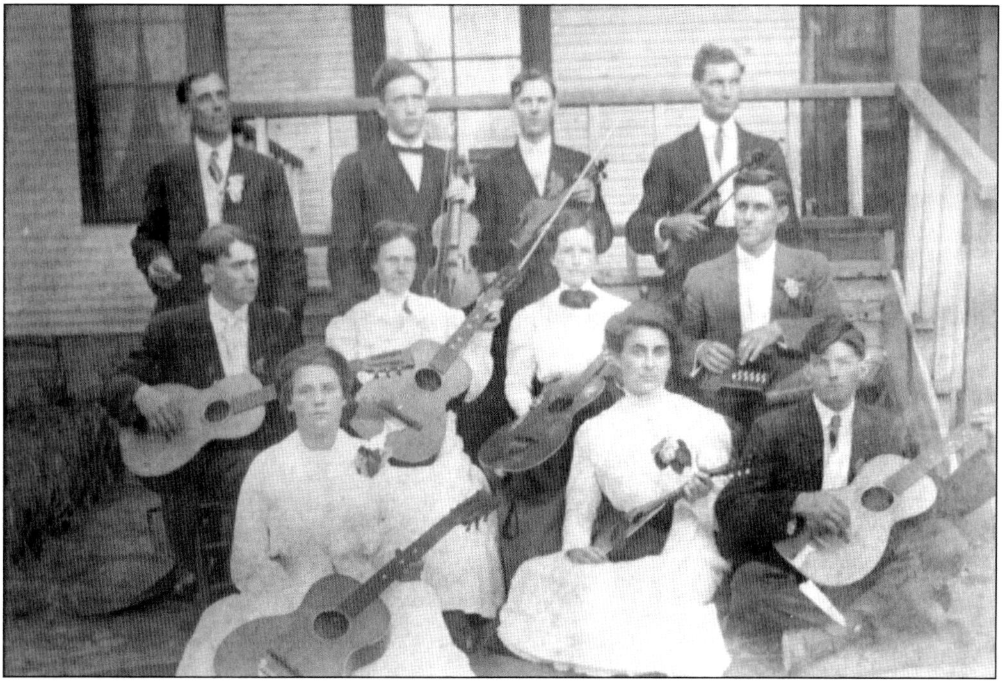

Mount Hebron Bible Institute offered instruction in many areas, including music. These unidentified students pose with their instruments in front of the upper building. The school taught all grades from primary to college and offered instruction in English, theology, Greek, literature, rhetoric, and philosophy. (Courtesy of Mount Hebron Wesleyan Church.)

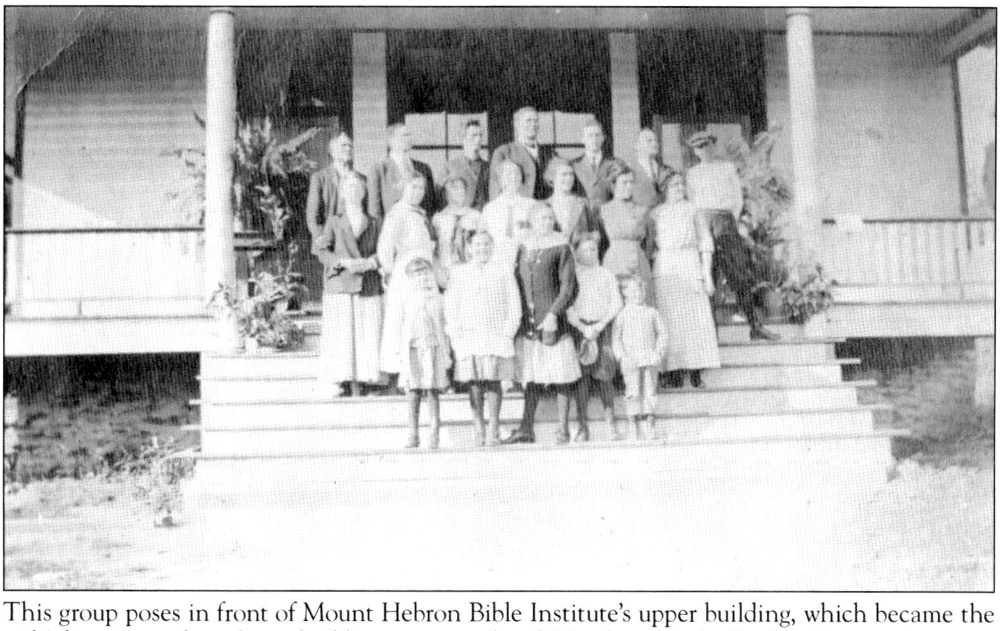

This group poses in front of Mount Hebron Bible Institute's upper building, which became the girls' dormitory after a lower building was completed. Nearby were the Beulah Cottage (a private residence) and a barn. To raise funds, the school sold apples raised on the grounds and water bottled from a nearby spring. The mineral-rich water became popular nationwide, especially in Asheville. (Courtesy of Barbara Meilhammer.)

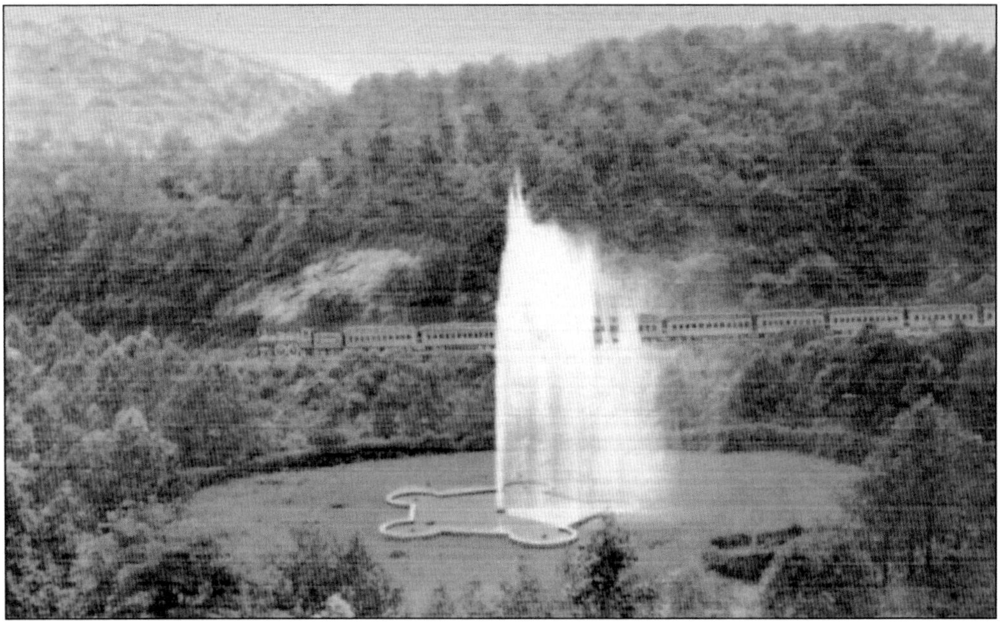

After Round Knob Hotel burned, its fountain fell into disrepair and ceased to flow. It was revived in 1911 and slightly relocated by influential businessman George F. Baker, who dedicated it in honor of his friend Col. Alexander Andrews of the Southern Railway. It soon became known as Andrews Geyser and is the focal point of this vintage postcard. (Courtesy of Mountain Gateway Museum.)

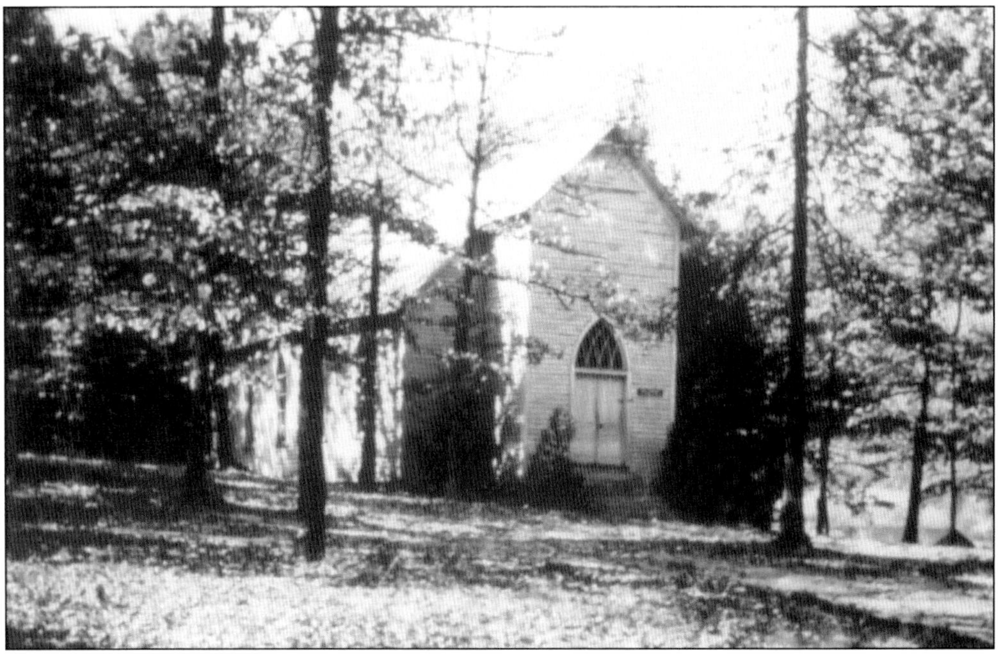

Siloam Presbyterian Church in the Greenlee community has one of the oldest Christian congregations in the county. The congregation came together in the 1780s, and church records begin in 1838. Pictured here is their fourth house of worship, built in 1903. (Courtesy of Historic Carson House Library.)

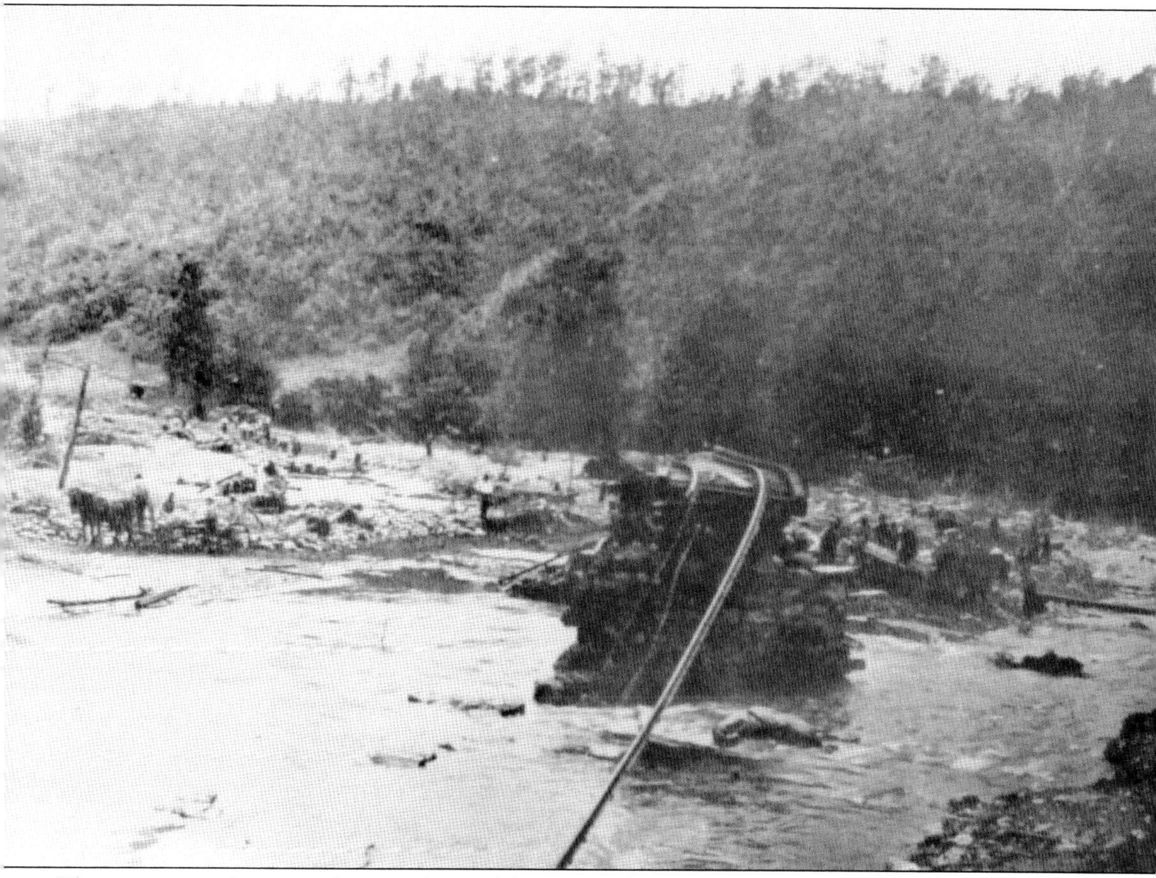

The remnants of a tropical storm thoroughly saturated the ground in Old Fort during the first week of July 1916. Then, on July 15 and 16, a hurricane dumped about 20 more inches of rain, causing widespread destruction. In this image, residents are moving debris from near the mangled remains of a railroad bridge. Bodies of drowned livestock still lie in the creek. (Courtesy of McDowell County Public Library.)

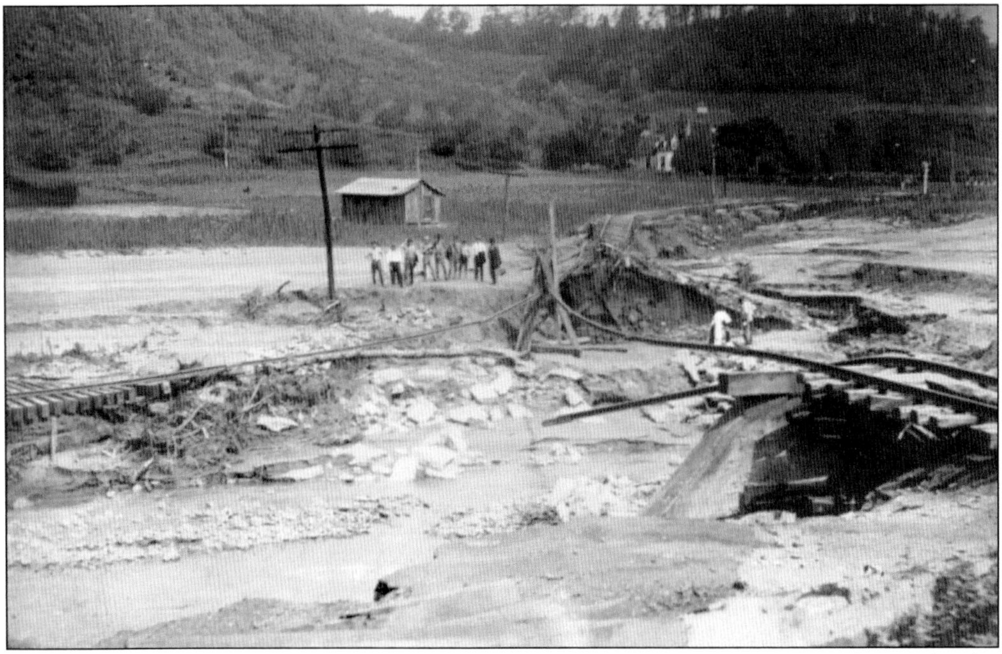

In this photograph taken in the days following the flood of 1916, Mill Creek is back in its banks, but the destruction that it wrought in the West Fort community is evident. The railroad bridge has been washed away, and the track has been twisted and mangled. The public road just beyond the men was washed away as well. (Courtesy of Mountain Gateway Museum.)

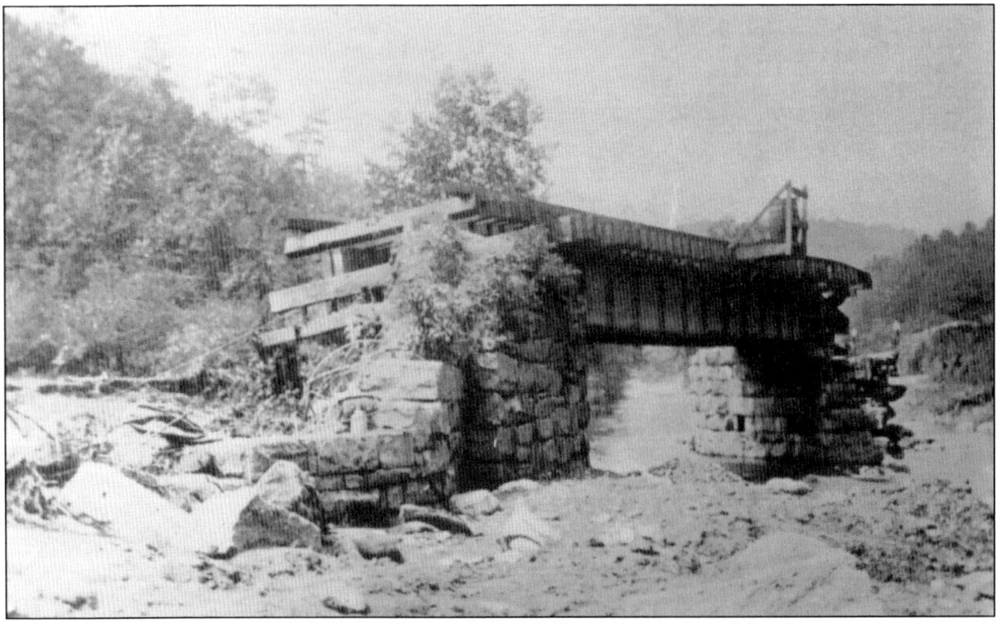

Stone abutments and crossties are all that remained of this railroad bridge over Mill Creek following the 1916 flood. The fill on both sides of the bridge was completely washed away by the raging waters. The *Old Fort Sentinel* said of the storm, "Rivulets became streams, streams became creeks, creeks became rivers, and rivers became frightful." (Courtesy of Historic Carson House Library.)

Nearly every cut along the Southern Railway line between Old Fort and Ridgecrest suffered tremendous mudslides like this one near Graphite. The slide was over 1,000 feet long. The material had to be manually removed by men working day and night with only shovels until the task was completed. Debris continued to slide down the slopes for seven weeks following the flood. (Courtesy of Historic Carson House Library.)

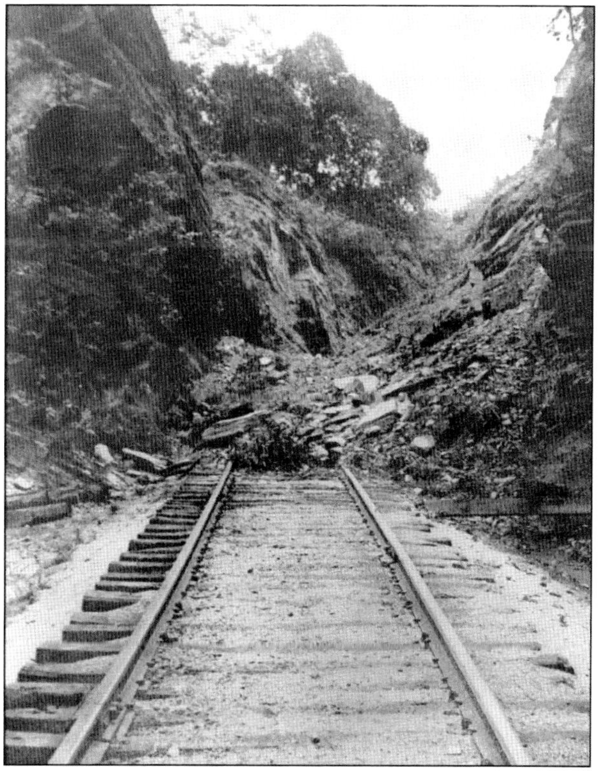

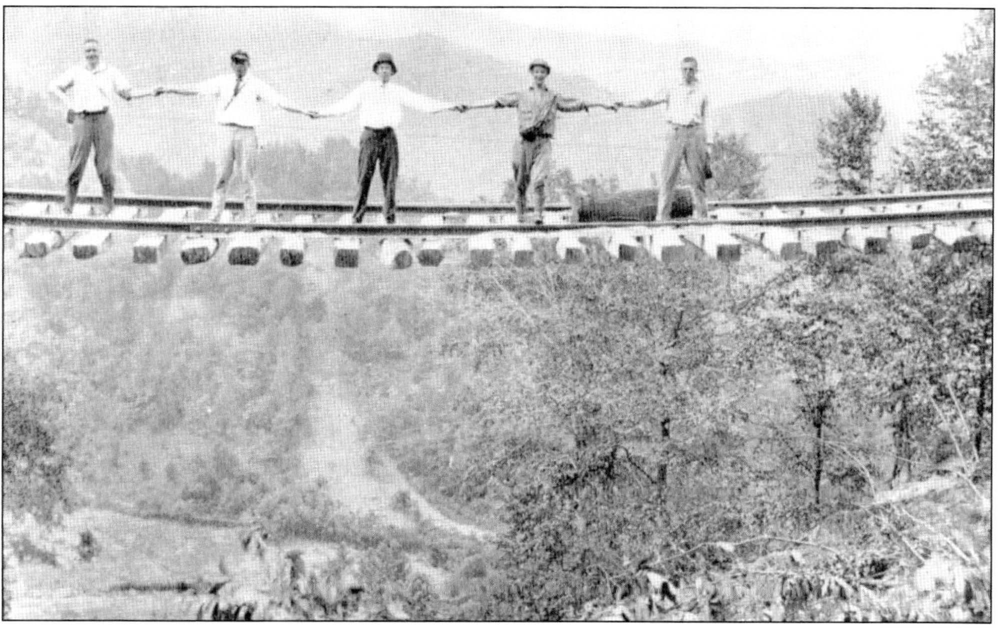

Daredevils stand on railroad tracks suspended in midair after the fill supporting them was washed away in the flooding. F.C. Abbot, who had been traveling by rail to Black Mountain and had to finish the trip on foot, wrote about crawling across this expanse. Where crossties were missing, he had to lie down and pull himself over the void to the next tie. (Courtesy of McDowell County Public Library.)

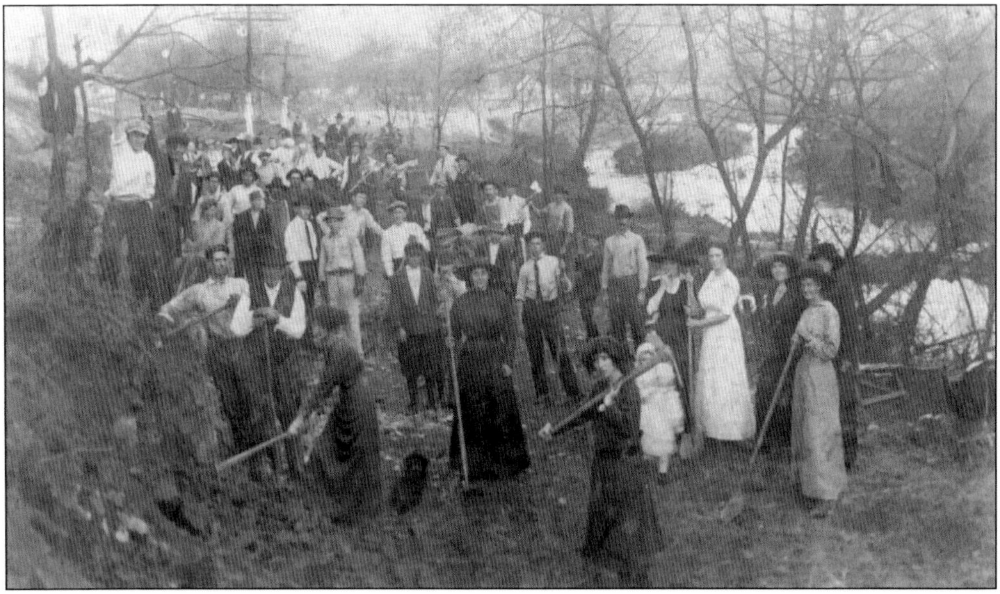

Old Fort residents of every age and description come together to dig out following the catastrophic flood. The course of Mill Creek had been altered and St. Gabriel's Episcopal Church had been destroyed by a landslide, but the town itself had emerged largely unscathed. The greatest damage was to the railroad and to public roads; many residents joined the repair efforts. (Courtesy of Mountain Gateway Museum.)

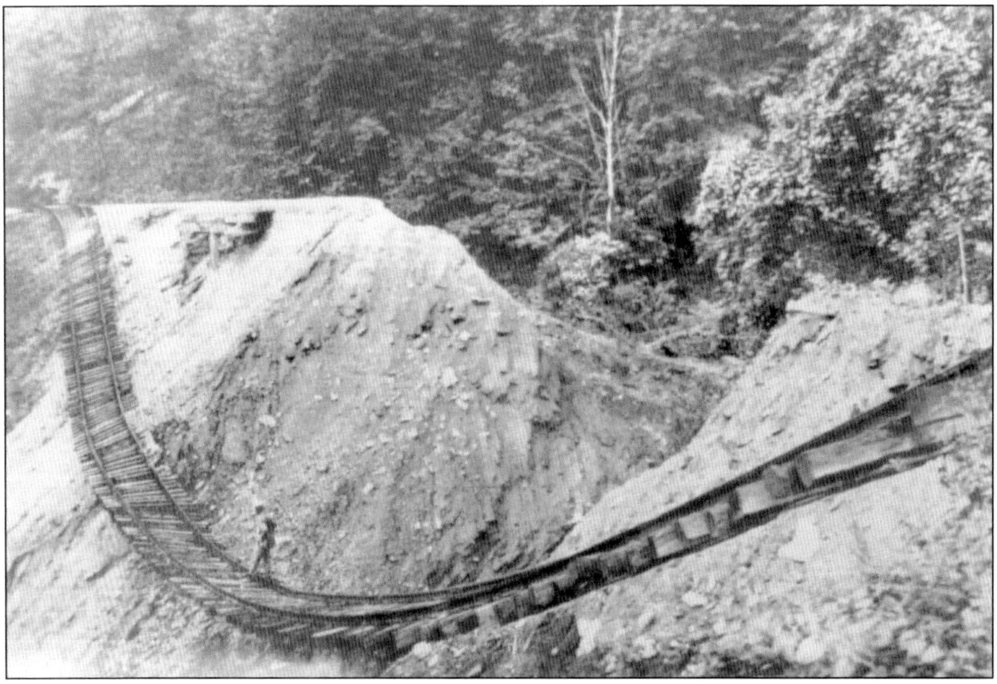

A Southern Railway inspector walks on a section of track dislodged from a fill in the Round Knob area. Following the July 1916 flood, the longest undamaged section of track between Old Fort and Black Mountain measured only a half a mile long. Through a heroic effort, rail service through the area was restored within six weeks. (Courtesy of McDowell County Public Library.)

Four

Moving Forward

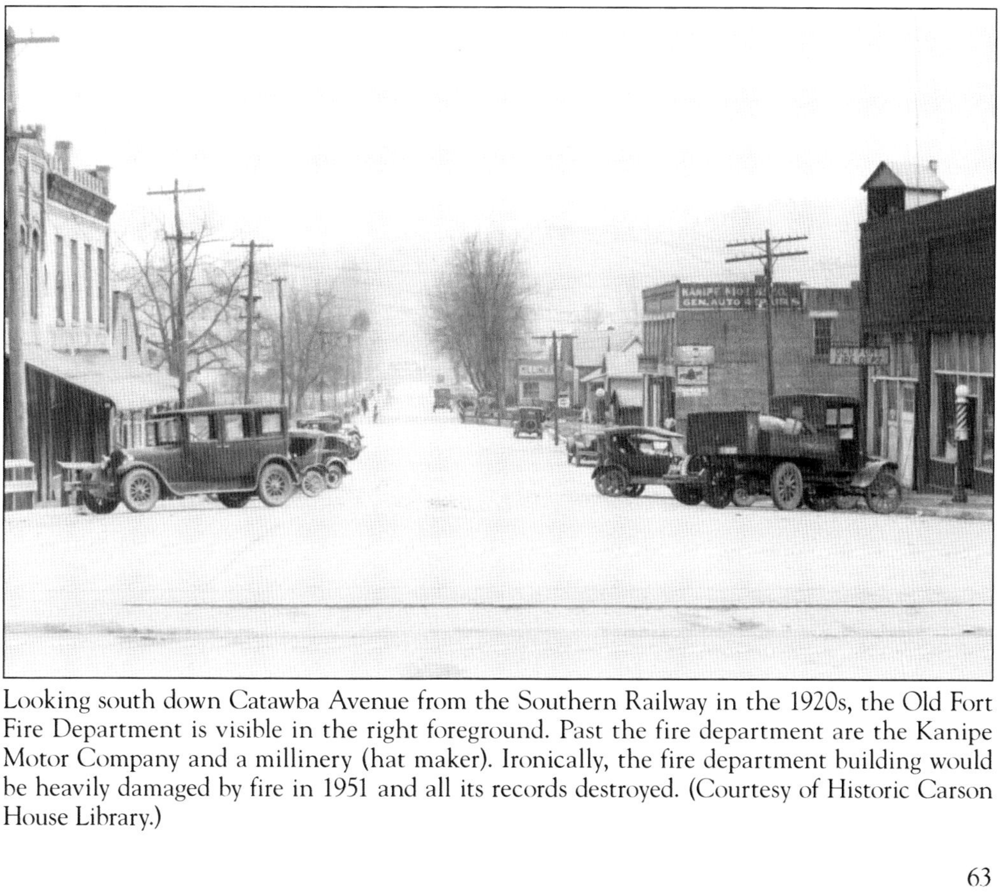

Looking south down Catawba Avenue from the Southern Railway in the 1920s, the Old Fort Fire Department is visible in the right foreground. Past the fire department are the Kanipe Motor Company and a millinery (hat maker). Ironically, the fire department building would be heavily damaged by fire in 1951 and all its records destroyed. (Courtesy of Historic Carson House Library.)

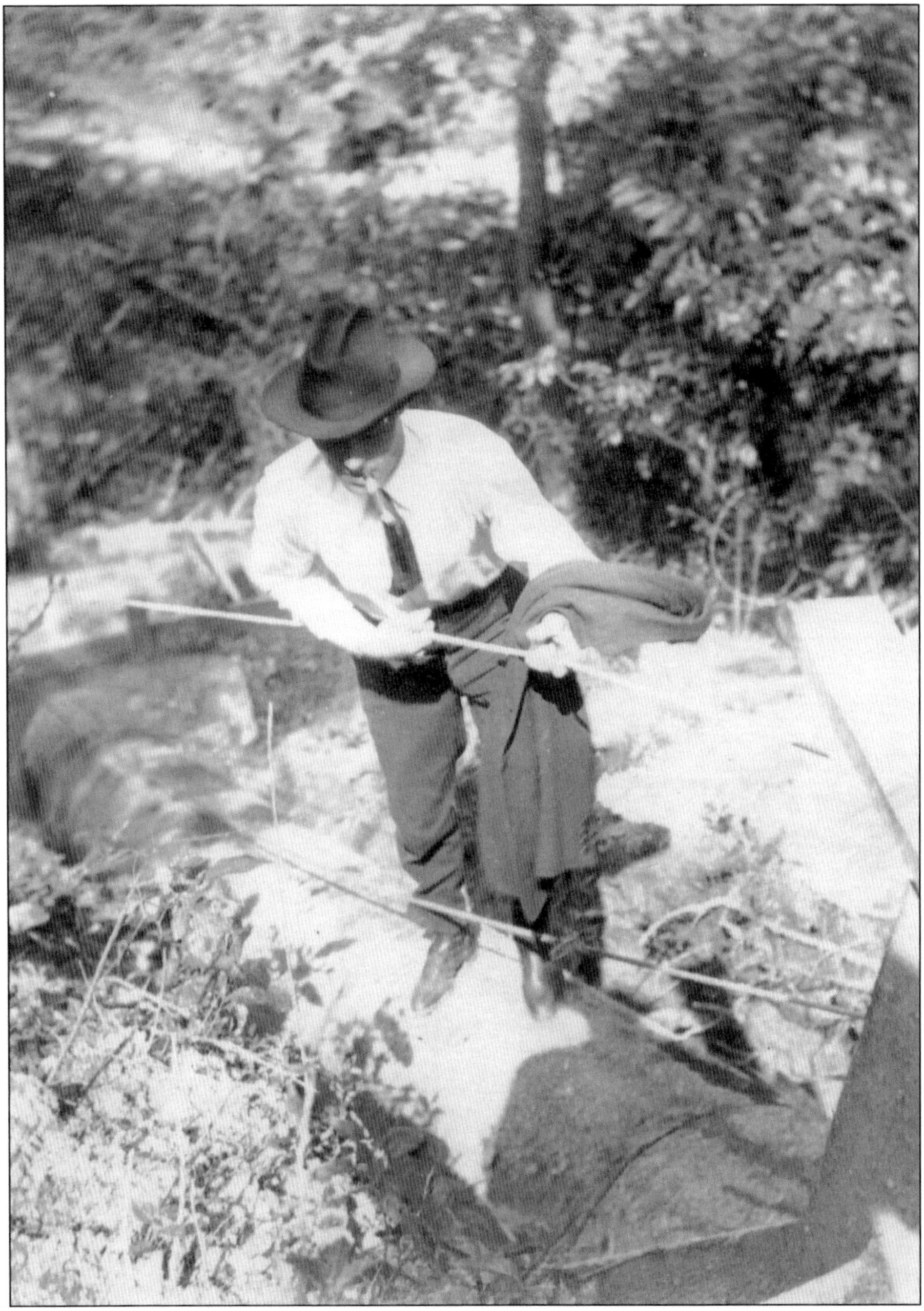

Col. Daniel W. Adams climbs one of the wooden water pipes running to his Catawba River dam. A remarkable man, Adams had risen to the rank of lieutenant colonel just 17 months after leaving officer training school during World War I. He designed and built the first fire tower in the United States and pioneered the triangulation fire-spotting system. Additionally, he invented the pilot ejection seat. Adams was an inventor, engineer, geologist, and explorer whose varied interests and talents greatly benefited Old Fort throughout his life. (Courtesy of Mountain Gateway Museum.)

Colonel Adams came to the Old Fort area in 1911 to survey the Curtis Creek forest tract for the US Forest Service. His work paved the way for the establishment of the Pisgah National Forest. He purchased the Westerman House just west of town and moved his family there in 1914. The house is visible in the background of this photograph. (Courtesy of Bill Nichols.)

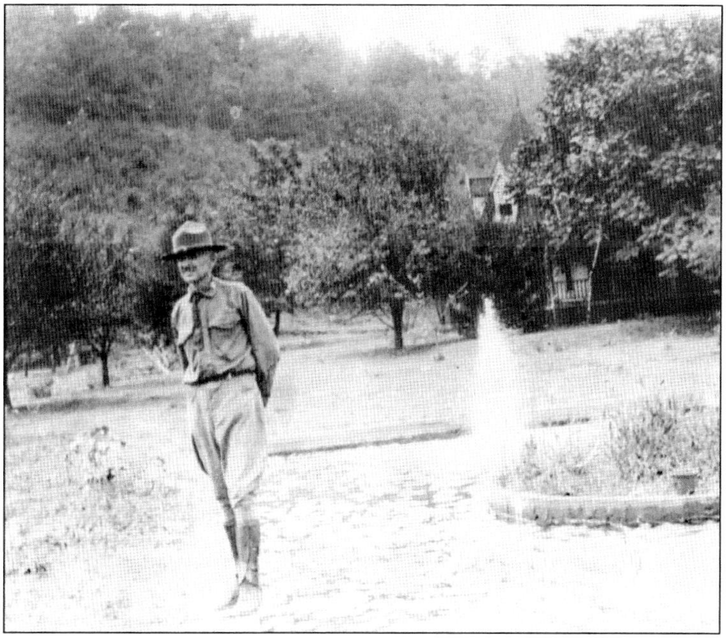

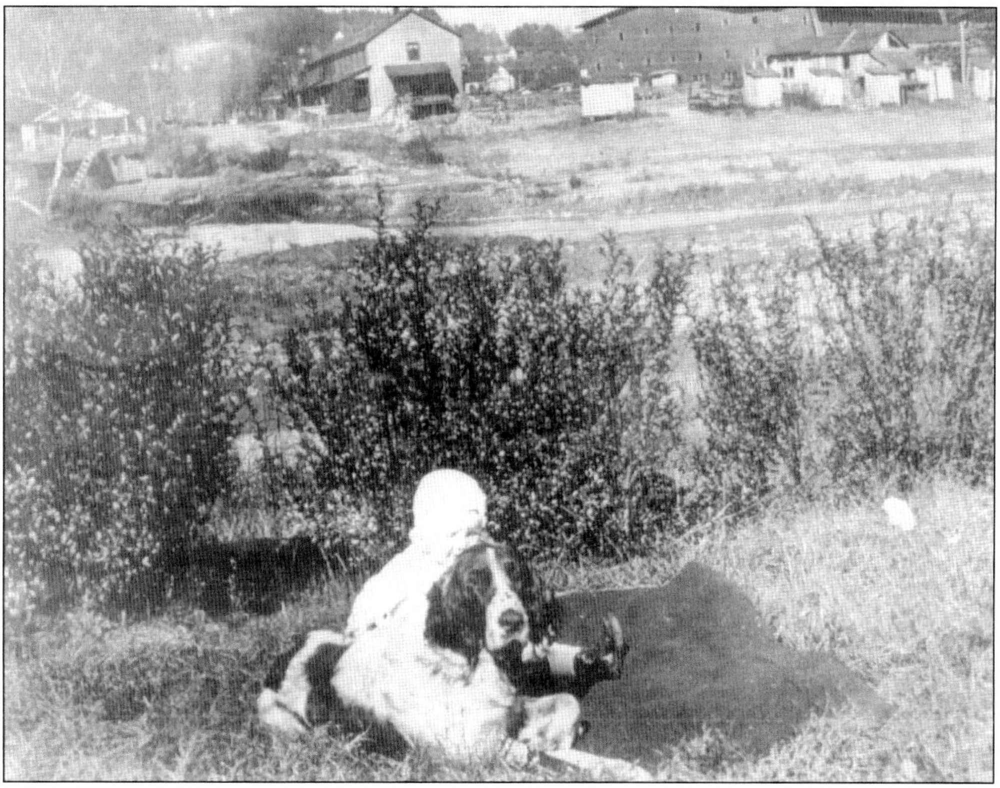

Little Doris Dalton and her canine friend are enjoying a sunny day in the late 1920s, with their blanket spread approximately where Old Fort Library is located today. Mill Creek is just behind them, and the large building in the right background is the Union Tanning Company bark shed. The building to the left facing Spring Street is the tannery boardinghouse. (Courtesy of Bill Nichols.)

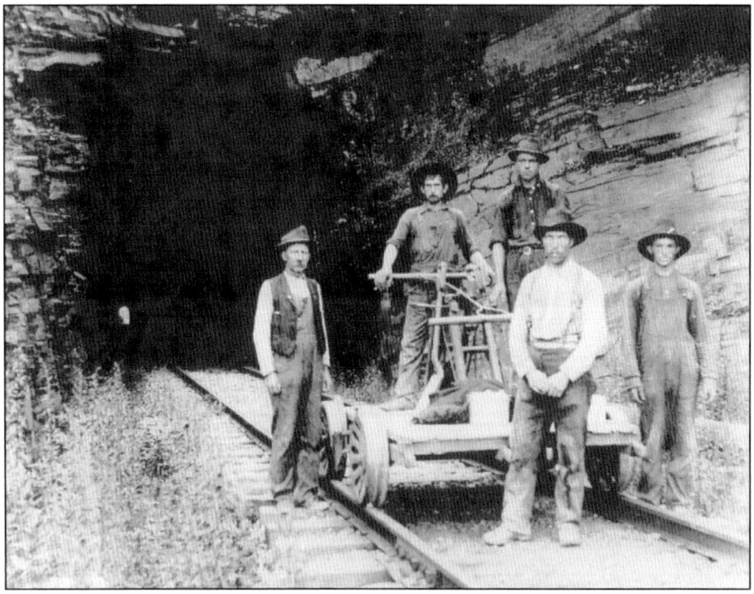

A local section crew, or gang, is seen at the Burgin Tunnel. The man on the left is John Lytle Stepp, a foreman. A section crew was responsible for a large section of track and rode handcars to look for and repair damaged ties, shaky spikes, and loose bolts. Many local men found jobs on these crews. (Courtesy of Mountain Gateway Museum.)

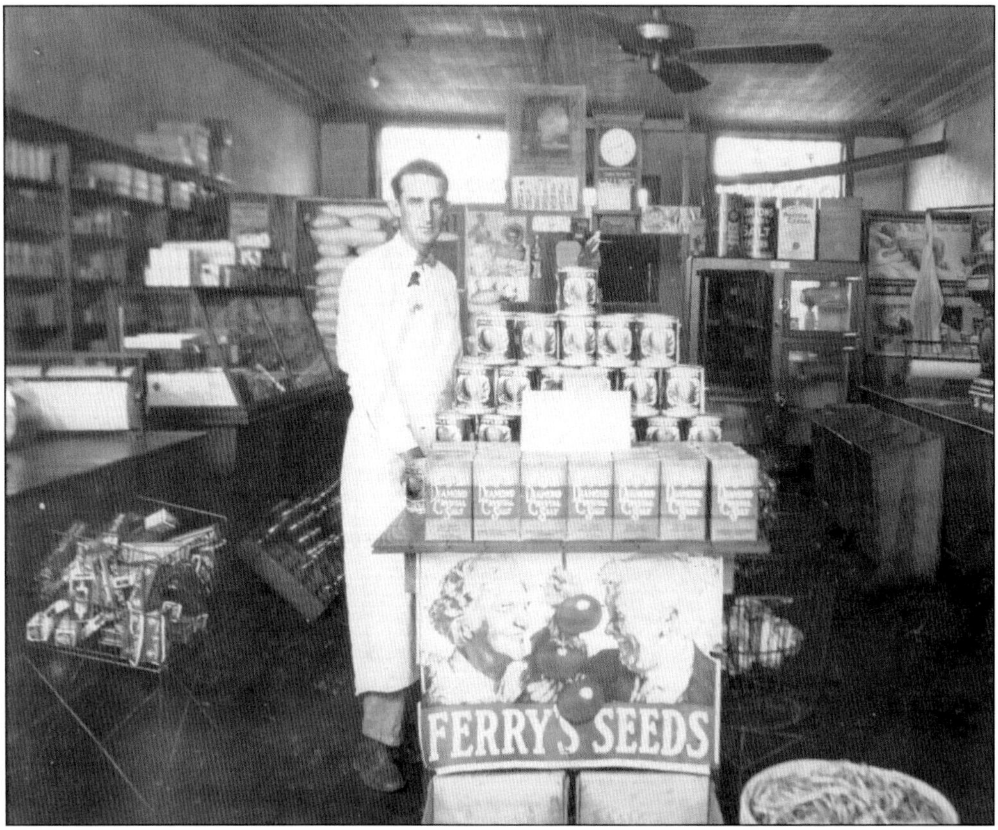

Grady Nichols operated a grocery store on Catawba Avenue next to the fire department for many years. Nichols was also a fireman and was elected as McDowell County sheriff in 1936. He went on to serve three terms. His father was Tyke Nichols, who worked for the Old Fort Post Office. (Courtesy of Bill Nichols.)

J.F. Harmon was Old Fort's longest-serving mayor. He was first elected in 1911 and served until 1917. He was elected again in 1921 and served until 1937. He was mayor for 22 total years in the early 20th century. (Courtesy of the Town of Old Fort.)

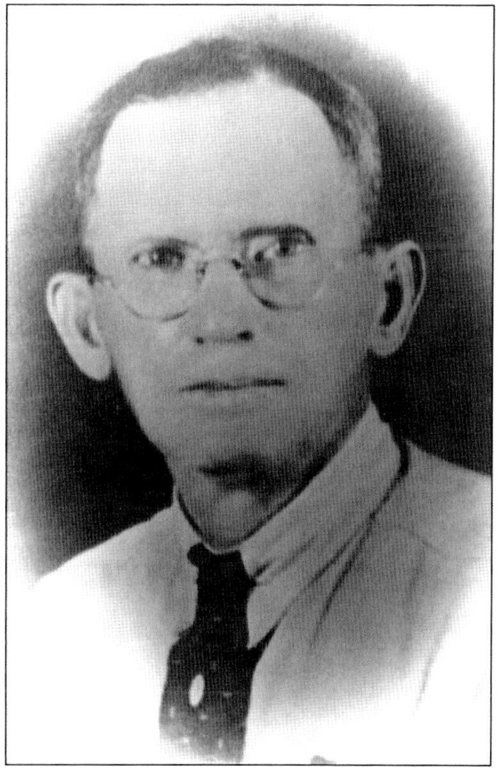

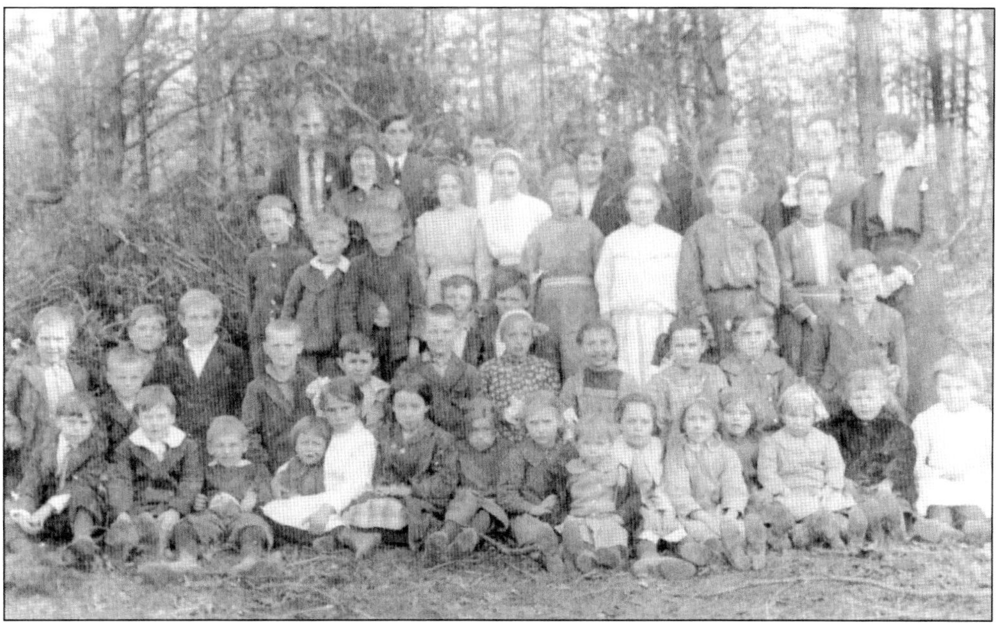

In this photograph of students at Belfont School, future Old Fort mayor Jack Lytle is third from left in the first row. Located in the Crooked Creek community, the school was built around 1850. It was a two-room frame building, with grades one through three in one room and grades three through six in the other. Water for the school was carried from a nearby house. (Courtesy of Nada Carroll.)

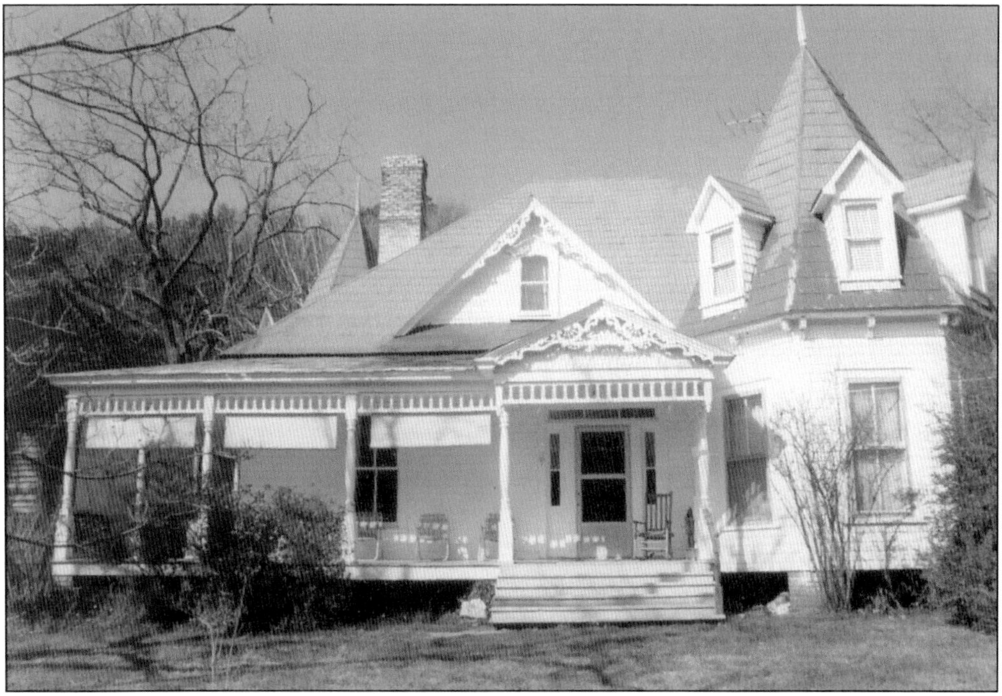

The Adams-Westerman House was built in 1887 by Henry A. and Ella Dula Westerman and purchased by Col. Daniel Adams in 1914. Flamboyantly Queen Anne in style, the house is eccentric, irregular, and eye-catching. It is located near the railroad track and Mill Creek just west of Old Fort. (Courtesy of Nada Carroll.)

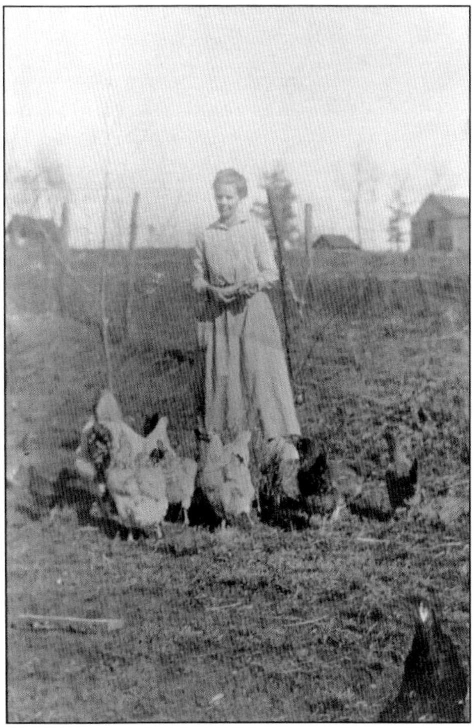

Rebecca Halford Burgin (1878–1938) is seen on the family farm on Bat Cave Road, just south of Old Fort town limits, some time in the 1920s. The wife of William A. Burgin, Rebecca is remembered as a principled, generous, and devout woman. She raised chickens and kept bees to augment the family income and to be able to help those in need should she be called to do so. (Courtesy of Nada Carroll.)

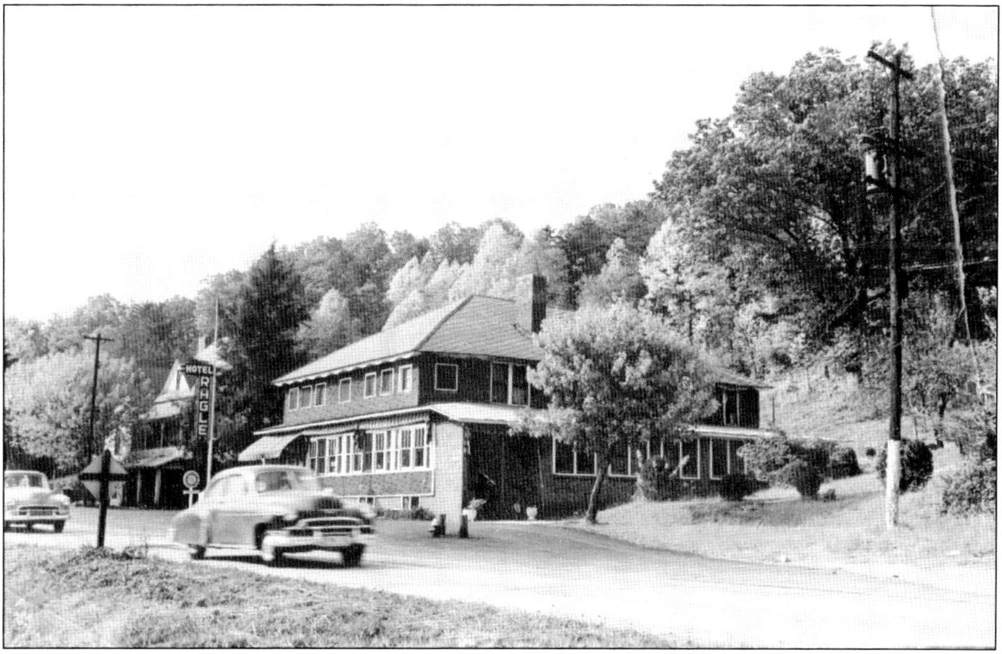

The Ragle Hotel was located on Highway 70 across from the depot. Built in 1852, it was owned and operated by Mr. and Mrs. H.A. Ragle from 1924 until 1933 when they moved to Point Lookout to operate a tourist stop there. Aunt Sue Sandlin was then the Ragle Hotel operator for many years. After becoming structurally unsound, the building was torn down in the early 1990s. (Courtesy of Nada Carroll.)

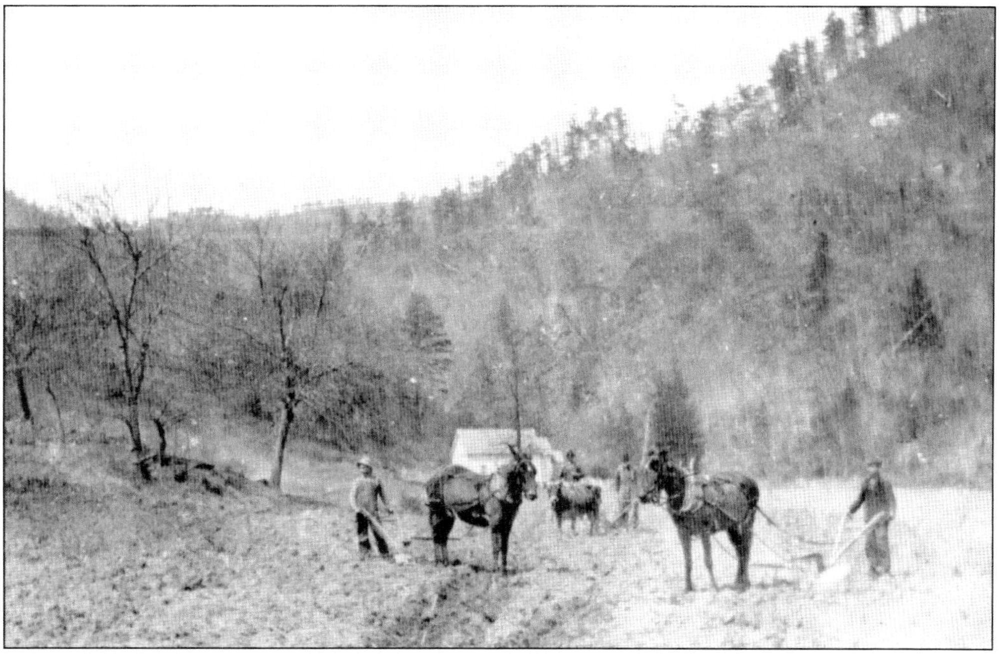

Plowing a field in the Curtis Creek area are, from left to right, Fate Woody, G.B. Woody, Milton Woody, and Russell Woody. The building in the background is the Curtis Creek schoolhouse. (Courtesy of Dee Daughtridge.)

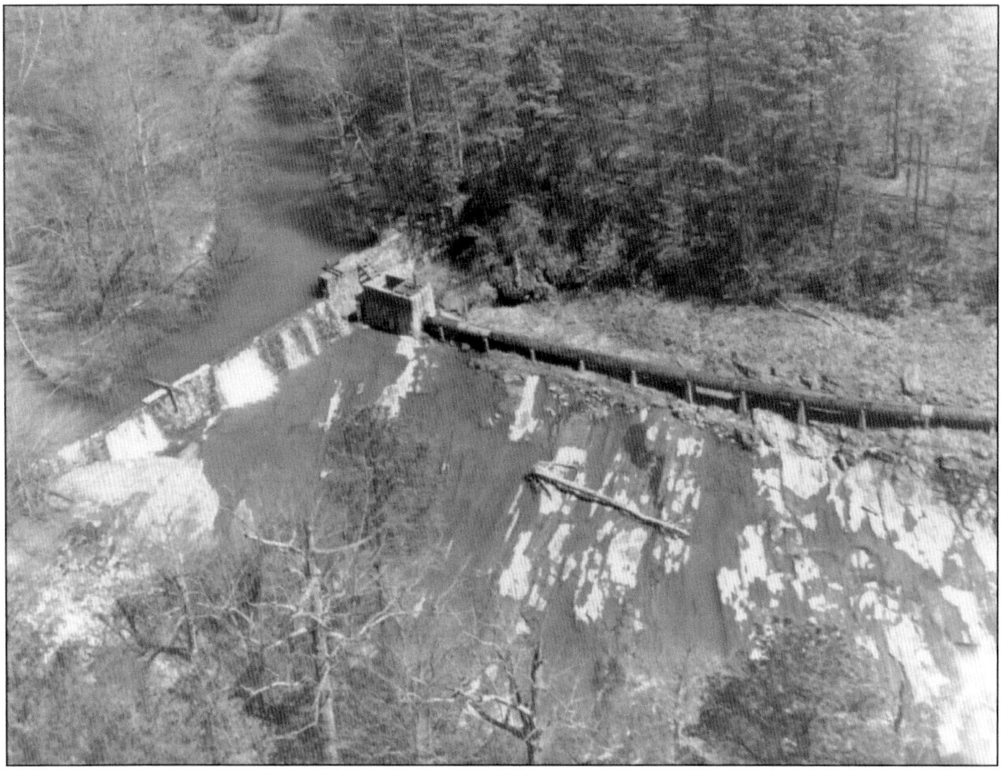

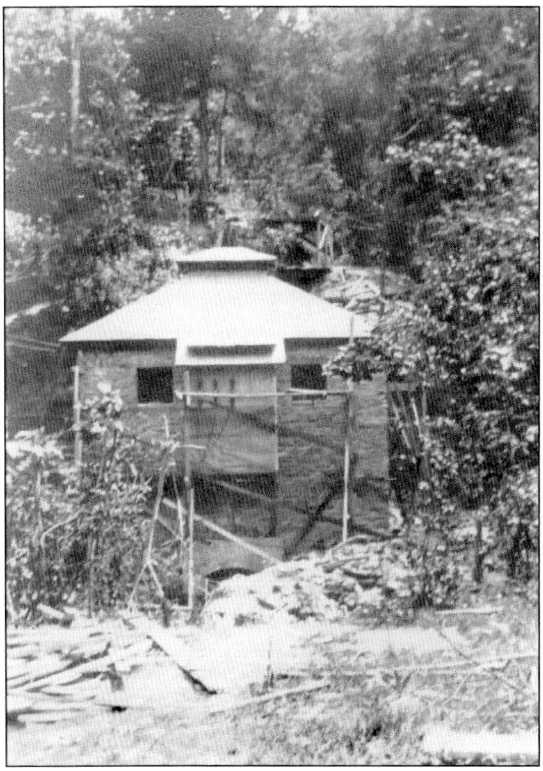

Colonel Adams built this dam on the Catawba River to generate electricity for the town of Old Fort. He started the project in 1924 and completed it three years later. It was the second civic engineering project that he had undertaken after moving to Old Fort. His first had been to build an intake on Jarrett's Creek to provide a municipal water supply. (Courtesy of McDowell County Public Library.)

The lower powerhouse at Colonel Adams's dam on the Catawba River is still under construction in this photograph. Shortly after the completion of the hydroelectric plant, the area entered a drought, which created problems meeting demand. Adams sold the power plant in 1928. It was eventually bought by Duke Power, which closed it and ran a line from Marion to Old Fort. (Courtesy of Mountain Gateway Museum.)

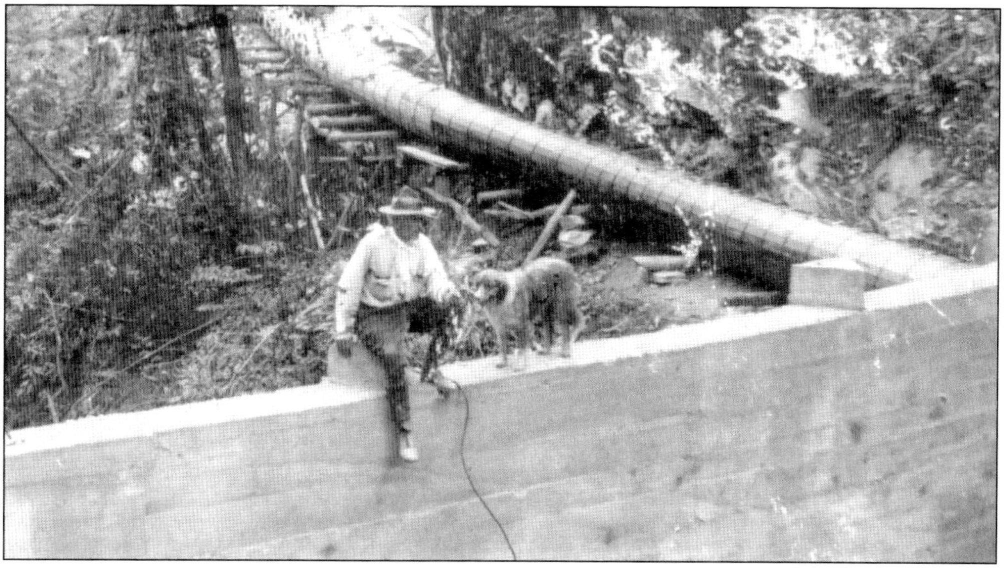

Colonel Adams and his dog Smoke survey construction of his hydroelectric dam near Catawba Falls. The large wire and wood stave pipeline seen in the background carried water down the mountain to the powerhouse that would furnish electricity to the town of Old Fort. Previously, only a few tannery employees had electricity, which was generated by burning coal. (Courtesy of Stuart Adams Robinson.)

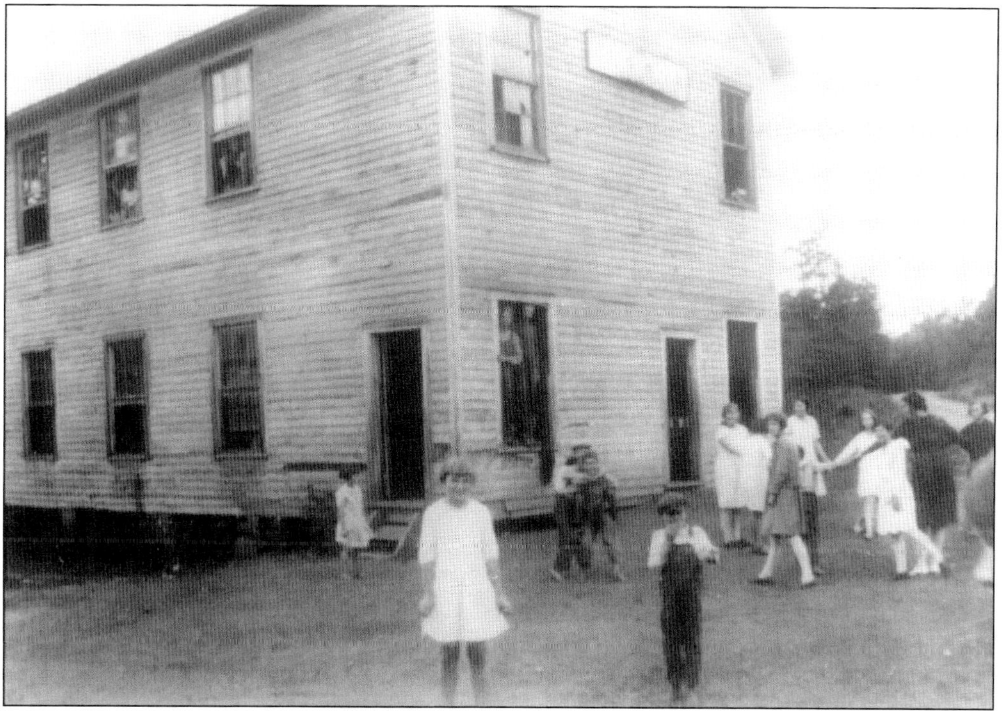

A group of students enjoy recess at the old Bethlehem School in the Crooked Creek community about 1928. To the right, teacher Florence Williams can be seen leading a game of Ring Around the Rosie. The school building burned down in 1933. (Courtesy of Historic Carson House Library and Shirley Lytle Anderson.)

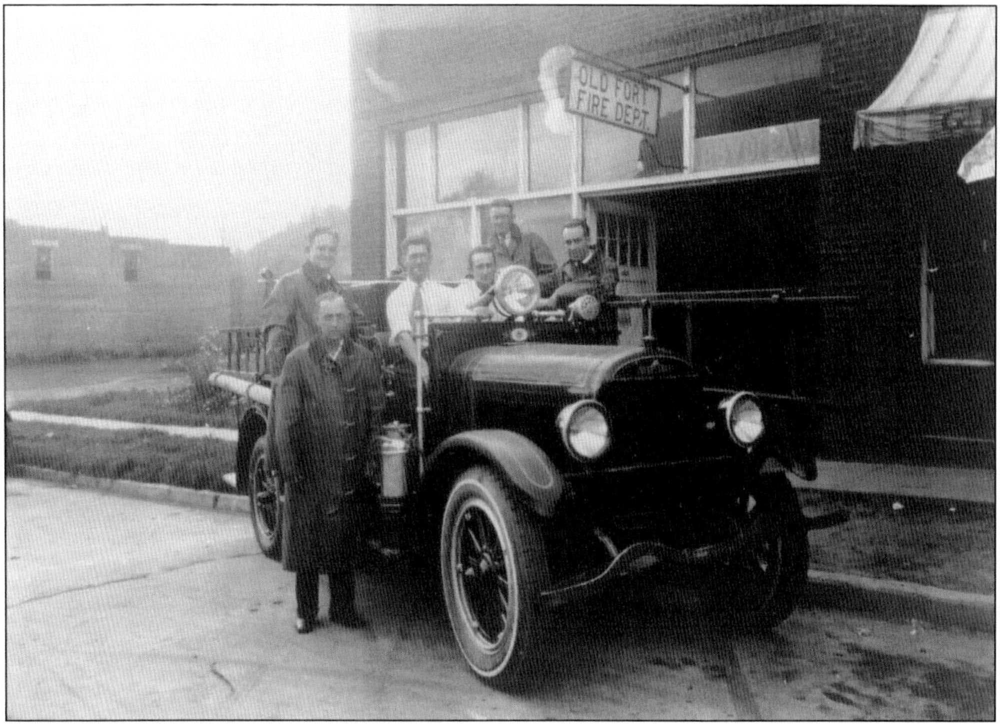

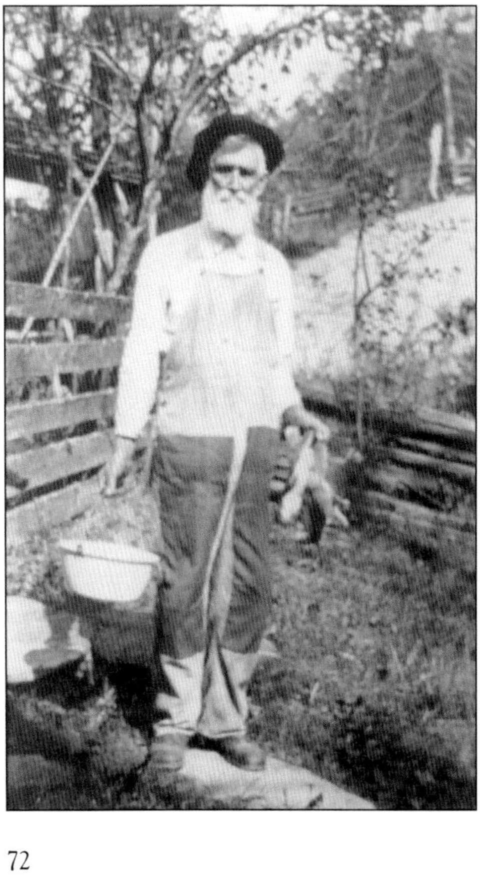

Old Fort firemen show off their new 1928 fire truck. William Hicks is standing, and behind him are, from left to right, Harry Noblitt, William L. Dalton, Grady Nichols, Kenneth Sawyer, and ? Swann. In addition to the truck, the department boasted 800 feet of hose and a 30-foot ladder. (Courtesy of McDowell County Public Library.)

In this photograph from 1926, Thomas Wilson Noblitt of the Crooked Creek community personifies the pioneer lifestyle that was prevalent in the Old Fort area well into the 20th century. The rugged farmland can be seen behind him, and he is holding two squirrels that he has killed for food. Noblitt carries a pot of water to be used in the skinning process. (Courtesy of Mountain Gateway Museum.)

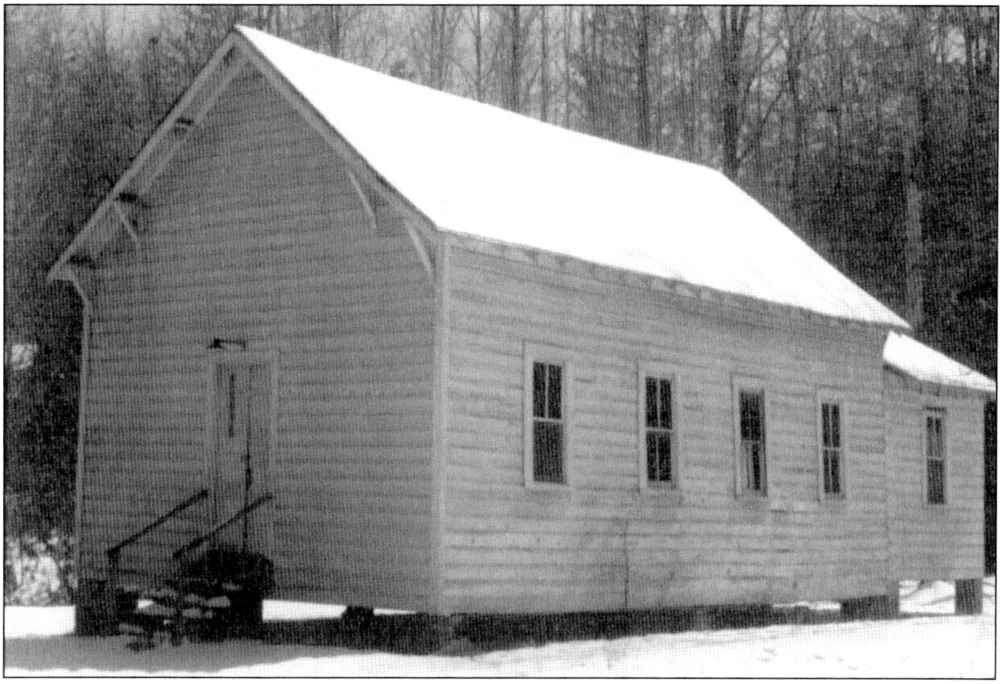

Mount Hebron Wesleyan Church was formed in September 1913. The congregation worshipped in the lower building of Mount Hebron Bible Institute until this structure was completed in 1927. Logs from the old Harvey Place were utilized, and a white ash from Sallie Knupp and R. Harvey's property was donated to make benches. An updated structure was completed in 1959. (Courtesy of Mount Hebron Wesleyan Church.)

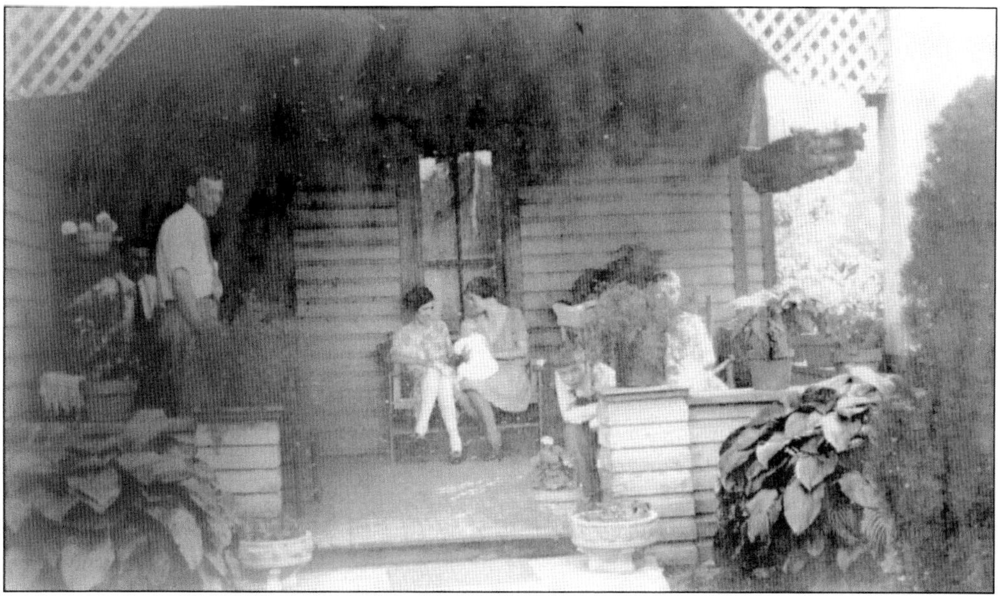

William Alexander Burgin purchased his home on Bat Cave Road just south of Old Fort in 1905. Pictured relaxing on the front porch in 1928 are, left to right, William Burgin, Grayson Bailey, Grace Burgin, Cassie and baby Rebecca, John Wilson Burgin, and William's wife, Rebecca Burgin. W.A. Burgin was a master carpenter and builder. (Courtesy of Nada Carroll.)

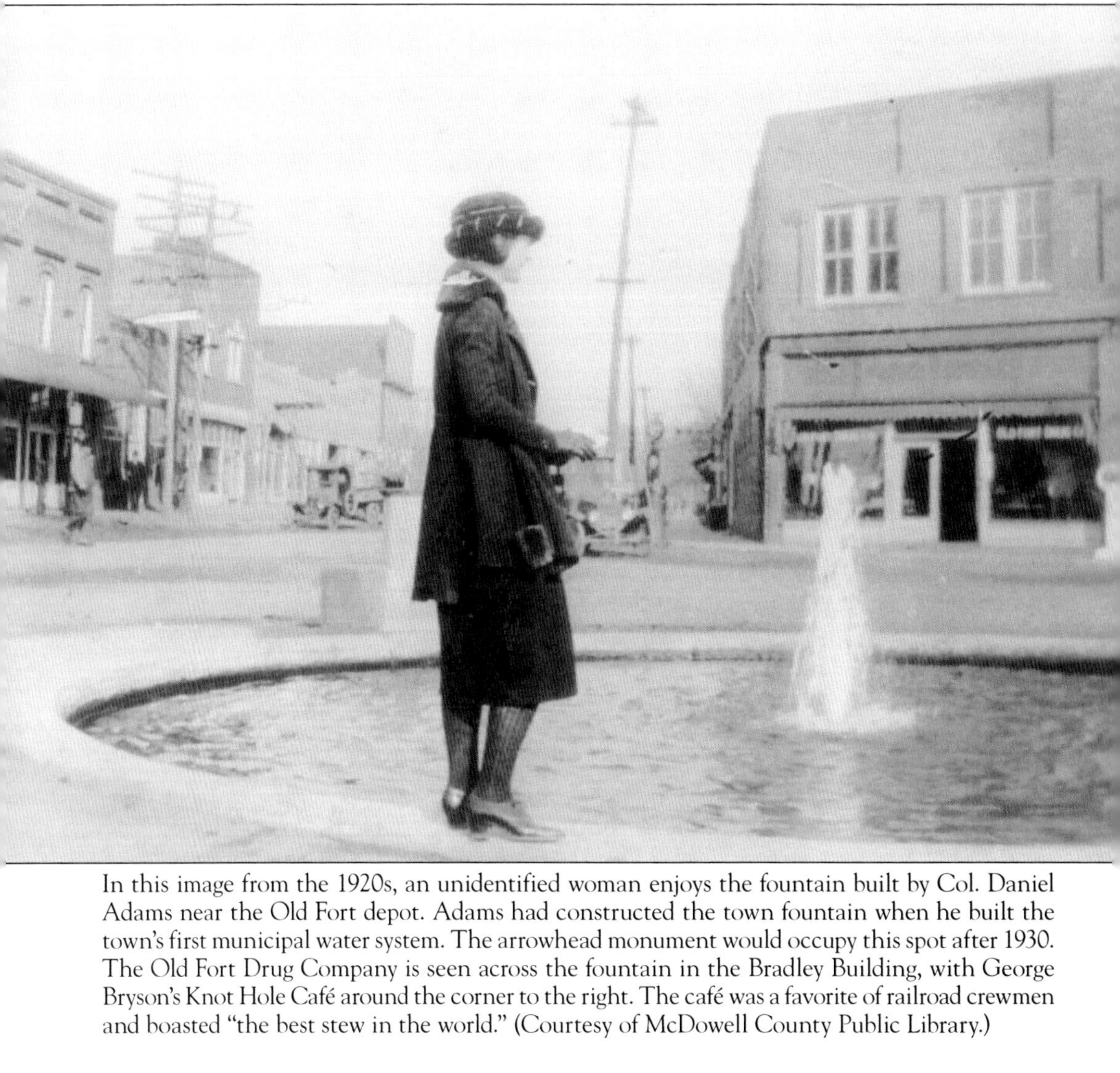

In this image from the 1920s, an unidentified woman enjoys the fountain built by Col. Daniel Adams near the Old Fort depot. Adams had constructed the town fountain when he built the town's first municipal water system. The arrowhead monument would occupy this spot after 1930. The Old Fort Drug Company is seen across the fountain in the Bradley Building, with George Bryson's Knot Hole Café around the corner to the right. The café was a favorite of railroad crewmen and boasted "the best stew in the world." (Courtesy of McDowell County Public Library.)

This house on Catawba Avenue is known as the Strickland House or Tate House, after the families who occupied it. It was built in 1910 by Witt Blackwelder. The distinguishing features are the long eight-paned attic windows, sloping roofed pediment, and the arrow design gable detail. It is a remaining example of the elegant simplicity of the homes on Catawba Avenue in the early 1900s. (Courtesy of Nada Carroll.)

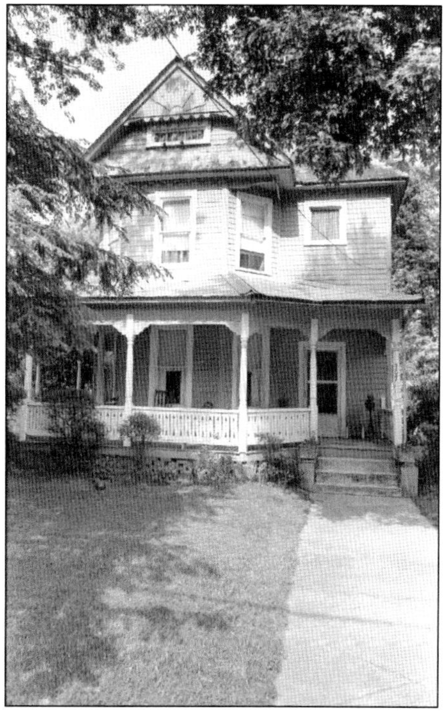

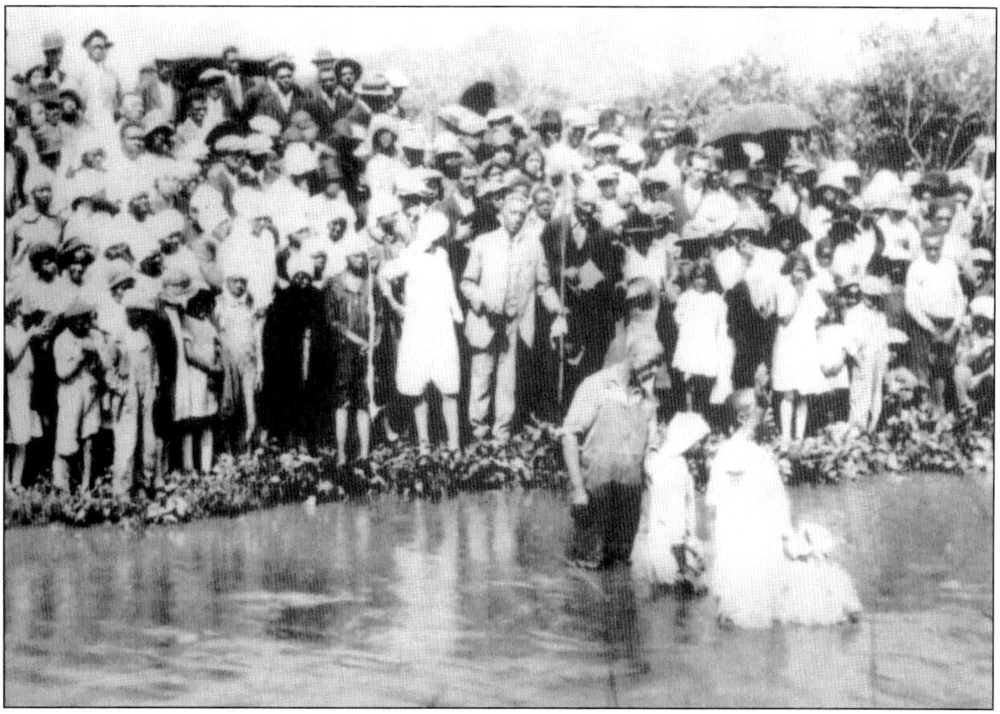

A 1925 Catawba View Church baptism takes place at Terrill Hole on the Catawba River, not far from the church. Reverend Camp, a visiting minister from Gastonia, is officiating. Floyd Brice's two children, along with Ed Morgan, are in the water. Those on the bank wearing white with white headpieces are waiting their turn in the water. (Courtesy of Mountain Gateway Museum.)

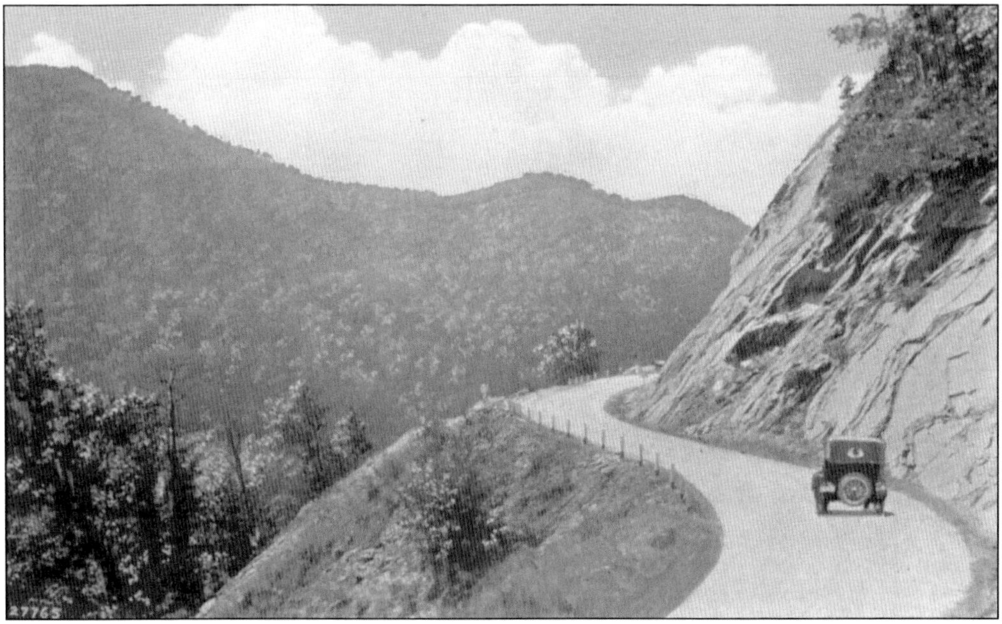

Highway 10 (later changed to Highway 70) through the Royal Gorge between Old Fort and Ridgecrest is shown in this vintage postcard. The eight-mile stretch accomplished a quarter-mile vertical rise with 98 curves, some of them hairpin. It would be replaced by a four-lane highway with a gentler climb in 1953. (Courtesy of Pack Memorial Public Library, North Carolina Collection.)

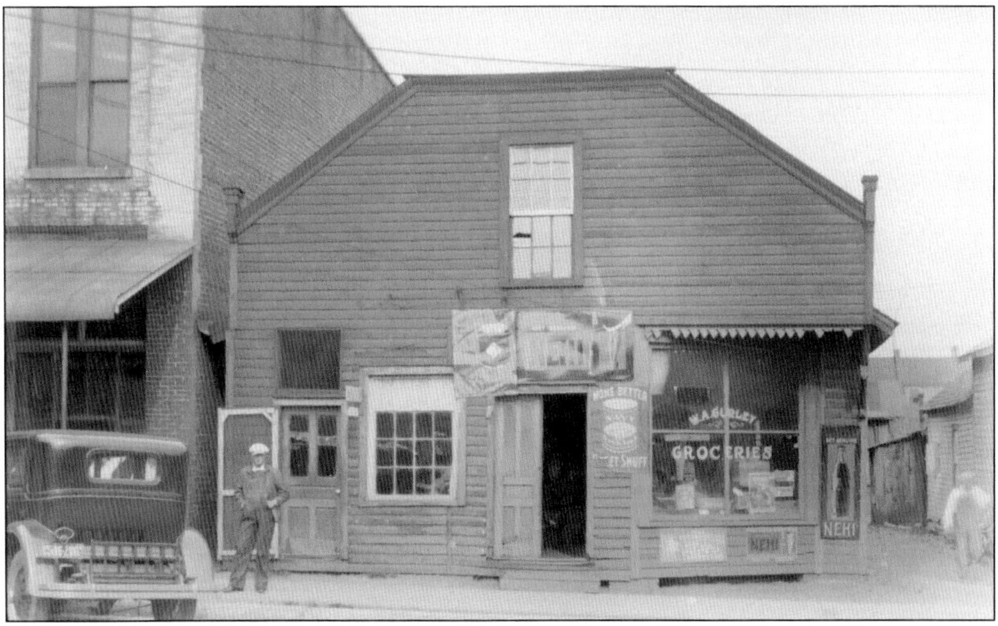

This building was located on the east side of Catawba Avenue and housed a grocery store owned by William Gurley (1856–1943). The popularity of snuff during the 1930s is demonstrated by the fact that two different brands are advertised on the front of the building. A grocery was in business on this site until 2012. (Courtesy of Mountain Gateway Museum.)

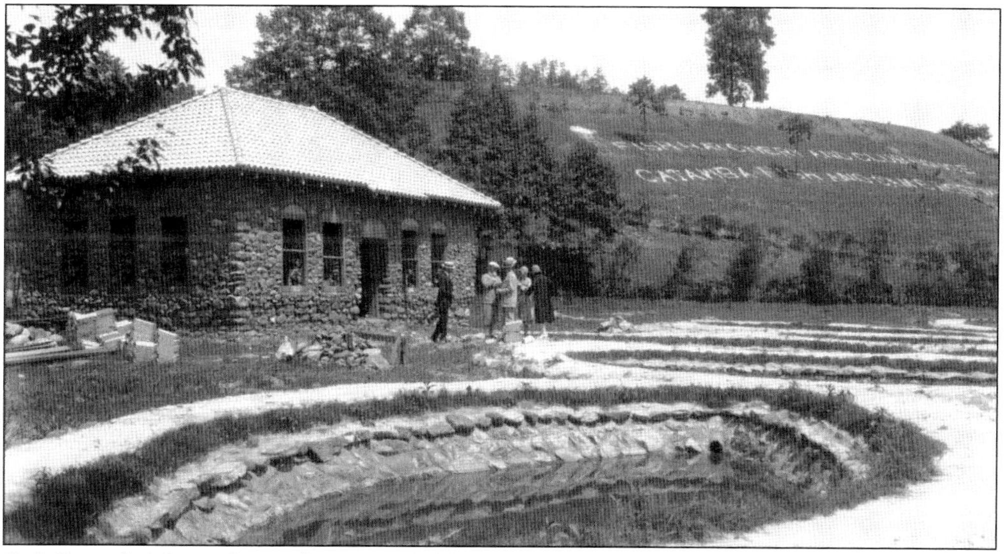

Col. Daniel Adams shows the stone clubhouse for his Catawba Fish and Game Preserve to visitors. The hillside sign was visible from the railroad and from Highway 70. His vision was to provide a weekend getaway for Asheville outdoor enthusiasts, even adding two wings to his home to accommodate guests. The stock market crash of 1929 ended the project. (Courtesy of Pack Memorial Public Library, North Carolina Collection.)

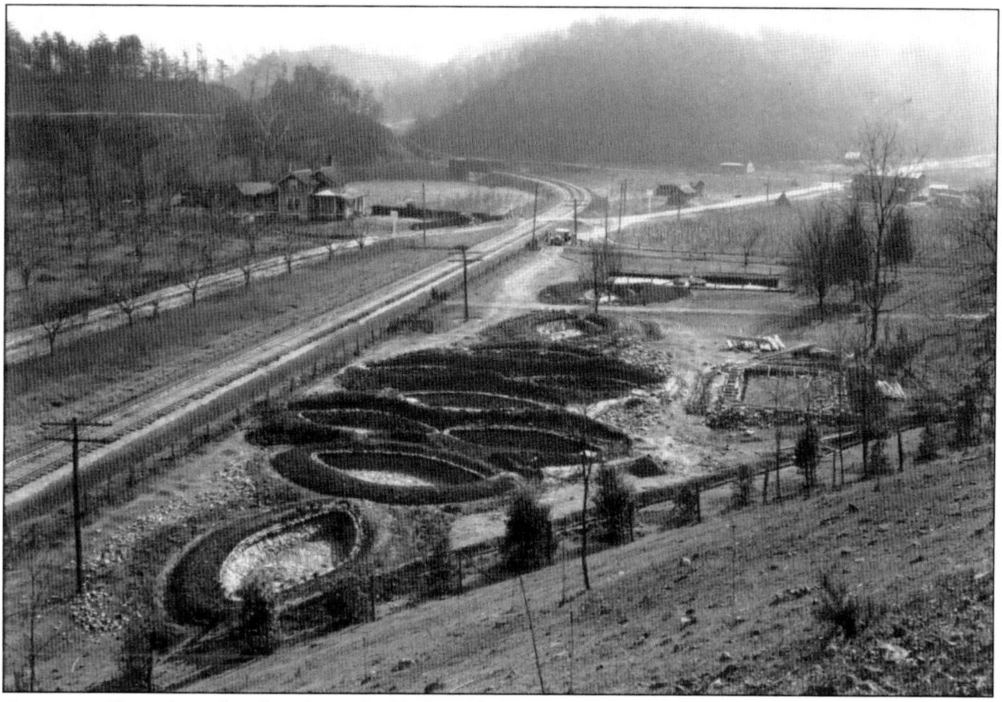

As part of his plans for the Catawba Fish and Game Preserve, Adams had nine fishponds dug on his property. Their construction is nearing completion in this image from around 1927 . He also had a horse trail cleared from his property all the way to Catawba Falls and released a herd of goats near the falls for amusement and occasional sport. (Courtesy of Historic Carson House Library.)

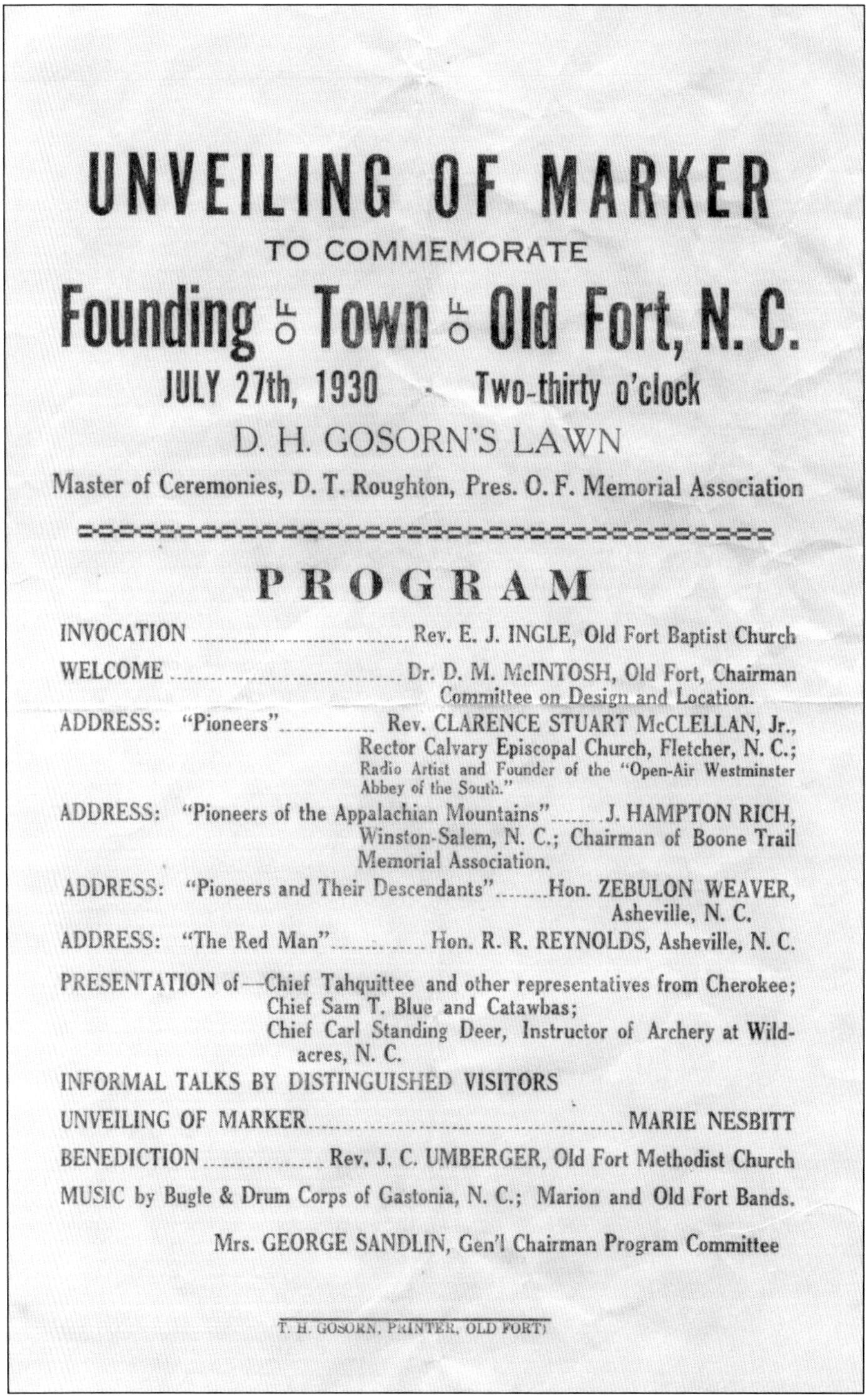

UNVEILING OF MARKER

TO COMMEMORATE

Founding of Town of Old Fort, N. C.

JULY 27th, 1930 · Two-thirty o'clock

D. H. GOSORN'S LAWN

Master of Ceremonies, D. T. Roughton, Pres. O. F. Memorial Association

PROGRAM

INVOCATION .... Rev. E. J. INGLE, Old Fort Baptist Church

WELCOME .... Dr. D. M. McINTOSH, Old Fort, Chairman Committee on Design and Location.

ADDRESS: "Pioneers" .... Rev. CLARENCE STUART McCLELLAN, Jr., Rector Calvary Episcopal Church, Fletcher, N. C.; Radio Artist and Founder of the "Open-Air Westminster Abbey of the South."

ADDRESS: "Pioneers of the Appalachian Mountains" .... J. HAMPTON RICH, Winston-Salem, N. C.; Chairman of Boone Trail Memorial Association.

ADDRESS: "Pioneers and Their Descendants" .... Hon. ZEBULON WEAVER, Asheville, N. C.

ADDRESS: "The Red Man" .... Hon. R. R. REYNOLDS, Asheville, N. C.

PRESENTATION of—Chief Tahquittee and other representatives from Cherokee;
Chief Sam T. Blue and Catawbas;
Chief Carl Standing Deer, Instructor of Archery at Wild-acres, N. C.

INFORMAL TALKS BY DISTINGUISHED VISITORS

UNVEILING OF MARKER .... MARIE NESBITT

BENEDICTION .... Rev. J. C. UMBERGER, Old Fort Methodist Church

MUSIC by Bugle & Drum Corps of Gastonia, N. C.; Marion and Old Fort Bands.

Mrs. GEORGE SANDLIN, Gen'l Chairman Program Committee

T. H. GOSORN, PRINTER, OLD FORT

This is a copy of the program that was handed out to attendees at the unveiling of Old Fort's arrowhead monument. The location is given as D.H. Gosorn's lawn, which refers to the yard of the Westerman House Gosorn had purchased, located across Main Street from the depot. The sloped lawn made it an ideal spot from which to stage the proceedings. (Courtesy of Mountain Gateway Museum.)

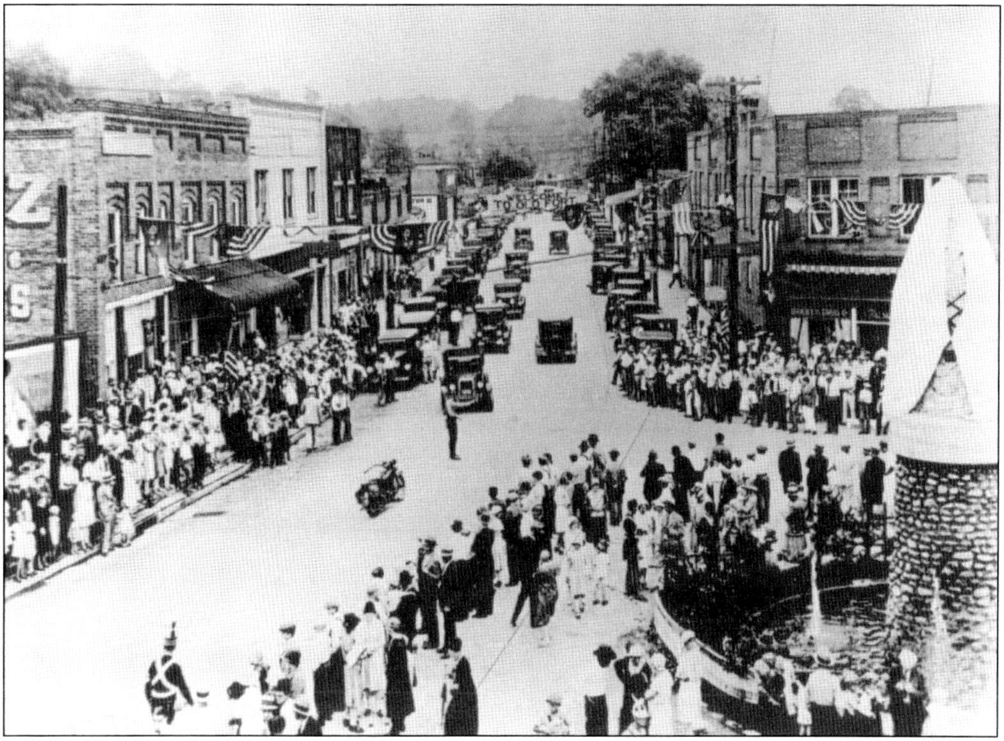

Dignitaries for the unveiling and dedication of Old Fort's arrowhead monument arrive for the event on July 27, 1930. The effort to install a marker to commemorate Davidson's Fort had begun in 1928 with the formation of the Old Fort Memorial Association. Members were P.H. Mashburn, Dr. D.M. McIntosh, Fred Bradley, Daniel W. Adams, Lula Ditmore Sandlin, and Gertrude Dula. (Courtesy of Mountain Gateway Museum.)

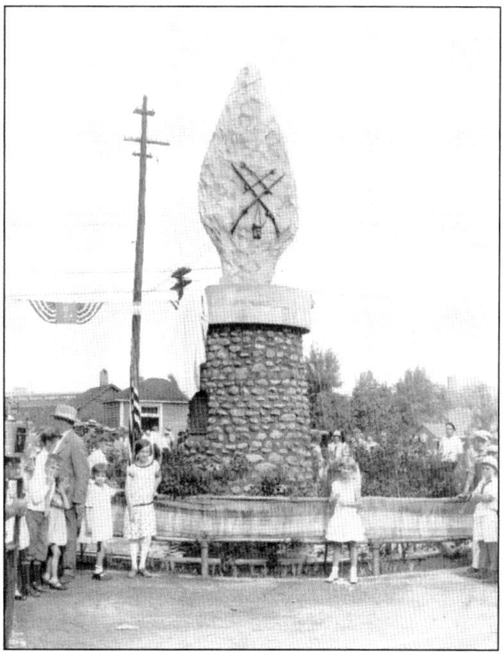

Marie Nesbitt was chosen to unveil the arrowhead monument because she was the great-great-great-granddaughter of Martha Burgin, the only white child born in the original fort from which Old Fort took its name. The base of the monument was built of native river rock, and the arrowhead itself was chiseled out of a slab of pink granite at the Salisbury Quarries. (Courtesy of Mountain Gateway Museum.)

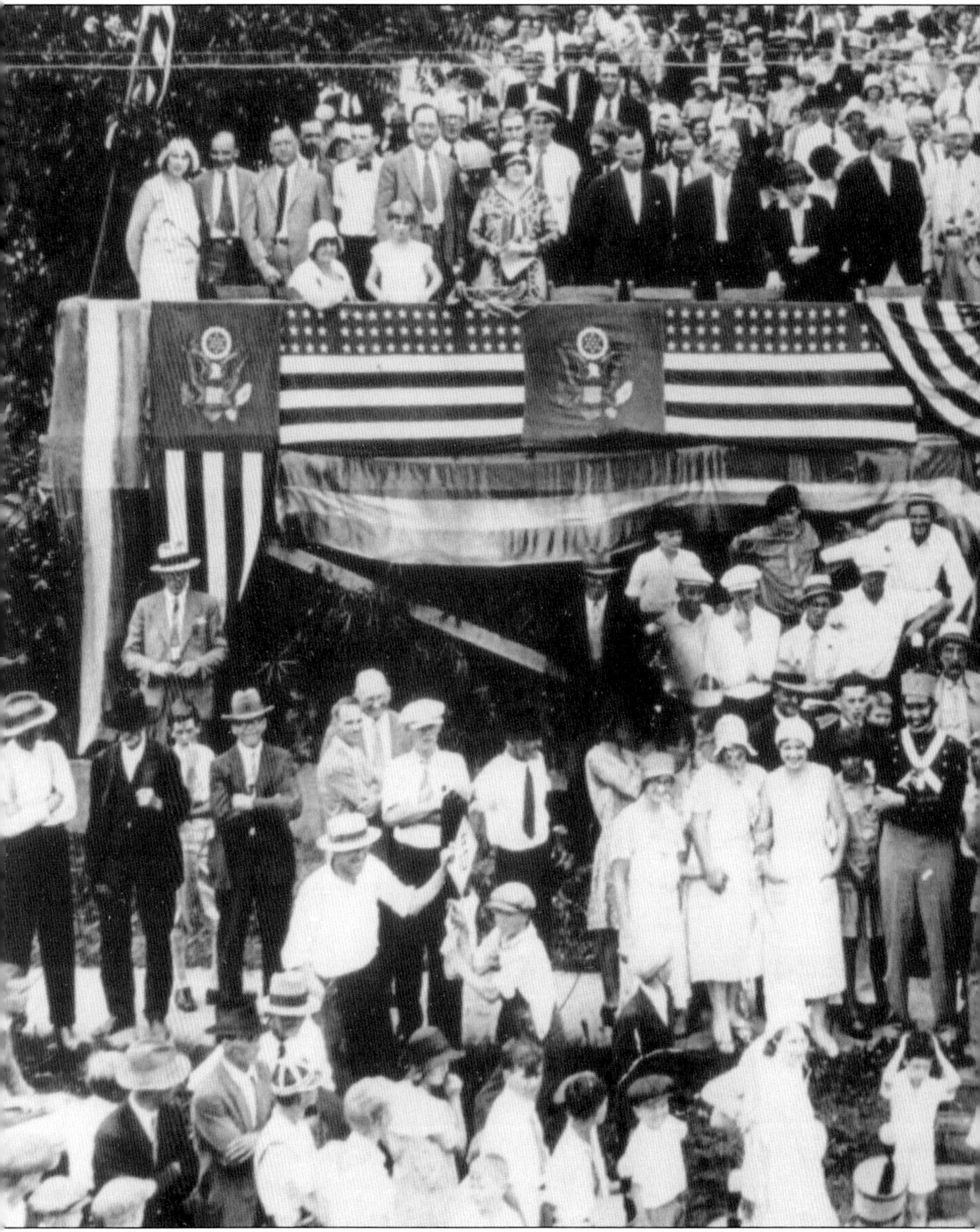

A festive mood is evident among those on and near the platform for the unveiling of Old Fort's arrowhead monument. Many of the Native American representatives participating in the event are standing on the right side of the platform. During the proceedings, a peace pipe was shared

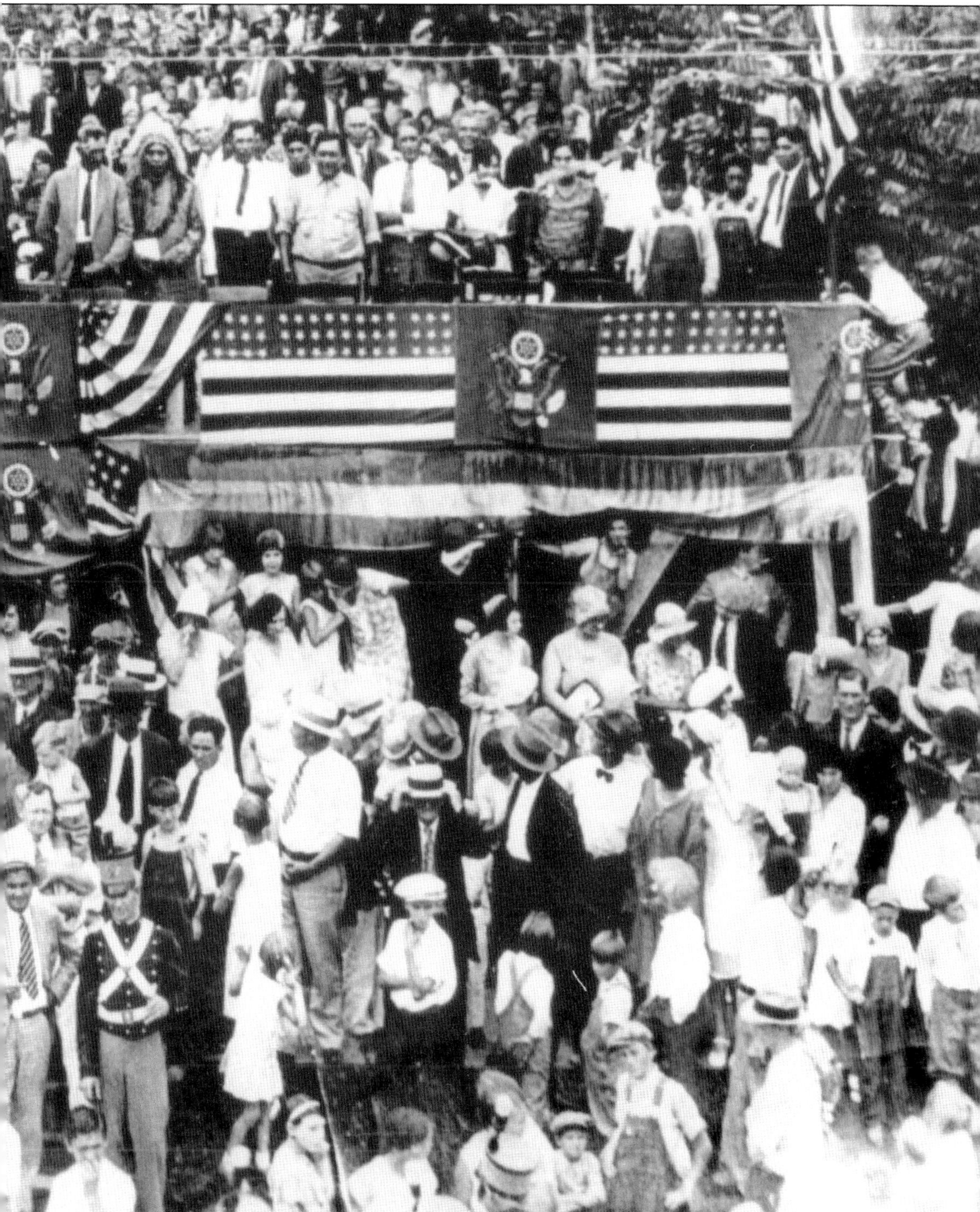

between members of the Cherokee and Catawba tribes for the first time in their history. Musicians from the performing bands can be seen mingling with the audience on the lawn. (Courtesy of Mountain Gateway Museum.)

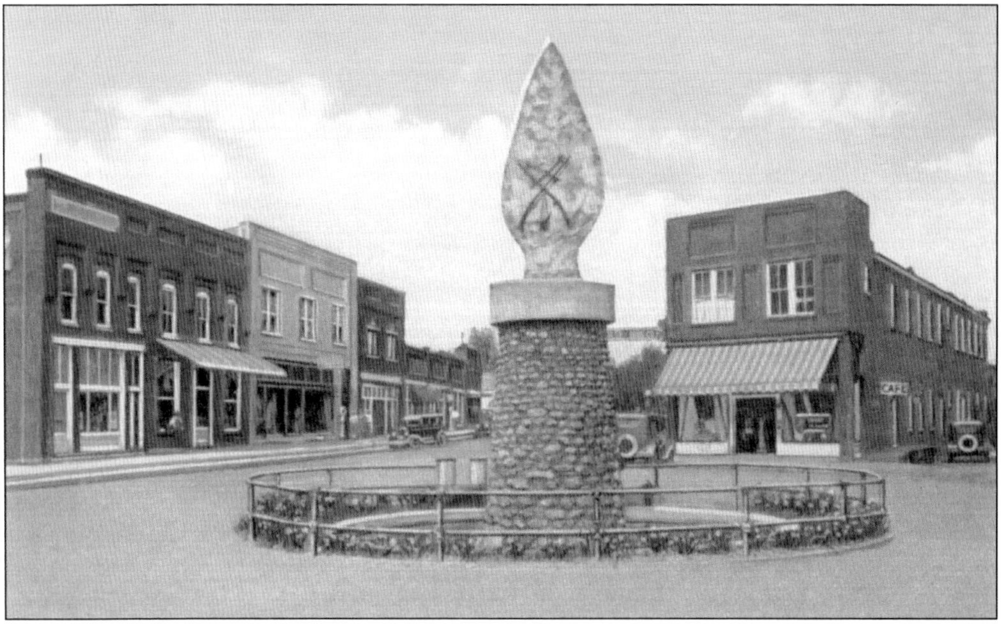

The arrowhead monument is depicted as it appeared shortly after its installation in this postcard from around 1931. The original adornments of crossed tomahawks, crossed muzzle-loading rifles, and a powder horn would soon be replaced by a plaque noting that the site was located on an old Native American trail. (Courtesy of Historic Carson House.)

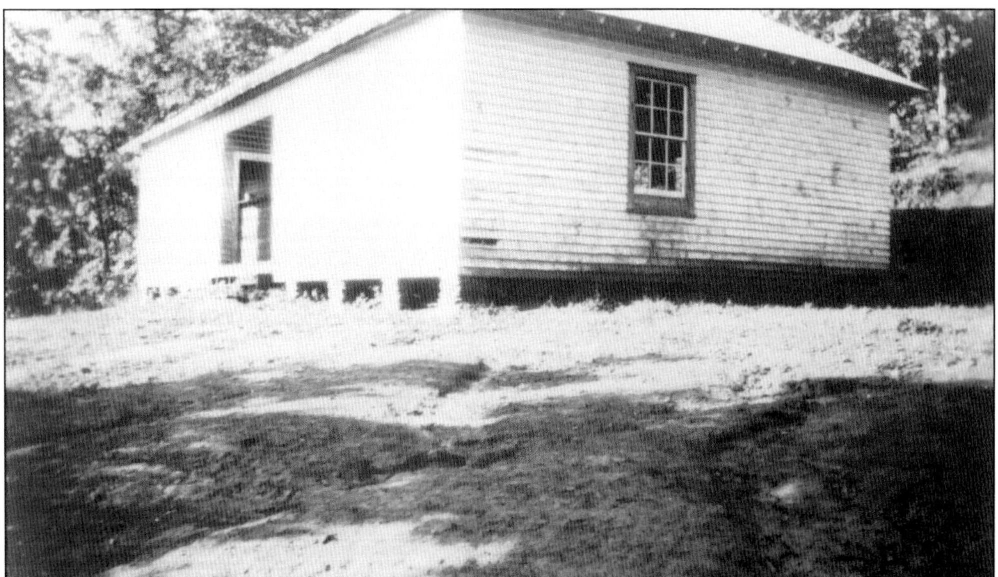

This photograph of the Cherry Springs schoolhouse in the Crooked Creek community dates to the 1920s. When the State of North Carolina assumed operation of the schools in 1933, the McDowell County Board of Education consolidated all of the rural schools in the area into Old Fort School. (Courtesy of Nada Carroll.)

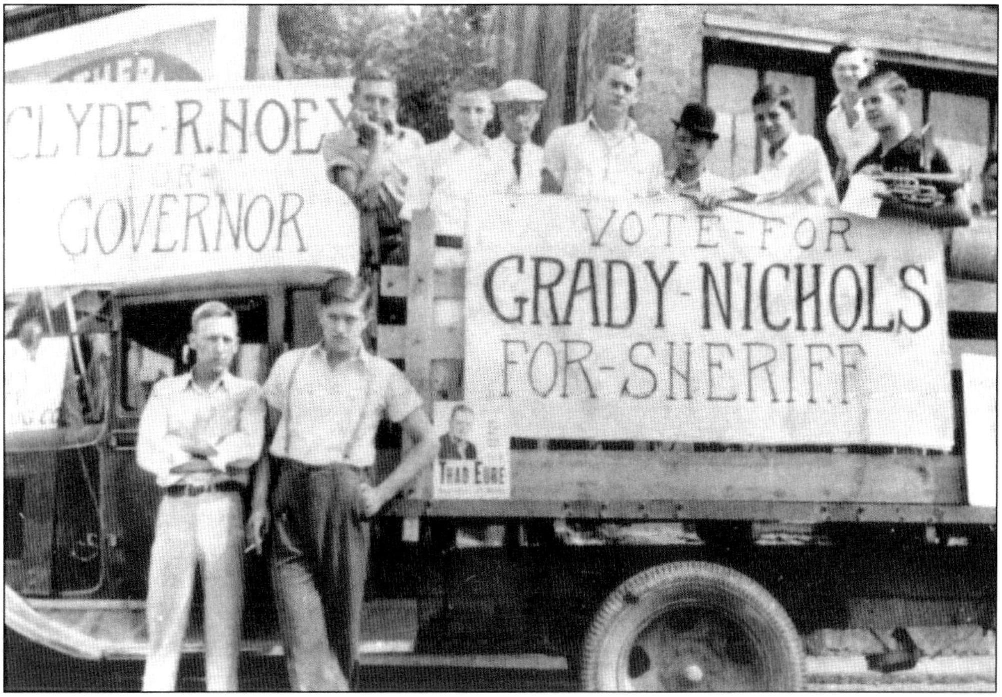

These men are on board in 1936 for Old Fort merchant Grady Nichols's successful campaign for McDowell County sheriff. Their favored candidates, Clyde R. Hoey of Shelby for North Carolina governor and Thad Eure for secretary of state, were successful as well in that year's Democratic sweep. (Courtesy of Bill Nichols.)

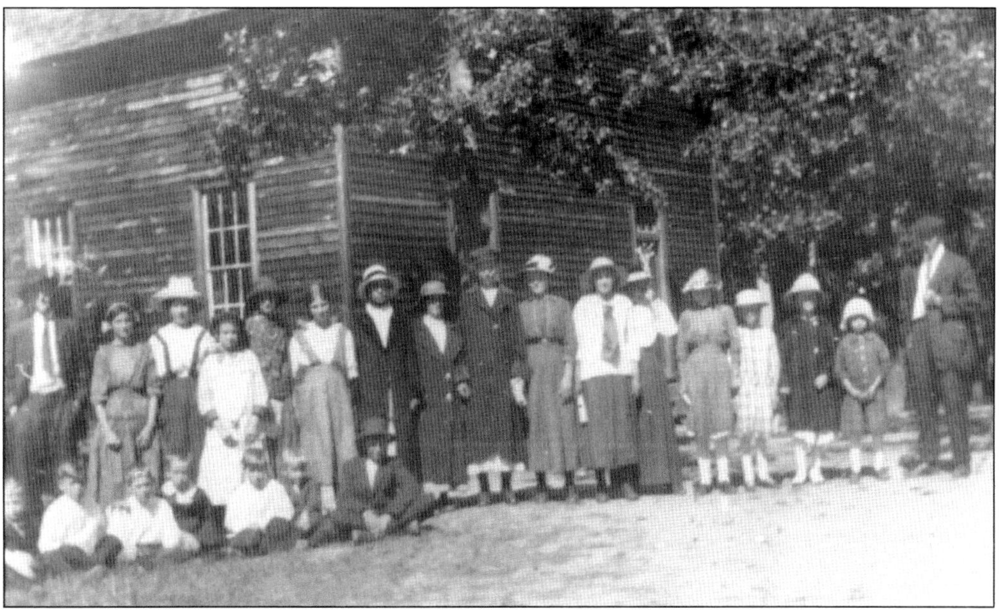

This unidentified group is standing behind what is probably the Cherry Springs Baptist Church building, constructed in the late 1800s in the Crooked Creek community. The name Cherry Springs was inspired by a nearby spring with a large wild cherry tree growing beside it. (Courtesy of McDowell County Public Library and Shirley Anderson Lytle.)

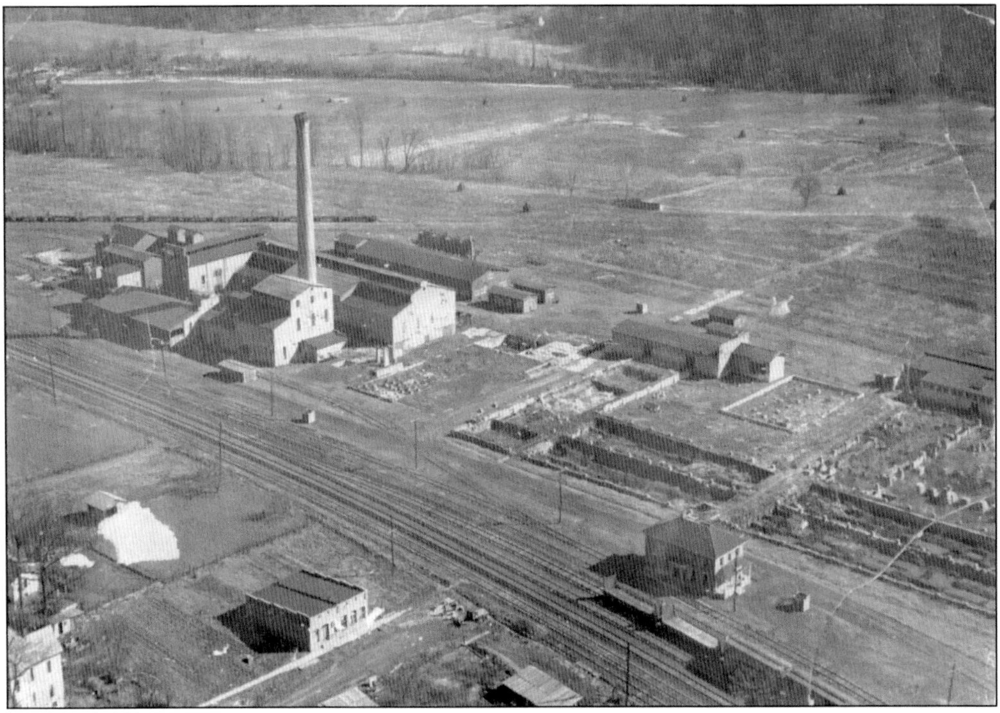

The foundation of the United Leather Company tannery building is all that remains following a disastrous 1931 fire started by lightning. The extraction plant and the frame building that housed company offices were all that survived. The disaster was so economically significant that it was announced on the news ticker in Times Square. Old Fort's economy was severely impacted. (Courtesy of Mountain Gateway Museum.)

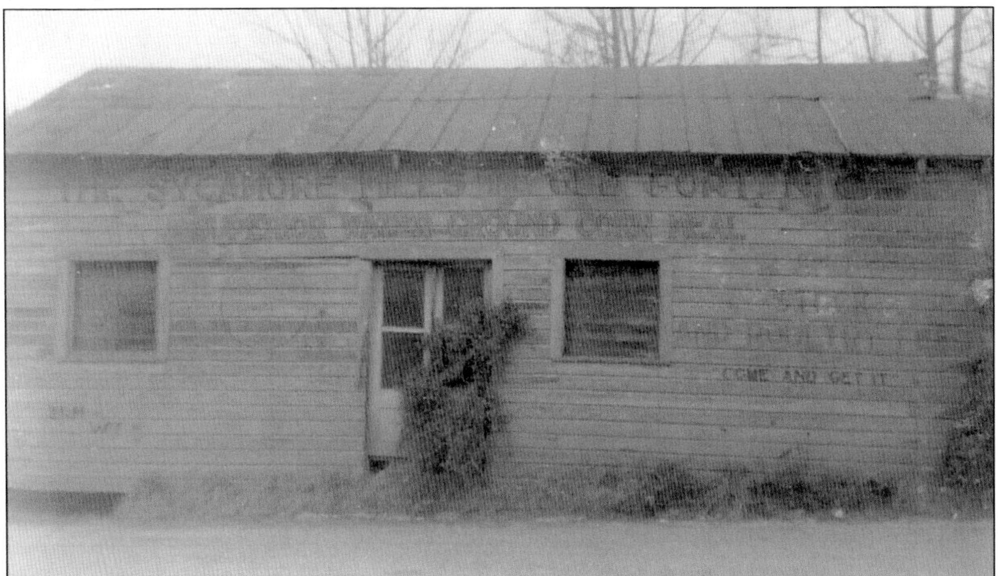

Sycamore Mill was built on Mill Creek by Will Silvers on the site of the old Davidson's Mill. It was powered by a dam built by Col. Daniel Adams. The mill used stone burrs to produce water-ground corn meal and had a capacity of 300 bushels per day. (Courtesy of Bill Nichols.)

An Old Fort group shows their solidarity with the Bonus Army that had set up camp in the nation's capital in 1932. Congress had voted to give a bonus to World War I veterans based on the number of days served during the war, but disbursement of the funds had been deferred until 1945. As the Great Depression deepened, veterans demanded immediate payment. (Courtesy of Bill Nichols.)

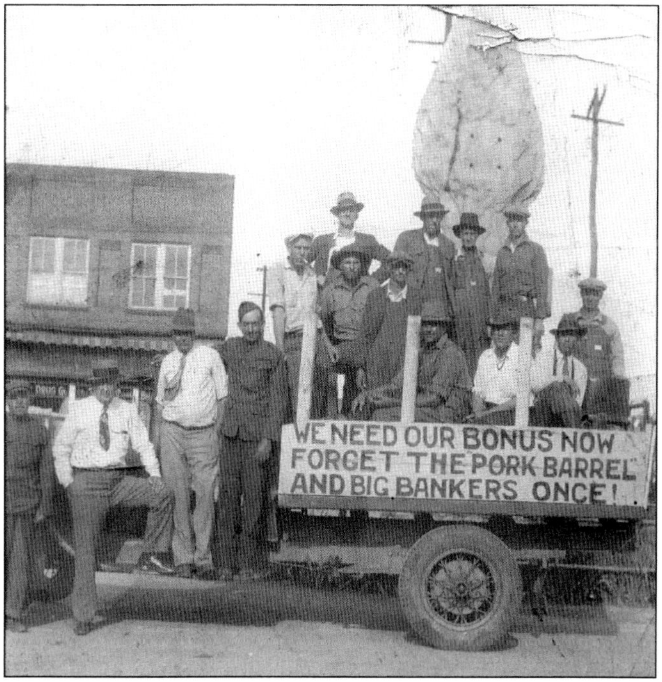

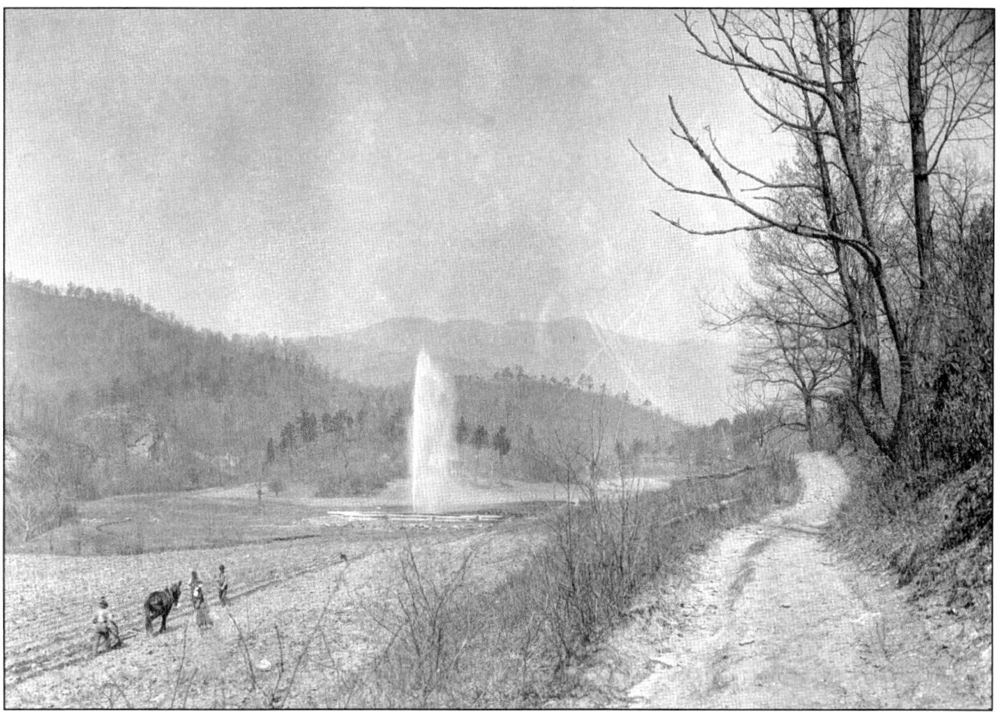

Farmers plow a field with a mule near Andrews Geyser beside Mill Creek Road in this image from the 1930s. The restored fountain had become a treasured part of the landscape and was bequeathed to the Southern Railway by George Baker with the stipulation that it be maintained in perpetuity. (Courtesy of the University of North Carolina Library at Chapel Hill, North Carolina Collection.)

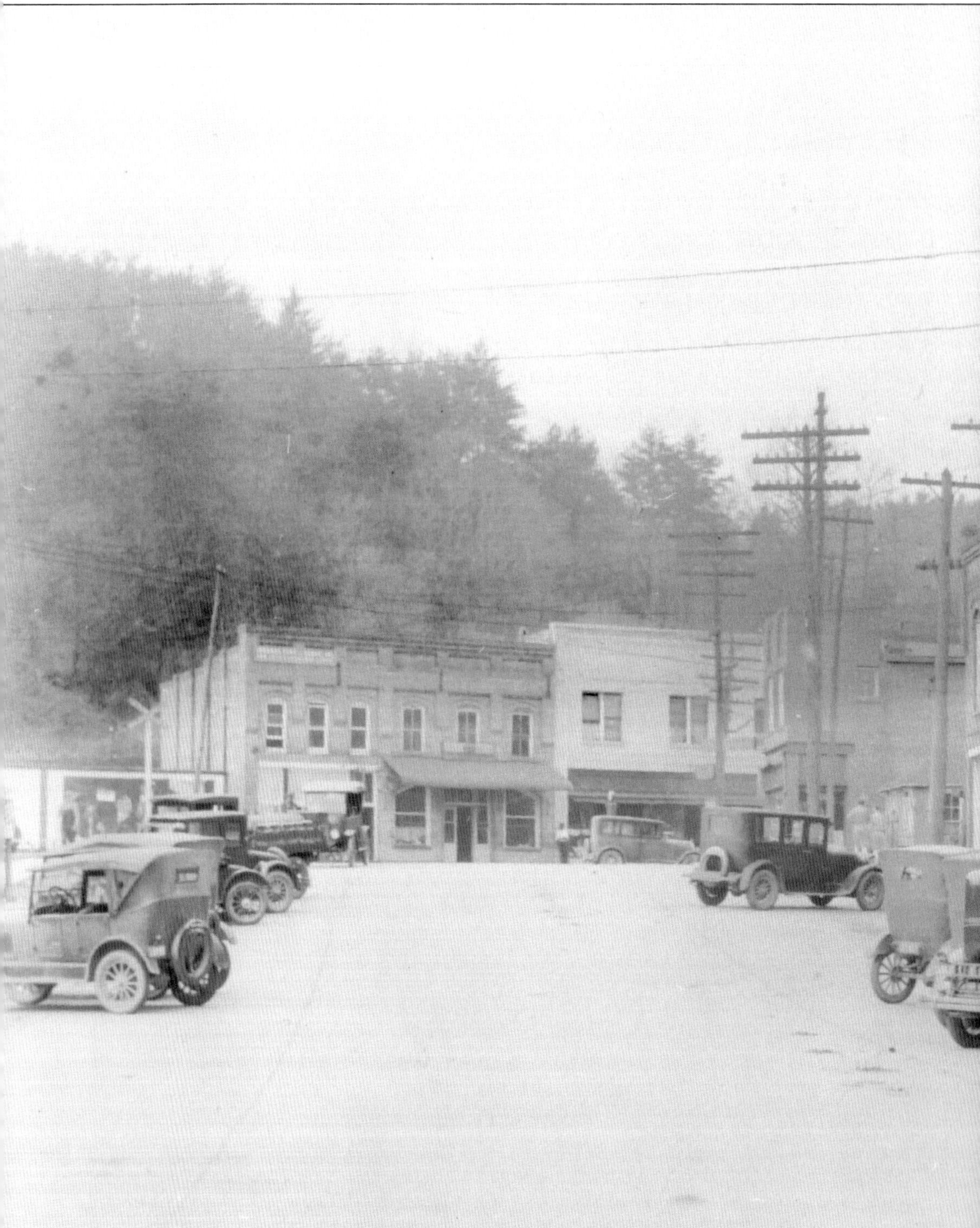

W.A. Gurley's grocery store is in the foreground of this 1930s-era view looking north on Catawba Avenue. Other businesses operating in downtown about that time were a millinery run by Gertrude Dula, Andrew Fortune's barber shop, P.H. Mashburn's drugstore, and the Arrowhead Tea Room,

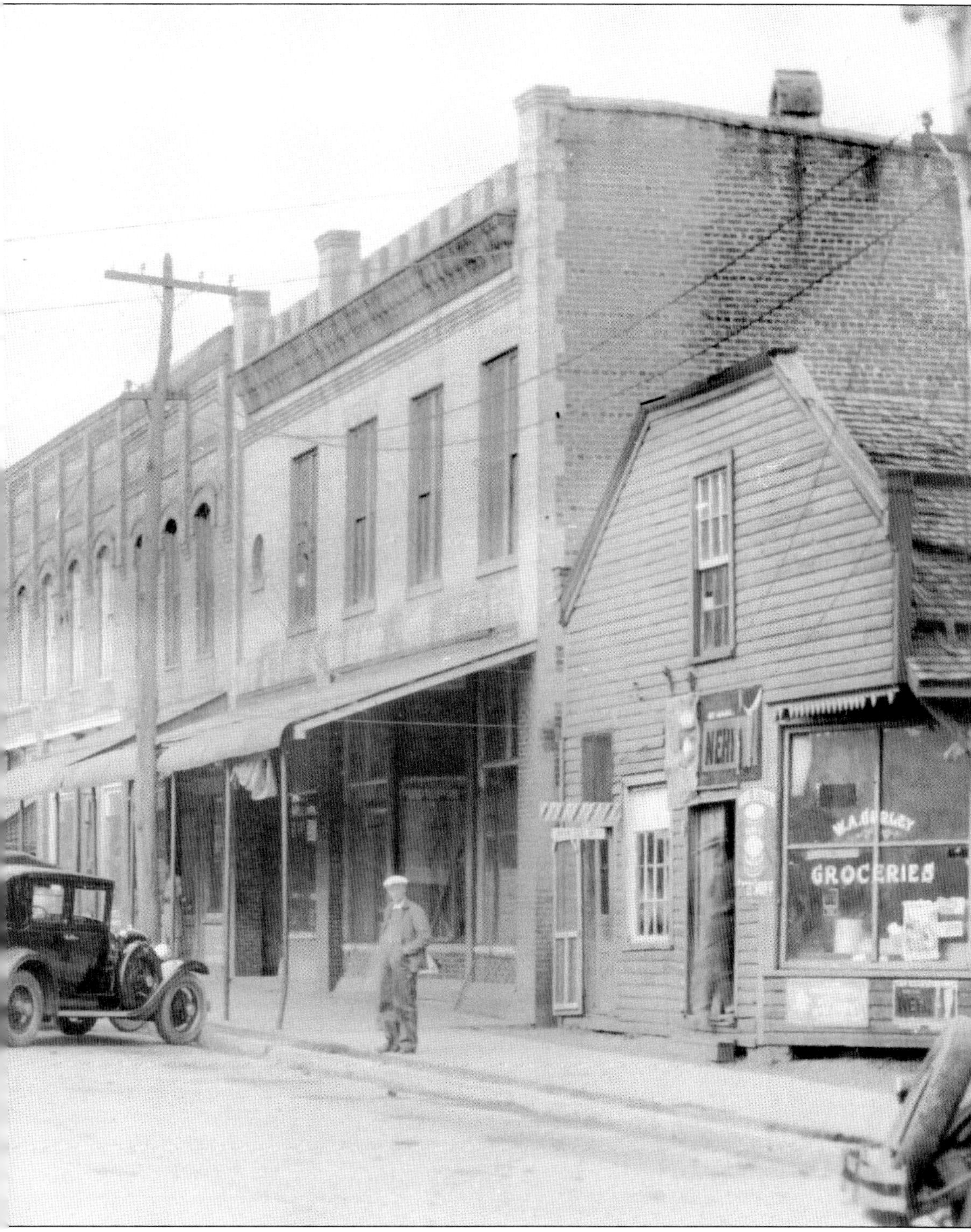

built of native stone and boasting fine dining in elegant surroundings. J.F. Harmon was mayor of Old Fort during the entire decade of the 1930s. Eight passenger trains per day were stopping at the depot. (Courtesy of Bill Nichols.)

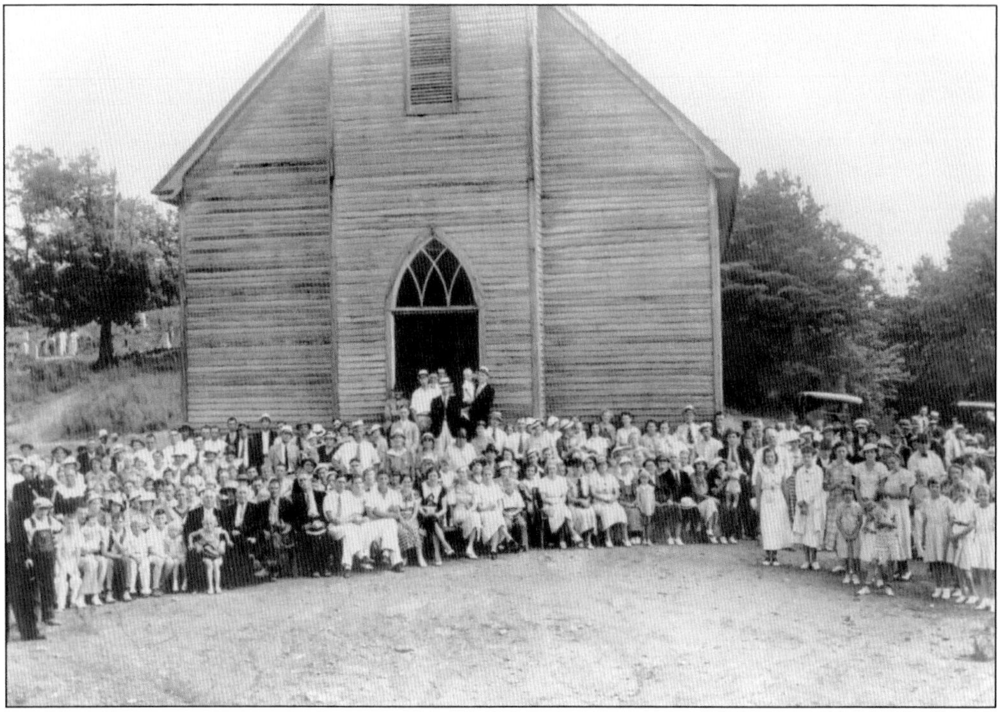

Attendees of the 1935 Burgin-Lytle reunion gather at Bethel United Methodist Church. The families are among the oldest in McDowell County and are linked by countless marriages. The first Burgin in the Old Fort area was Benjamin Burgin, who arrived around 1770. Lytle ancestor Capt. Thomas Lytle received a land grant from Queen Elizabeth for a tract on Bat Cave Road about the same time. (Courtesy of Nada Carroll.)

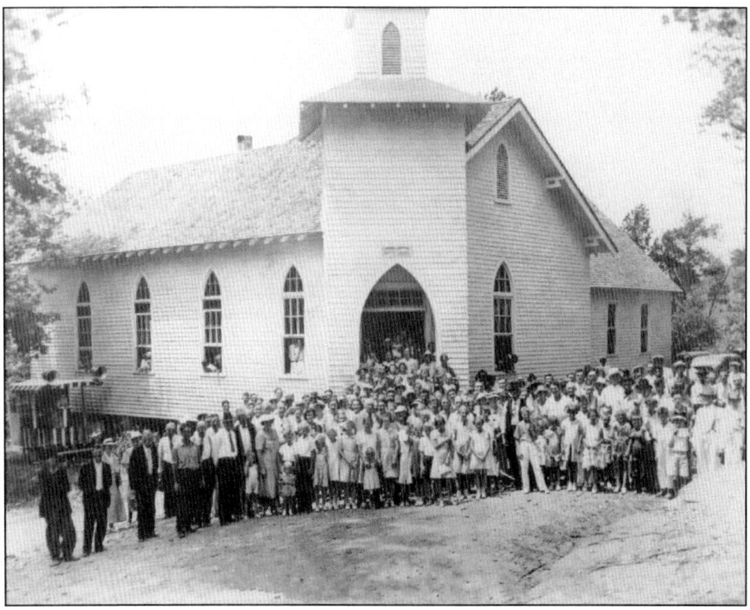

The 1936 Burgin-Lytle reunion participants pose in front of Cherry Springs Baptist Church, six years after their first gathering. Most of the Burgin families in North Carolina are descended from Phillip Burgin, grandfather of Pioneer Ben. (Courtesy of Peggy Silvers.)

Mary Virginia "Binkie" Adams, seen here in 1939, was Col. Daniel Adams's oldest daughter by his wife, Pearl Cross Adams. Binkie married John Vernon Robinson in 1943 during his deployment in the US Navy in World War II. While he was away, Binkie helped build Camp Lejeune Marine Base. She became an Old Fort character in her own right and was an avid historian. (Courtesy of Stuart Adams Robinson.)

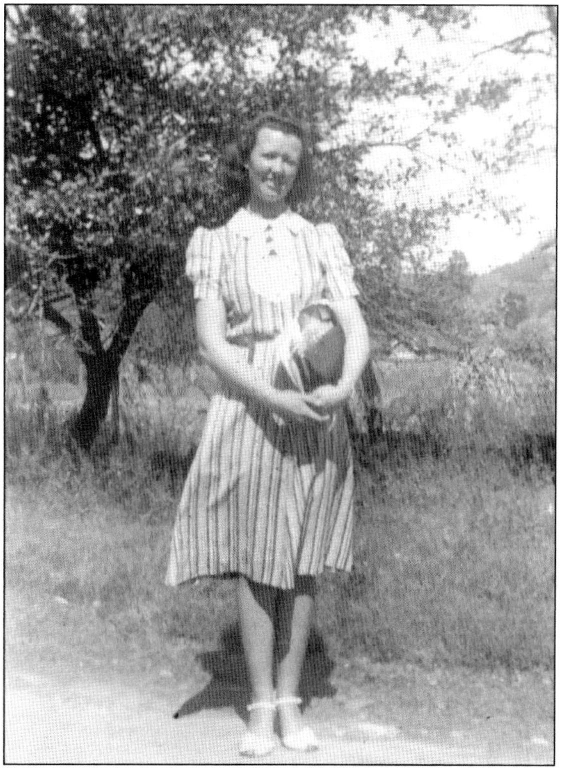

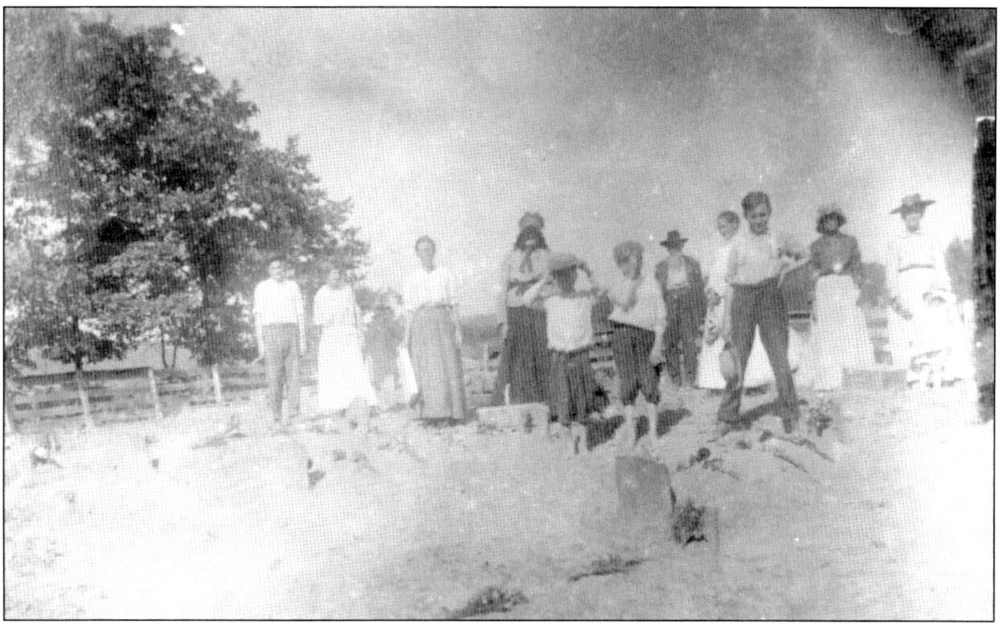

The Harris cemetery on Old Fort-Sugar Hill Road has 33 graves and is representative of the many private cemeteries in the county. Three people in the photograph have been identified: Jess Lackey and Edna Hogan Lackey at far left and Lettie Nesbitt Hogan Harris, second from right. This photograph was taken on Decoration Day. (Courtesy of McDowell County Public Library and Shirley Lytle Anderson.)

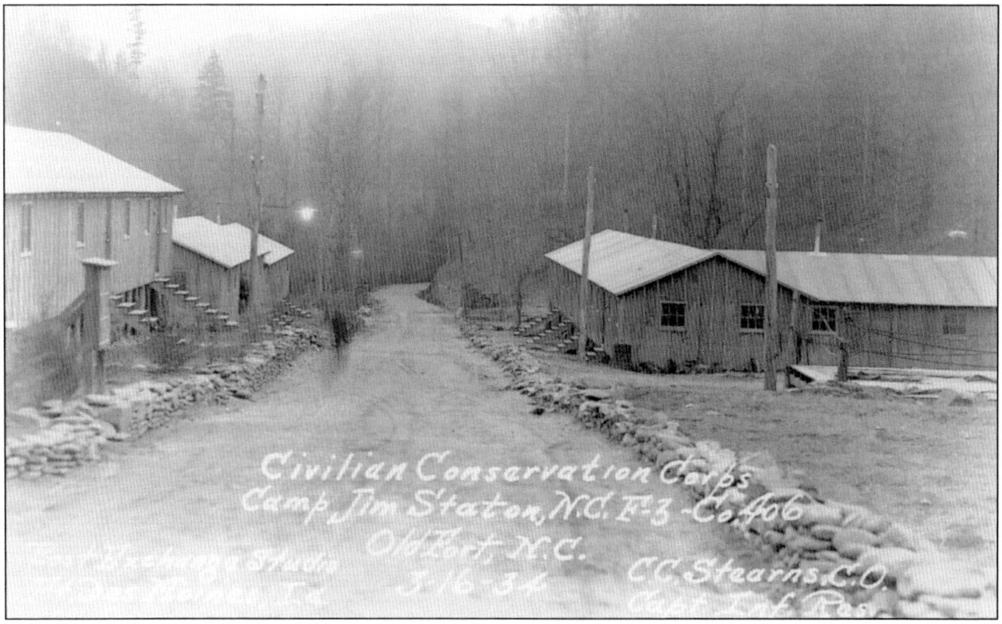

Camp Jim Staton was a Civilian Conservation Corps (CCC) camp located on Curtis Creek. The CCC was a relief program in effect from 1933 to 1942, when the national unemployment rate hovered at around 20 percent. A part of President Roosevelt's New Deal, the program provided meaningful work for the young men involved and allowed them to earn enough money to help support their families back home. (Courtesy of Bill Nichols.)

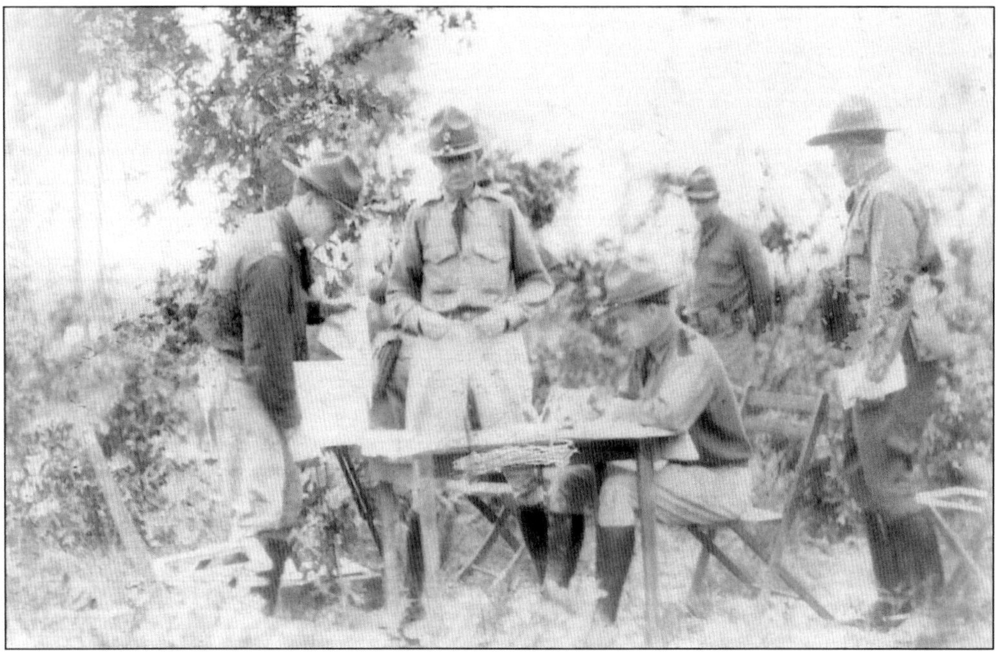

Capt. Clyde C. Stearns (seated) was the commander at Camp Jim Staton from 1933 to 1935. Commander Stearns planned and coordinated the activities of the men stationed at the CCC camp on Curtis Creek. Projects included improving Curtis Creek Road, clearing a road bed for the Blue Ridge Parkway, and building bridges. (Courtesy of Mountain Gateway Museum.)

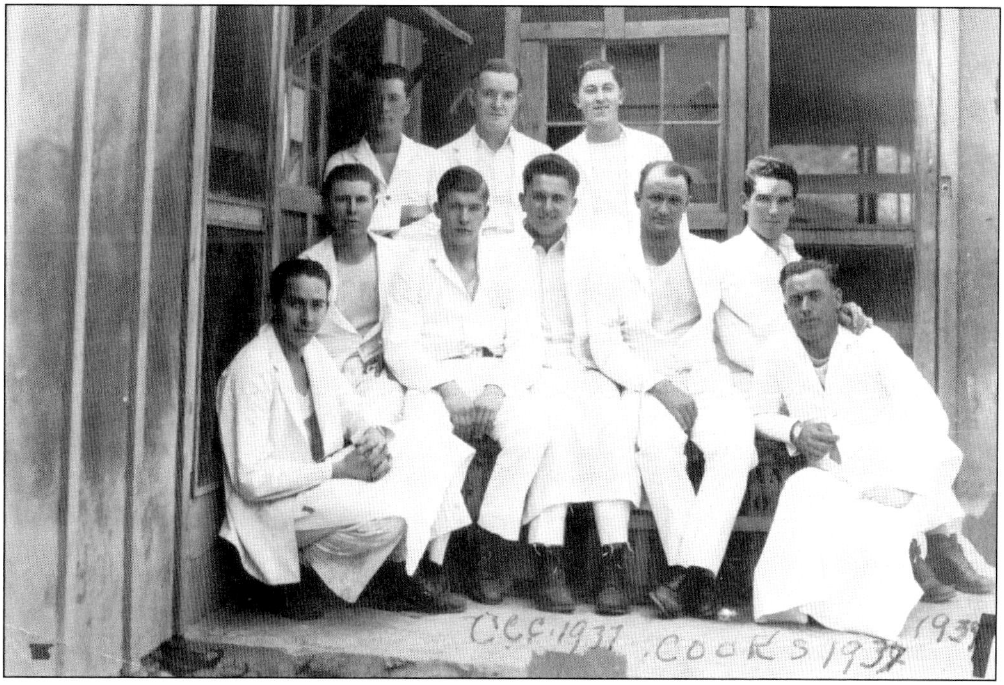

The cooks at Camp Jim Stanton relax outside the mess hall. Providing "three squares and a cot" was a prime objective of the CCC program. It gave young unemployed men three nutritious meals a day and a place to sleep in addition to employing them to provide community improvements. (Courtesy of Dee Daughtridge.)

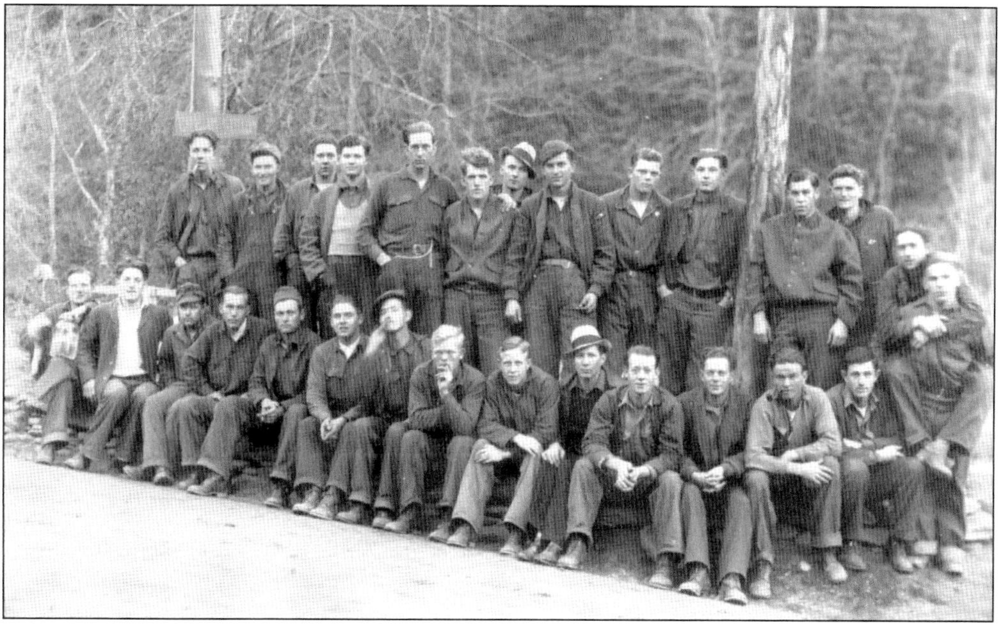

The CCC camps like the one at Curtis Creek were primarily designed for men aged 18 to 24, although veterans could serve with no restrictions. The men were paid $1 a day and were required to send $25 home per month to help support their families. Many enrollees learned to read and write in the camps. (Courtesy of Dee Daughtridge.)

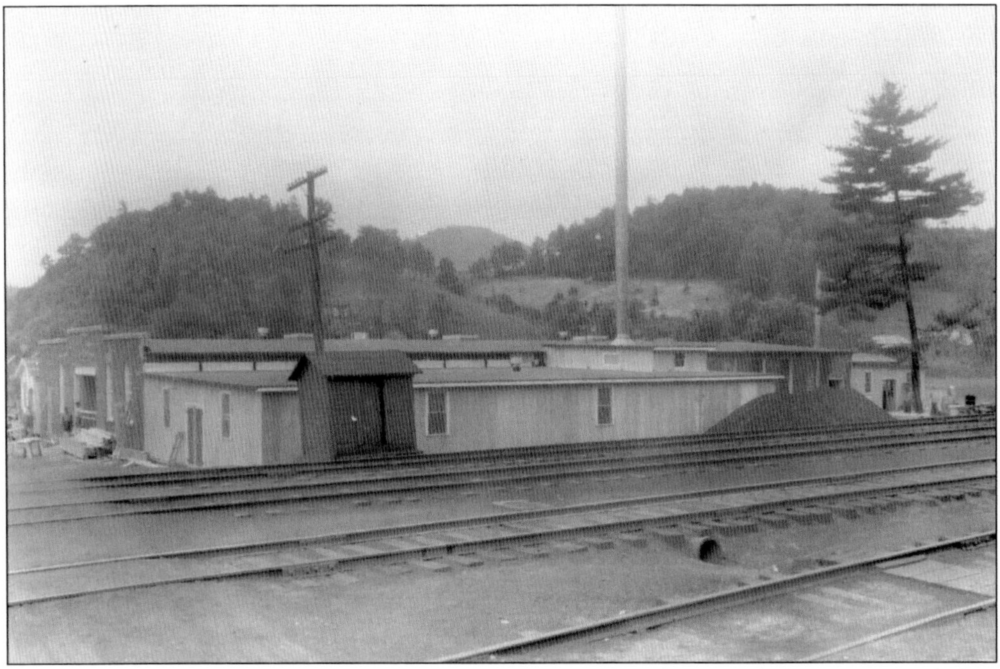

The ERH Tannery is under construction in Old Fort in this photograph from 1935. Built four years after the Union Tannery had burned, the ERH Tannery was a smaller-scale operation. The Old Fort area was attractive to tanneries due to the abundance of tanbark in the surrounding forests. (Courtesy of the North Carolina Department of Cultural Resources.)

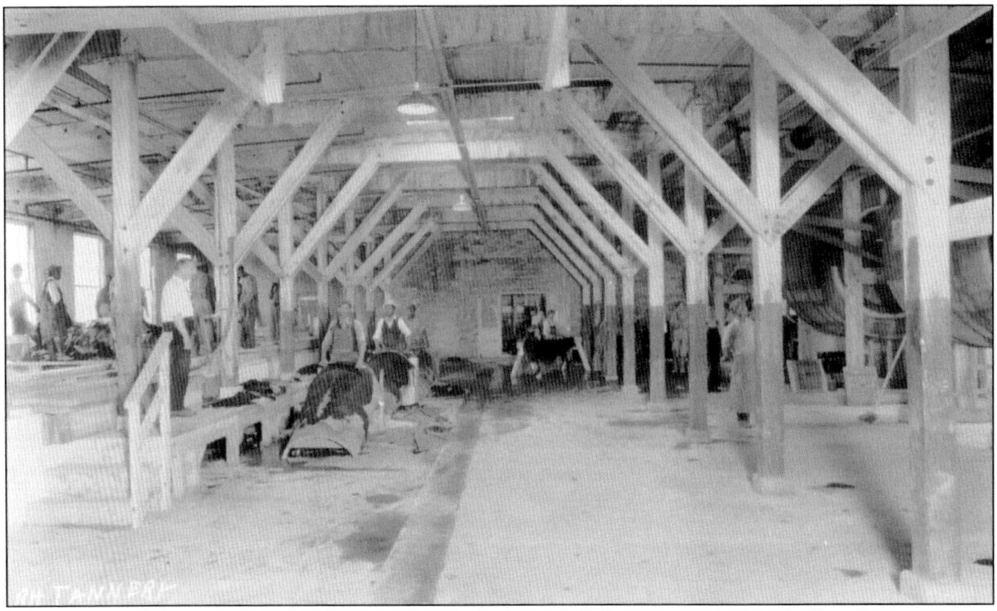

Workers inside the ERH Tannery are processing animal hides shipped in by train. These men are working with hides that have soaked in a solution to loosen the hair. They are performing the next step in the process, which is to scrape the hides and shave them into a uniform thickness. The hides will then be placed in tanning vats. (Courtesy of the North Carolina Department of Cultural Resources.)

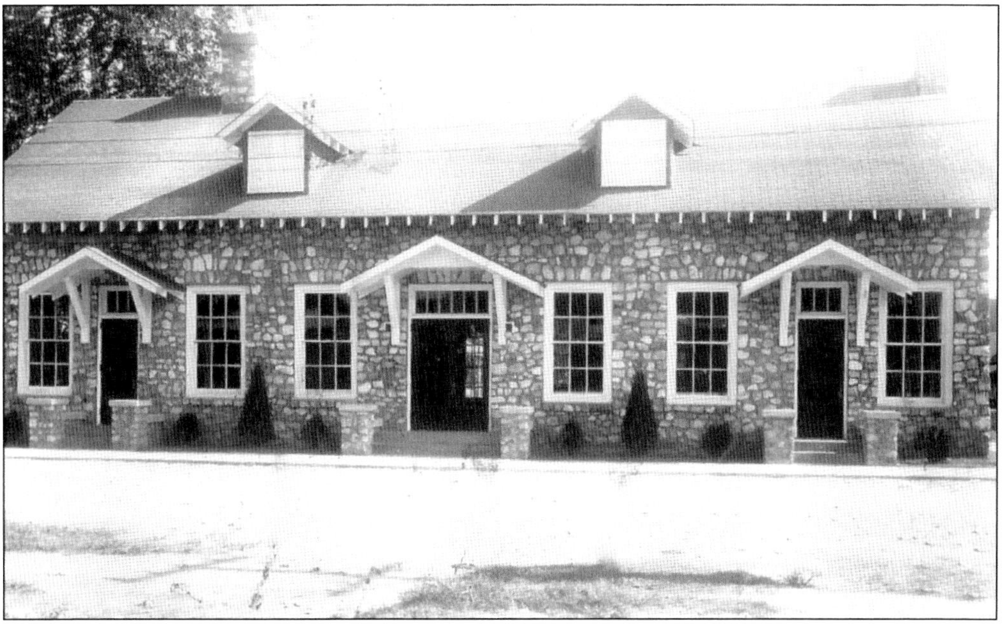

The Old Fort Community Center was built by the Work Projects Administration (WPA) in 1937 using native river rock. It was later used as an inn before the town gave it to the nonprofit Old Fort Historic Sites, Inc., for a museum. When the building was first constructed, it had these three entrances on Water Street. They were later filled in to give the museum more wall space. (Courtesy of Mountain Gateway Museum.)

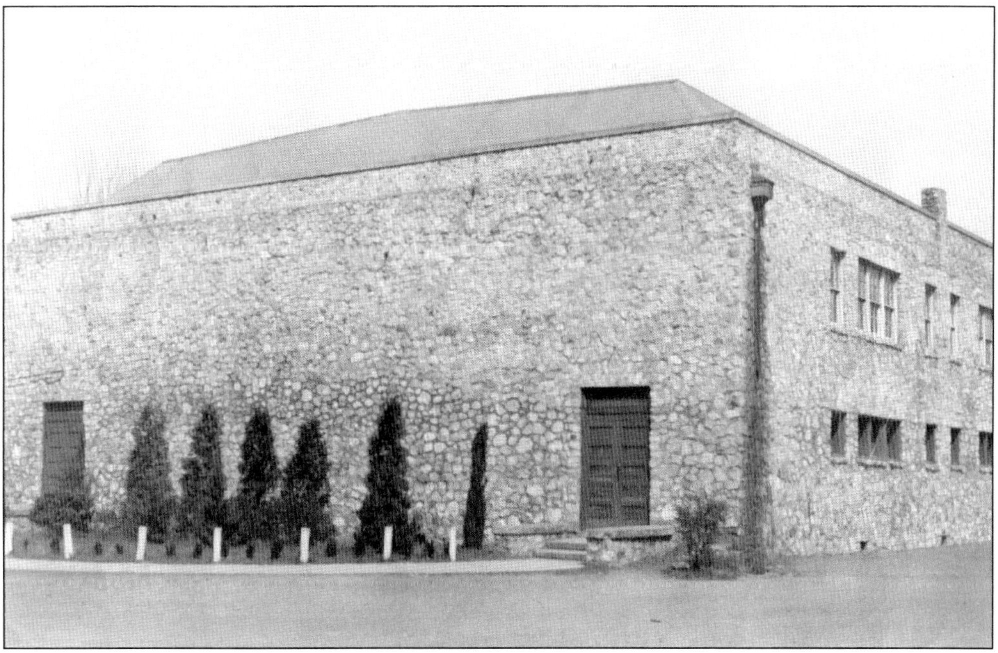

The gymnasium building at Old Fort School was built by the WPA during the Great Depression. Other McDowell County WPA projects included the Old Fort Community Center and the Marion Community Center. Local and state government provided land, trucks, and supplies for the projects, while the WPA was responsible for wages. (Courtesy of McDowell County Public Library.)

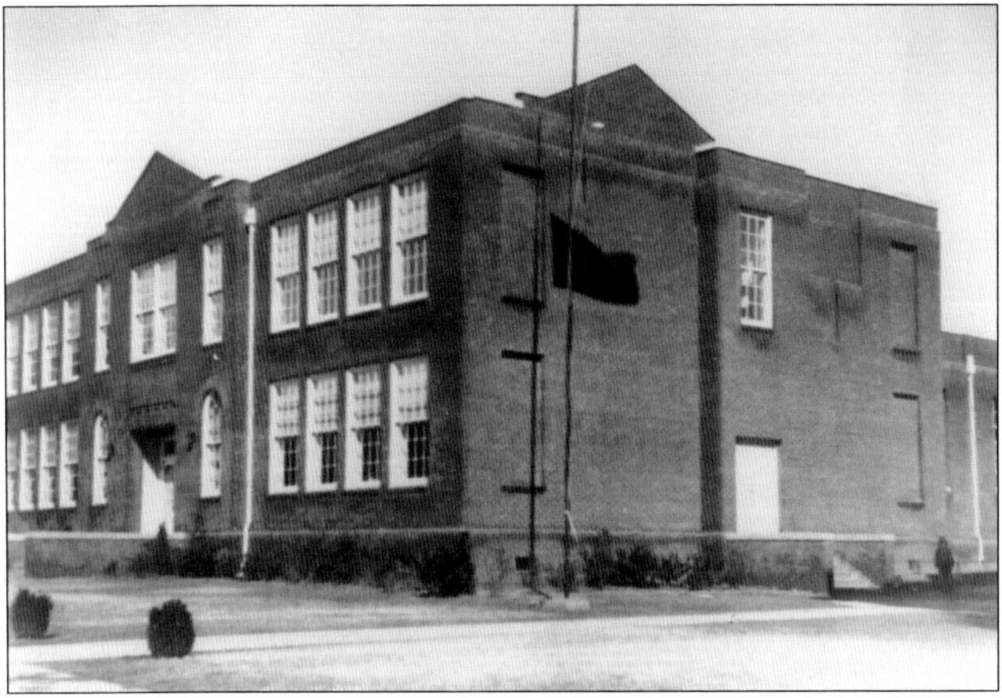

This high school building was constructed from 1935 to 1937 with the aid of the WPA and contained five classrooms, an auditorium, and an office. The updated facilities became necessary when enrollment surged as a result of the consolidation of the numerous rural schools into one Old Fort facility. (Courtesy of Historic Carson House Library.)

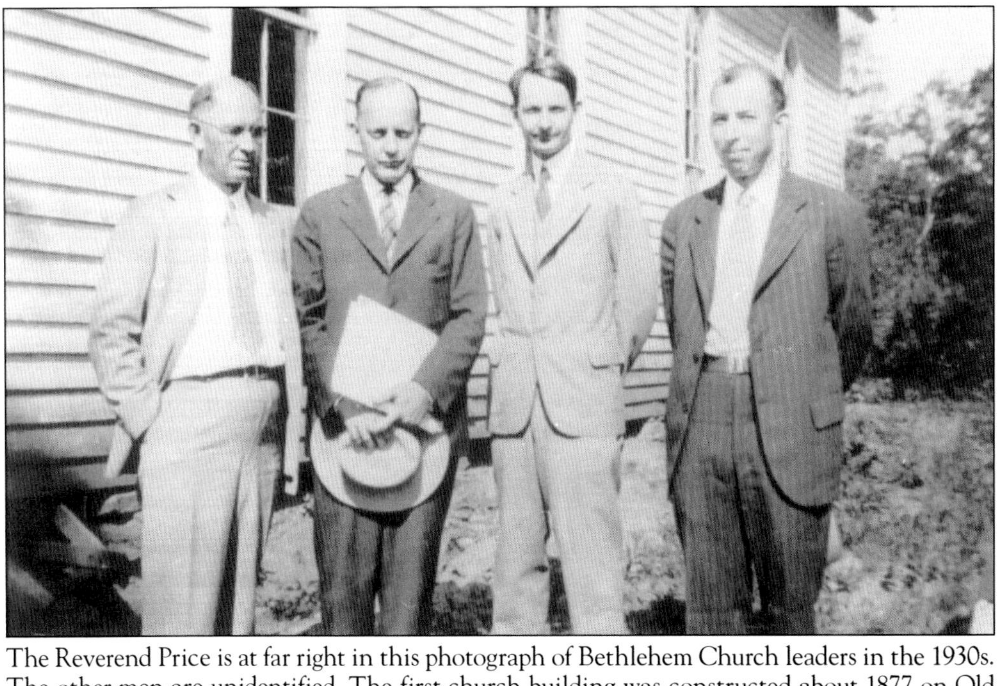

The Reverend Price is at far right in this photograph of Bethlehem Church leaders in the 1930s. The other men are unidentified. The first church building was constructed about 1877 on Old Fort-Sugar Hill Road (Courtesy of McDowell County Public Library.)

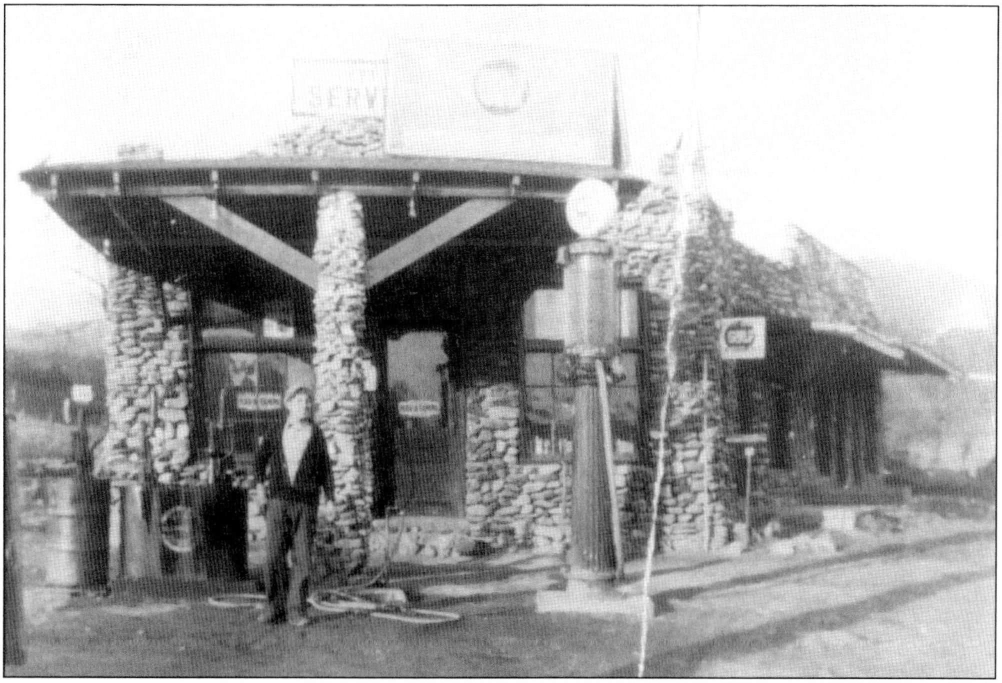

The Big Rock-Little Rock Service Station was located east of Old Fort on Highway 70. The man seen in this 1930s image is unidentified. The eccentric building style and the use of local river rock helped make the station a popular stop for tourists as well as locals. Some of its popularity can be attributed to the fact that it was also a beer joint. (Courtesy of McDowell County Public Library.)

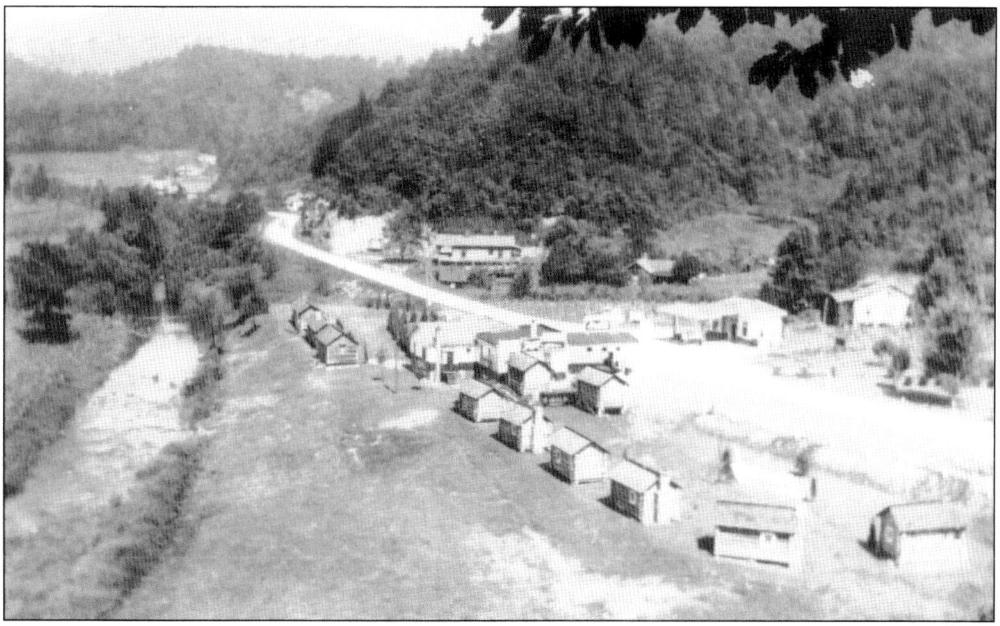

Shanty Town was Old Fort's first tourist court. Ed and Dorsey Silver built it in the early 1930s, just west of town on Highway 70 when that road was the main thoroughfare to Asheville and beyond. Shanty Town consisted of 10 log cabins, a restaurant, and a filling station. The property changed hands several times before it was finally abandoned. (Courtesy of Bill Nichols.)

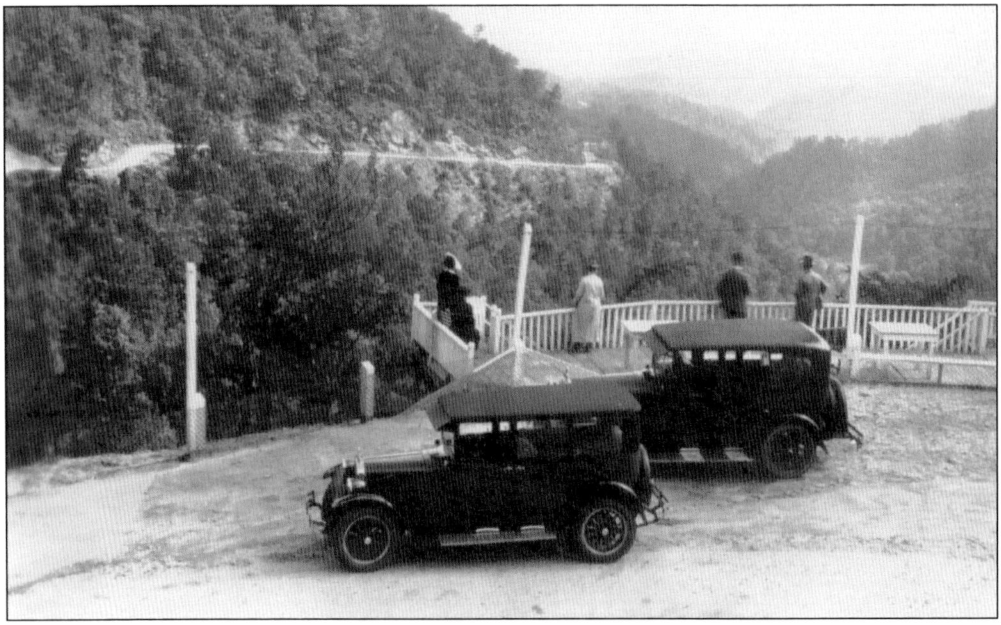

Motorists pull over at Point Lookout west of Old Fort around 1930 to appreciate the view of the Royal Gorge from Highway 70. At this time, there were no retail facilities at the site. H.A. Ragle, who had previously operated the Ragle Hotel in Old Fort, would purchase the land and make it into a full-fledged tourist trap. (Courtesy of Pack Memorial Public Library, North Carolina Collection.)

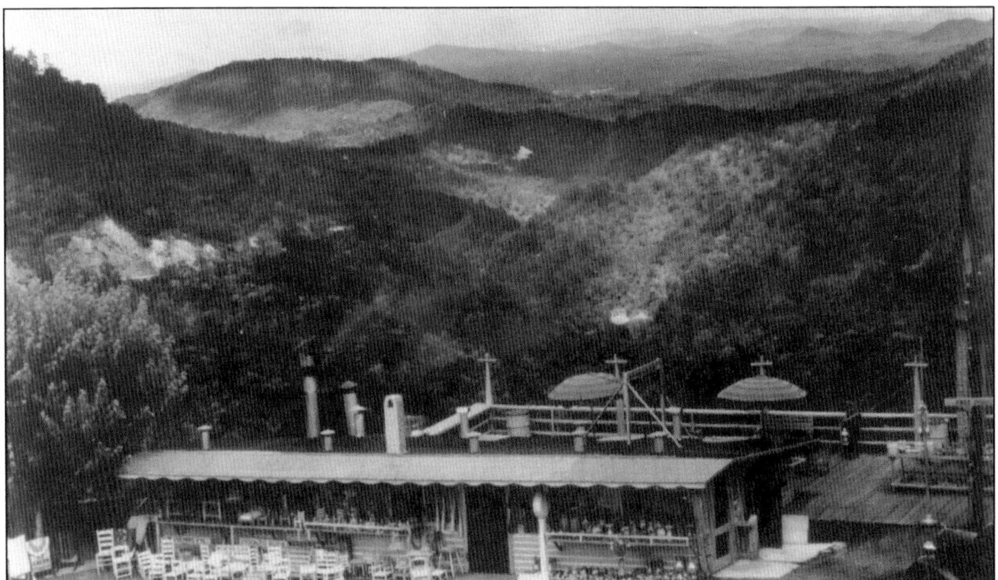

By 1936, Point Lookout had been expanded to include a café, gift shop, filling station, motel rooms, and rest stop. The prime attractions were the hot dogs, fresh apple cider, and Sally the bear, who drank sodas straight from the bottle. Proprietor H.A. Ragle sold Point Lookout in 1947. (Courtesy of Pack Memorial Public Library, North Carolina Collection.)

Five

Times of Change

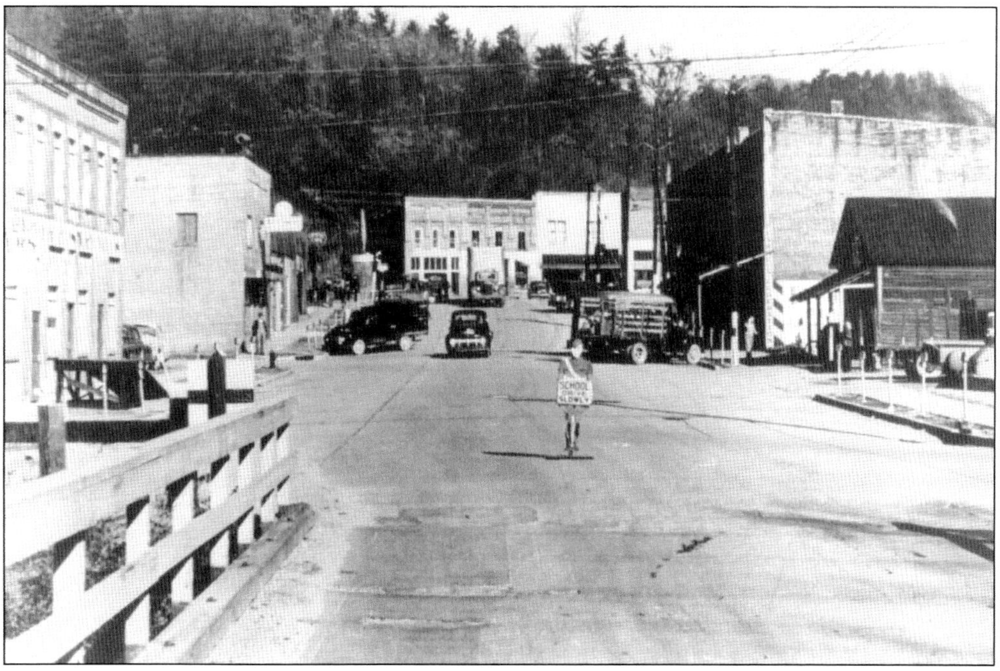

This view looking north from the bridge across Mill Creek in the early 1950s shows Parker Hosiery Mill and Norton's Furniture on the left. To the right are the Farmer's Federation building and the small wooden structure occupied by W.O. Nichol's store. The Nichols family operated a grocery store on this spot until 2012. (Courtesy of Historic Carson House Library.)

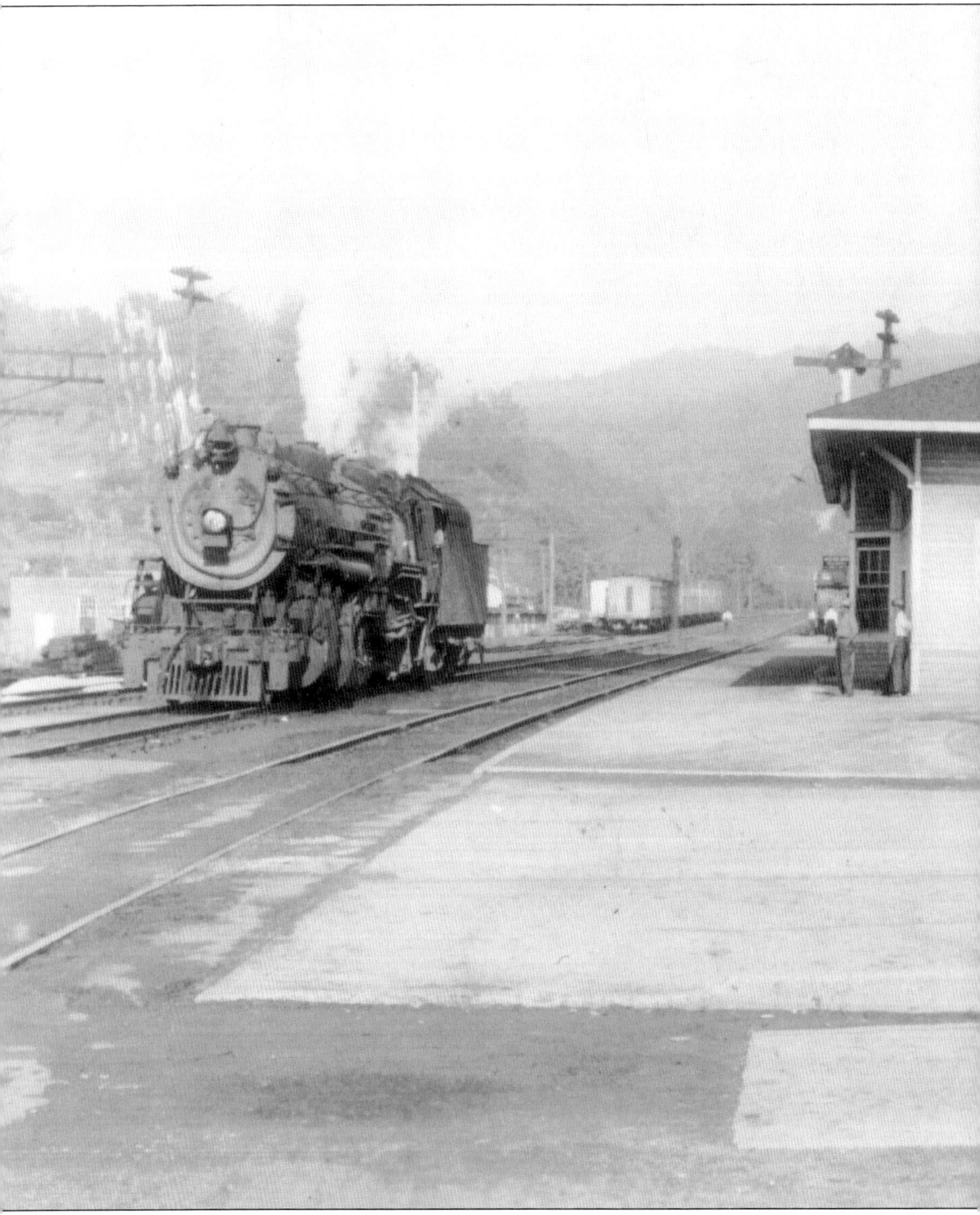

The Old Fort depot was built in 1892. When this photograph was taken in the 1940s, eight passenger trains served Old Fort daily, four eastbound and four westbound. People traveling in the day coaches bought sandwiches, fruit, and candy from Old Fort vendors who made the transactions through the open windows. A "news butch" sold newspapers and magazines. A

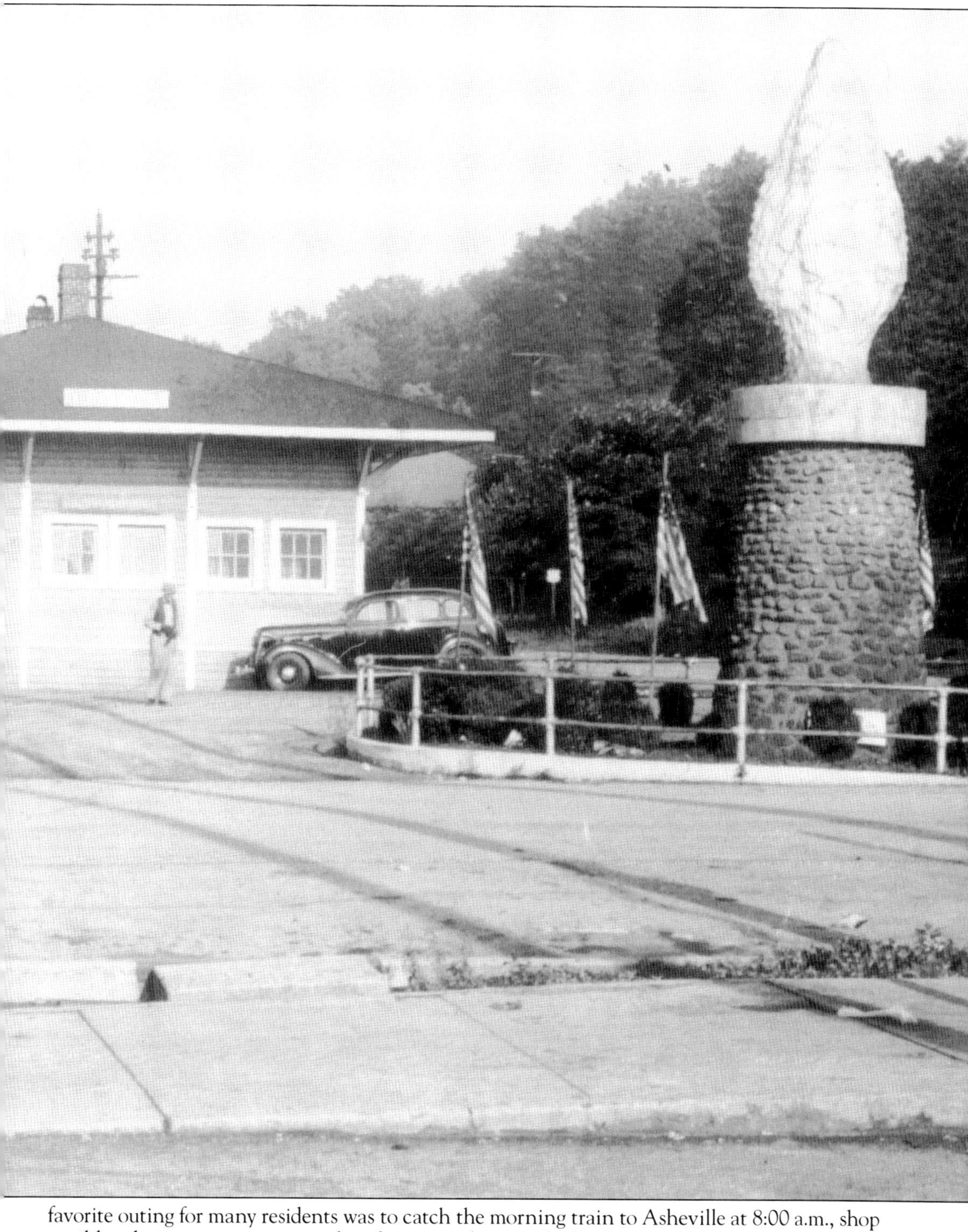

favorite outing for many residents was to catch the morning train to Asheville at 8:00 a.m., shop until lunchtime, see a movie in the afternoon, then catch the 5:00 p.m. train to arrive back in Old Fort by 6:00 p.m. The depot also housed a Western Union telegraph office. (Courtesy of Mountain Gateway Museum.)

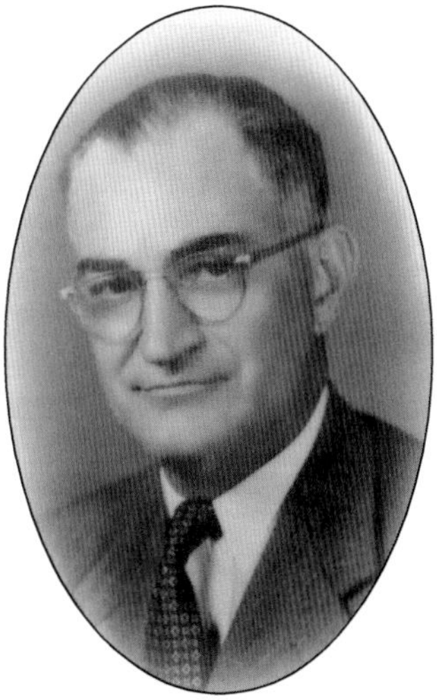 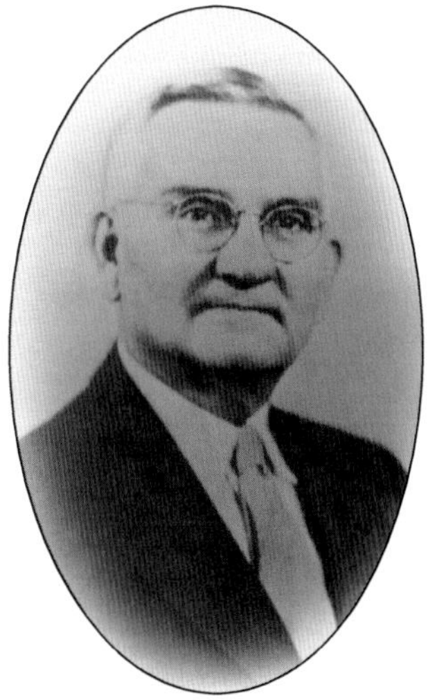 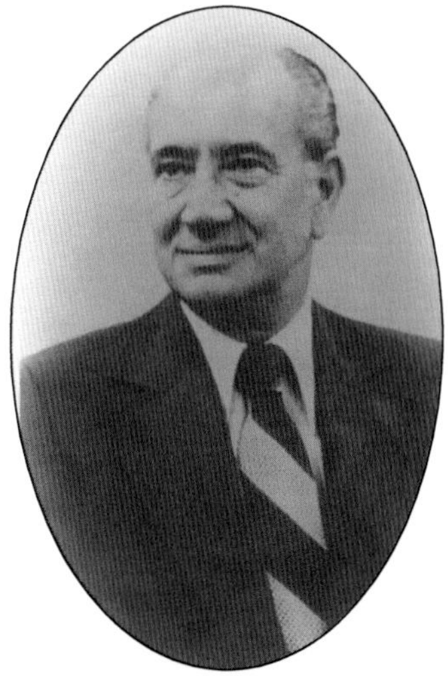

Three prominent Old Fort mayors and businessmen are pictured here: On the left is H.J. Rockett, owner of Rockett Motors and mayor from 1943 to 1947. In the center is I.L. Caplan, who ran Caplan's Drug Store and was mayor from 1951 to 1952 and 1961 to 1969. Vann Hughes is on the right. He was in office from 1959 to 1961 and operated Hughes' Department Store. (Courtesy of the Town of Old Fort.)

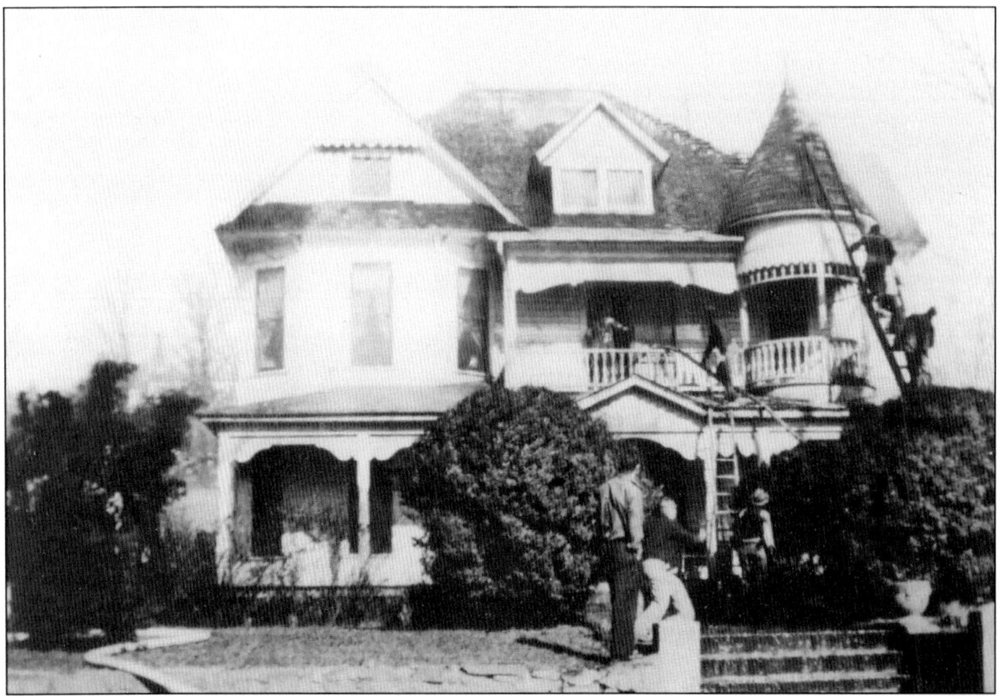

Members of the Old Fort Fire Department battle a blaze on the second floor of the Mashburn House in this undated image. By 1937, the volunteer company consisted of a chief and 25 men and had updated their equipment to include an REO Speedwagon. During World War II, with most of the regular firefighters serving in the military, the town's older men and young boys took over their duties. (Courtesy of Nada Carroll.)

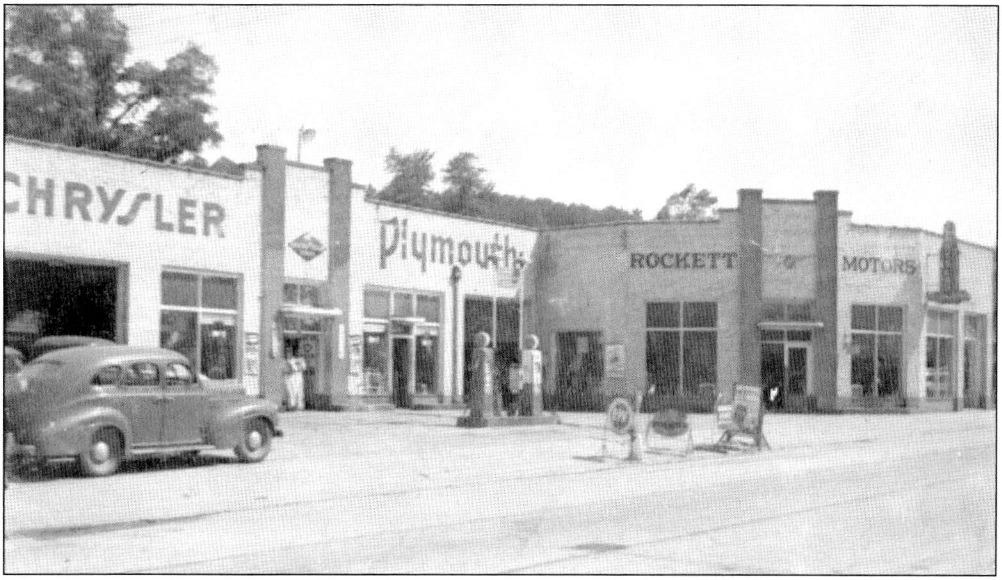

Rockett Motors, located on Main Street, was an authorized dealer for Chrysler and Plymouth automobiles. Mo Par parts and accessories were offered, and Rockett mechanics were advertised to have "the know-how." In the late 1980s, the Rockett Building became the site of Old Fort Mountain Music, a weekly bluegrass and old-time music jam session. (Courtesy of Pack Memorial Public Library, North Carolina Collection.)

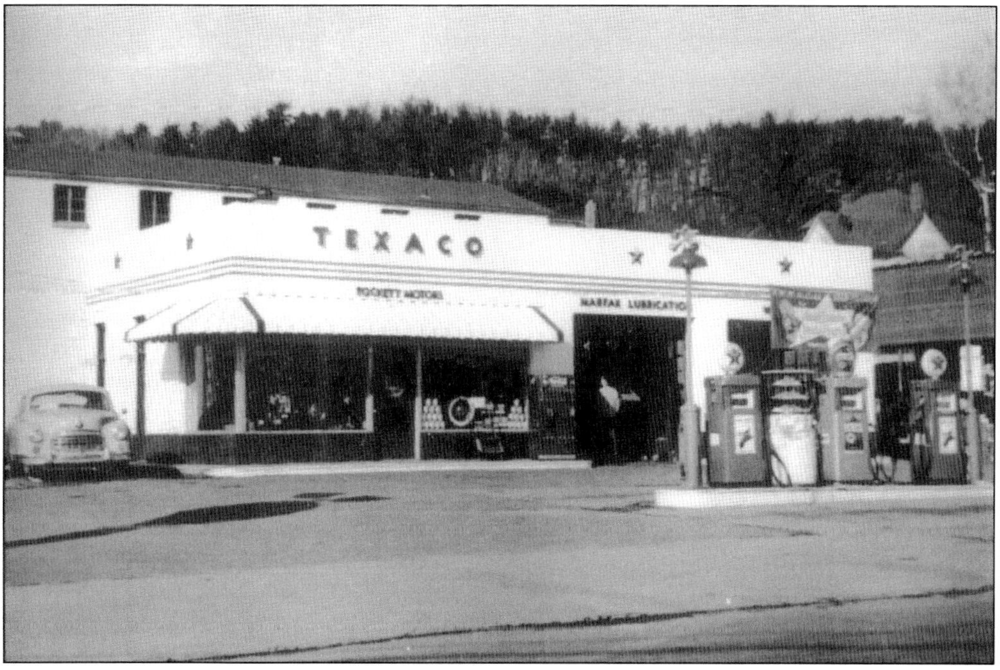

Rockett Motors operated this full-service gas station on the corner of East Main and Spring Streets. The building is an example of a Teague Texaco designed by industrial architect Walter Dorwin Teague. The modern, streamlined, gleaming look revolutionized filling station design across postwar America. An automotive repair business continues to operate in this original Old Fort building at the time of this writing. (Courtesy of Bill Nichols.)

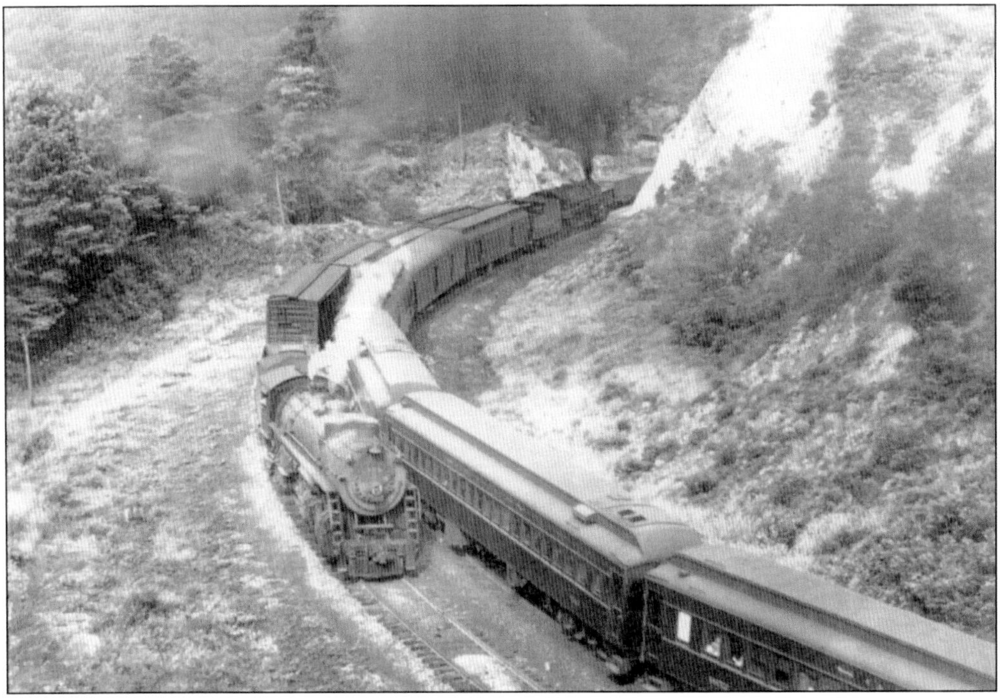

A freight train passes passenger train No. 15 in 1944. No. 15 was the Asheville-Salisbury morning local. In addition to the passenger cars, it is pulling a baggage car and a mail car. (Courtesy of Mountain Gateway Museum.)

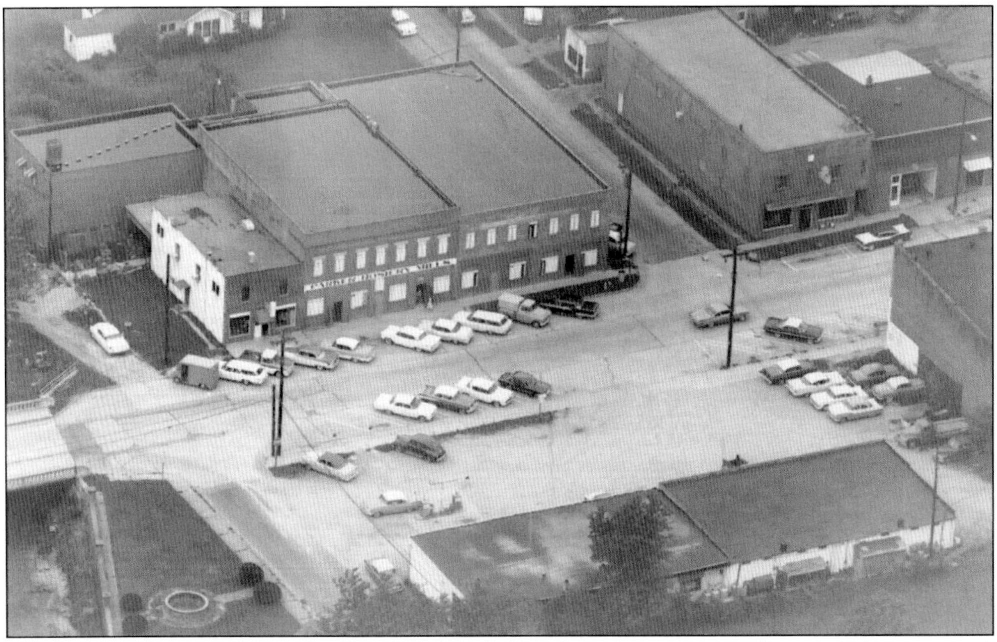

Knitting machine mechanic E.W. Parker founded Parker Hosiery in 1946 to manufacture men's crew socks. By the 1970s, over 300 workers producing a variety of men's and ladies' hosiery were employed at the 100,000-square-foot plant. With the rise of automation and inexpensive imports, the number of employees fell substantially beginning in the late 1980s. (Courtesy of Bill Nichols.)

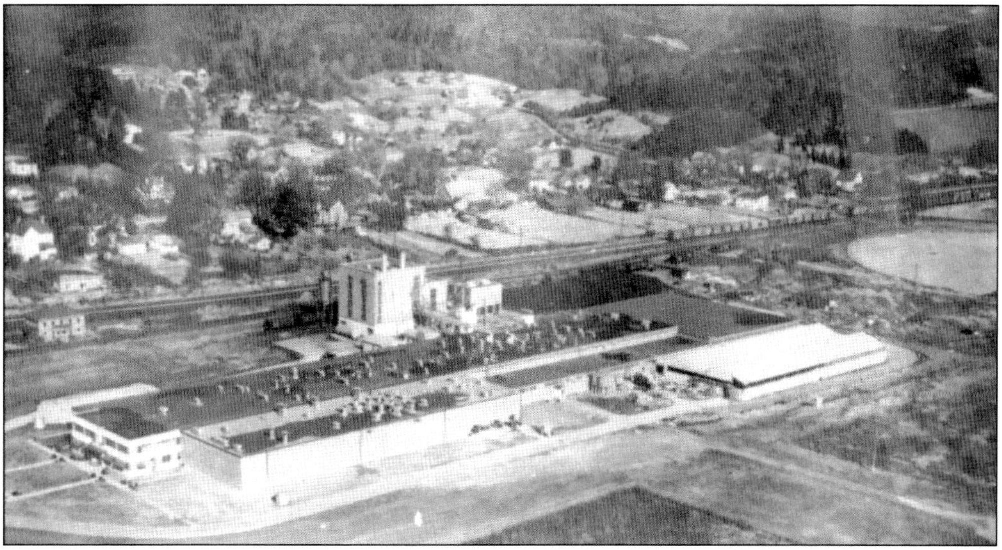

The Old Fort Finishing Plant was built in 1946 as a subsidiary of United Merchants and Manufacturers, Inc., for dyeing and finishing rayon fabrics. At its peak, the Old Fort plant employed 1,000 people and was processing up to two million yards of fabric daily. The closing of the plant in 1984 dealt a huge economic blow to the town. (Courtesy of McDowell County Public Library.)

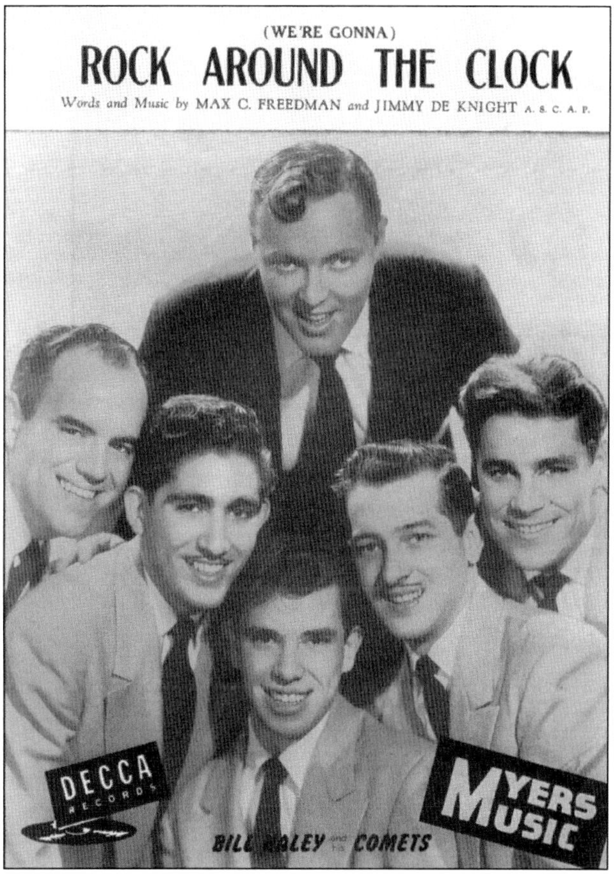

Marshall Lytle, pictured second from right, was an Old Fort native and the original bass player for Bill Haley & His Comets. He performed on "Rock Around the Clock" and other seminal rock and roll recordings by the group. Lytle pioneered an athletic and playful upright bass performance style and was inducted along with the other original Comets into the Rock and Roll Hall of Fame in 2012. (Author's collection.)

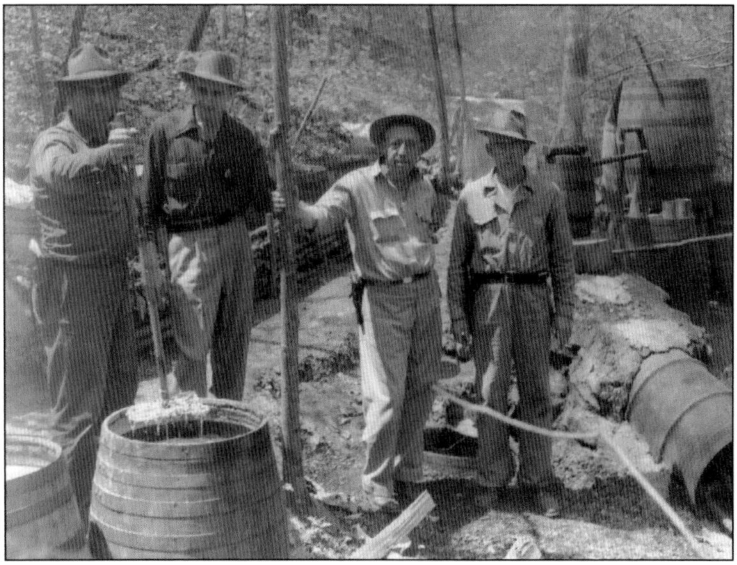

McDowell County sheriff Ashby Robinson (second from left) and three deputies examine an illegal still discovered in the Old Fort area. One of the deputies displays the mash from a barrel. Robinson was sheriff from 1950 to 1958 and had served three terms as mayor of Old Fort before that. (Courtesy of Stuart Adams Robinson.)

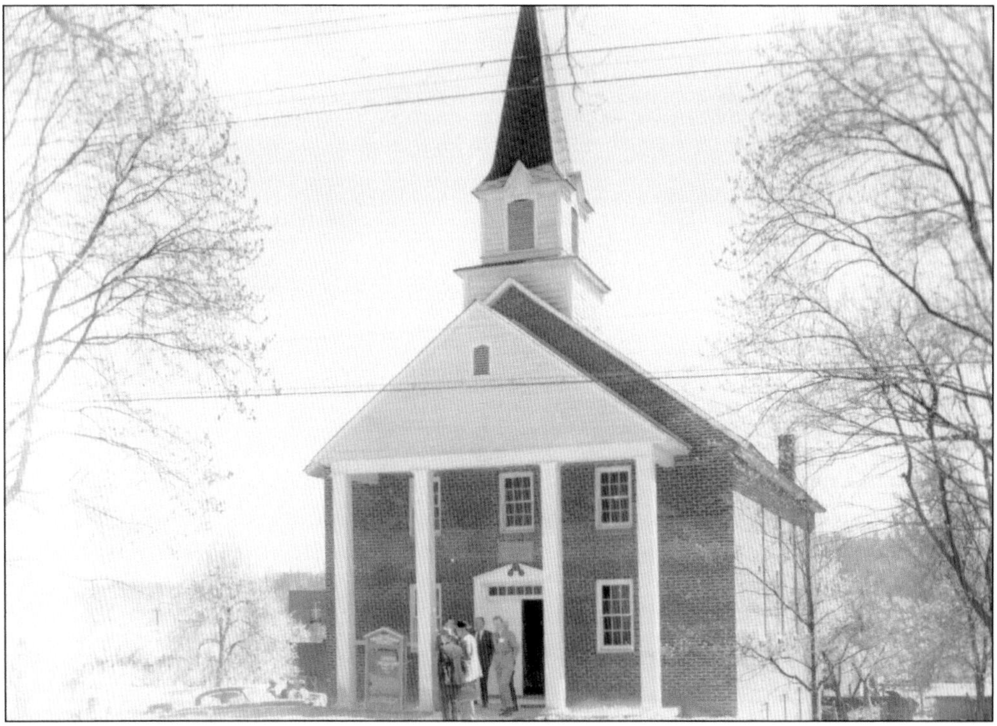

In 1883, Old Fort Presbyterian Church was built on land donated by Joseph Burgin, and the structure was erected under the leadership of Rev. C.A. Moore. This view shows the building after additions were made and exterior brick added in 1950. (Courtesy of McDowell County Public Library.)

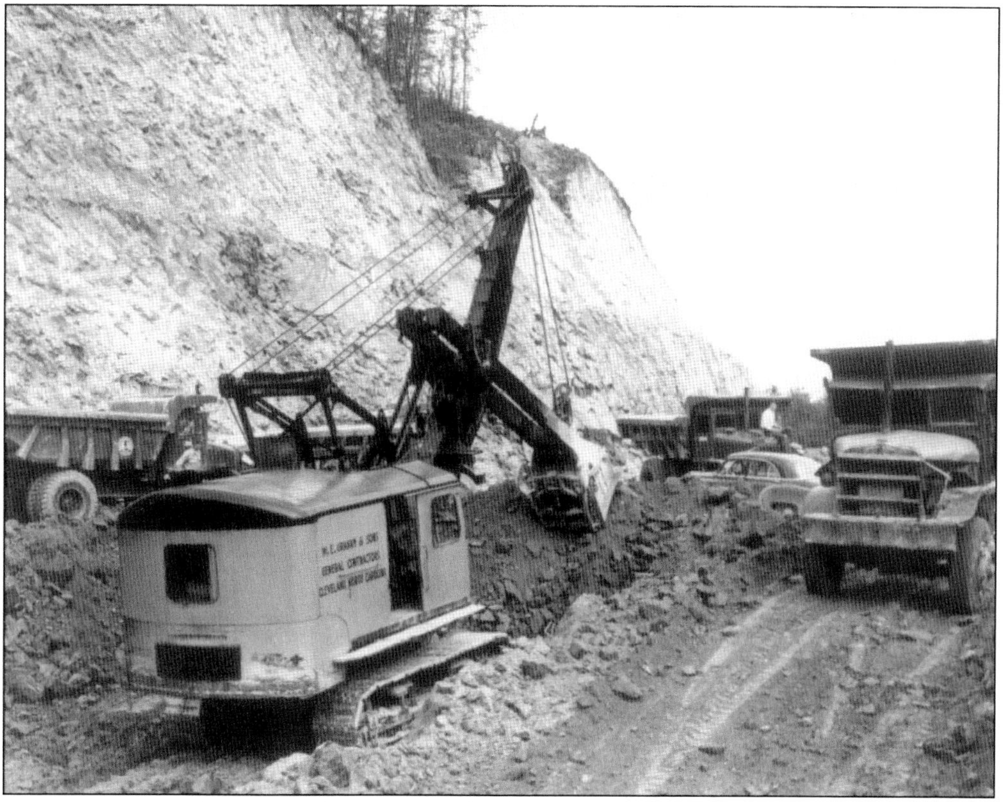

The construction of a dual-lane highway up Old Fort Mountain in 1953 provided engineering and earth-moving challenges just as the building of the railroad had in the previous century. The big fill about a mile west of Old Fort was claimed to be the largest in the United States. Interstate 40 would later follow this route. (Courtesy of the University of North Carolina at Chapel Hill, North Carolina Collection.)

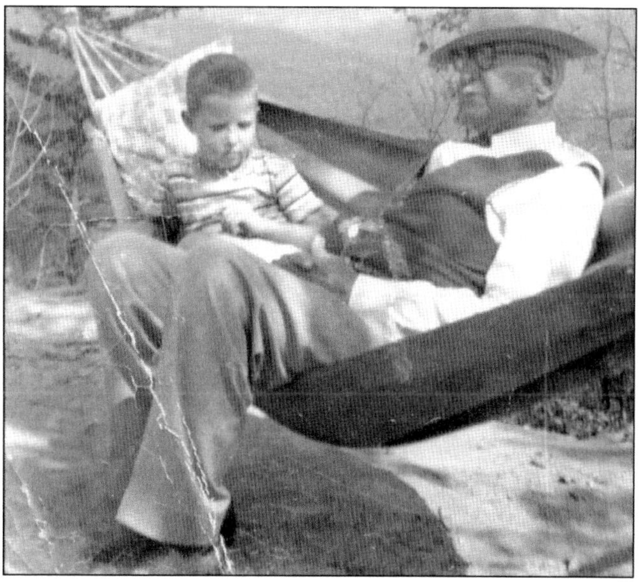

Col. Daniel Adams relaxes with his grandson Stuart on the mountaintop he called "High Windy," near present-day Interstate 40. Adams planned a tourist complex adjacent to the roadway when a divided highway was first built up the mountain, but the state later disallowed it due to safety concerns on the steep grade. (Courtesy of Stuart Adams Robinson.)

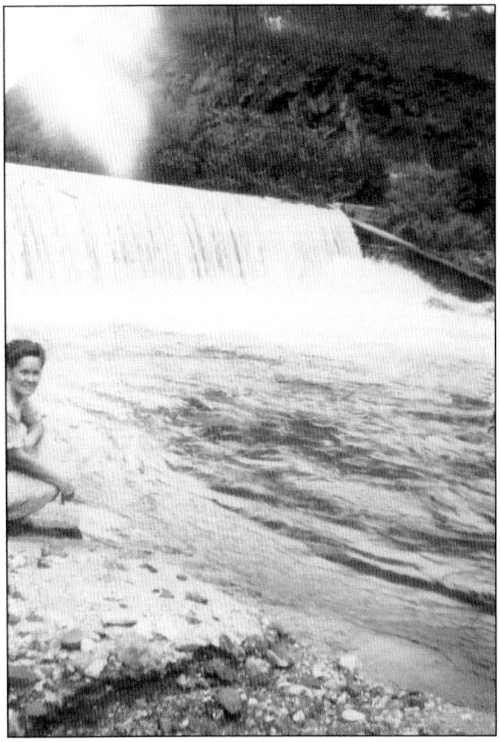

This dam on Mill Creek was built by Adams in 1914 to power the Sycamore Mill and another gristmill. Agnes Creasman is the woman seen in this image from the 1950s, when the area had become a recreational spot. When the dam was demolished, it took numerous charges of dynamite to break it up, a testament to the quality of its construction. (Courtesy of Mountain Gateway Museum.)

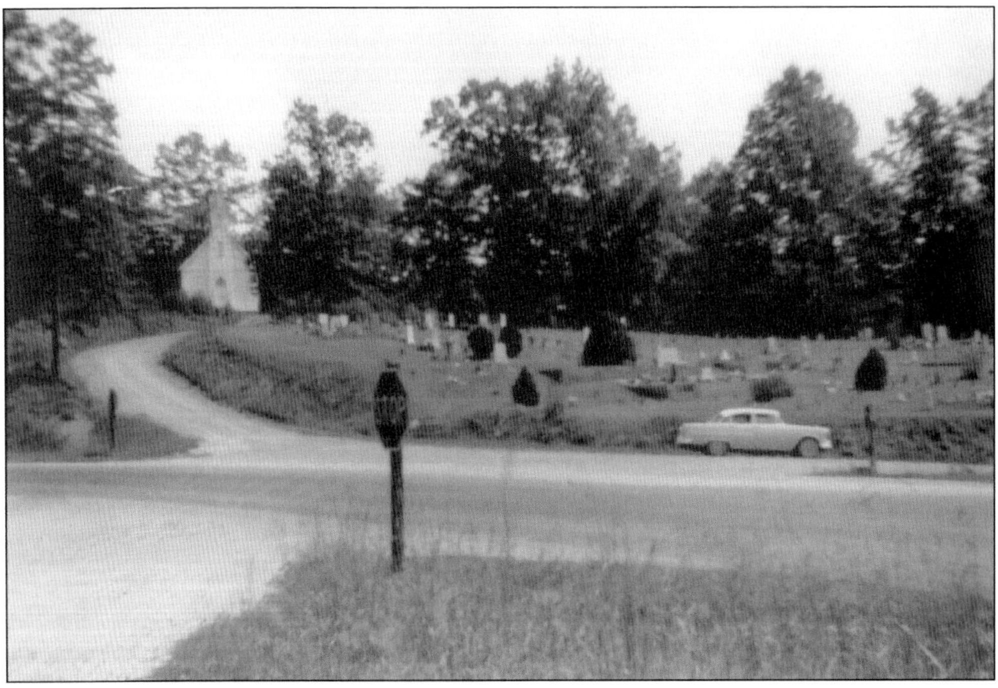

The old Bethlehem Church building is seen in this photograph taken in the 1950s, when the church was located across Old Fort-Sugar Hill Road from its present location. The oldest graves in the cemetery date to the 1860s, with members of the Burgin, Lytle, Lavender, Parker, and Souther families most numerous among those interred there. (Courtesy of Barbara Meilhammer.)

Caplan's Drug Store, located in the Bradley Building on town square, was a social center in the 1950s and particularly popular with teenaged students from Old Fort School. This photograph also shows the Appalachian Indian Road plaque that had been added to the arrowhead in 1932. According to some research, Highway 70 through Old Fort follows an ancient Native American trail. (Courtesy of Bill Nichols.)

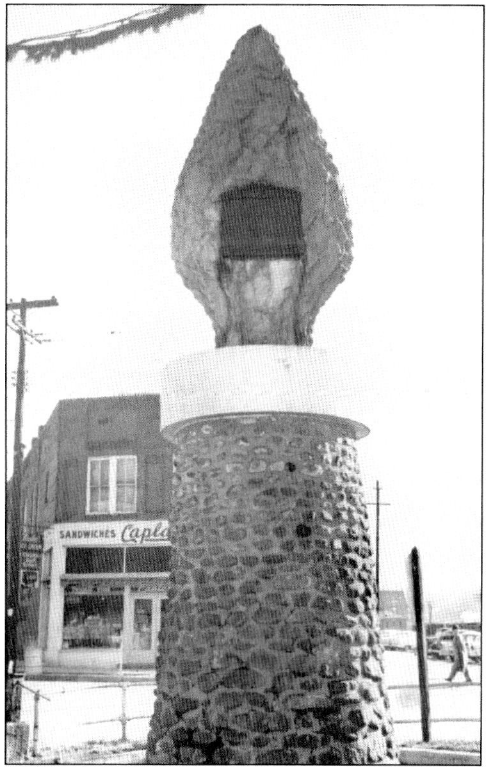

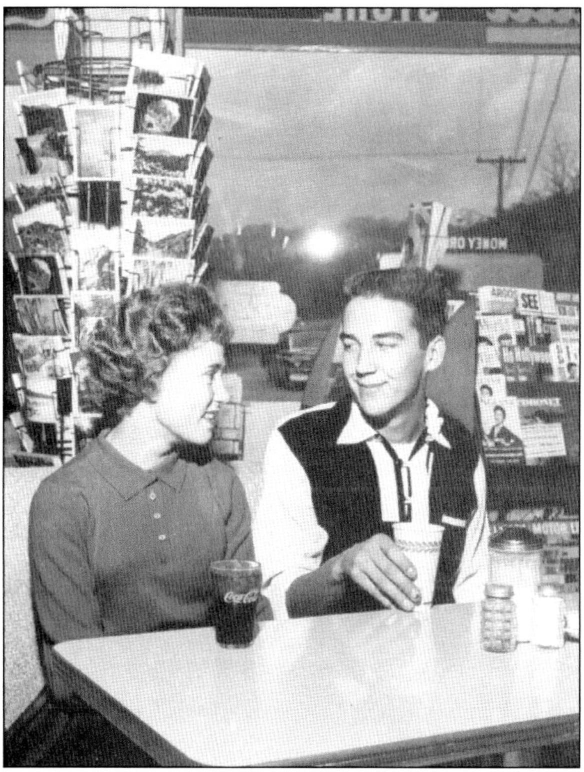

In 1958, Old Fort School seniors Betty Sue Bryant and David Setzer enjoy a soft drink at Caplan's Drug Store, located in the Bradley Building. Caplan's was a popular afterschool gathering place. (Courtesy of McDowell County Public Library.)

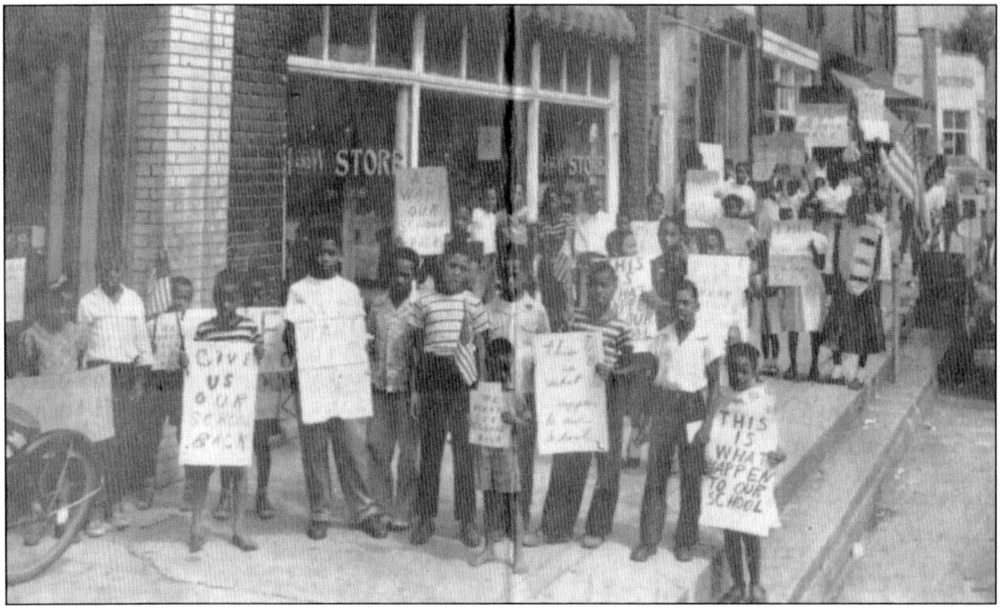

This is the only known photograph of the protest that occurred on Main Street on September 17, 1950. These Catawba View students protested the closing of their school and subsequent bussing to a consolidated African American school in Marion. Officials refused to reconsider, and tensions built over the next few years, culminating in a confrontation at the all-white Old Fort School in 1955. (Courtesy of McDowell County Public Library.)

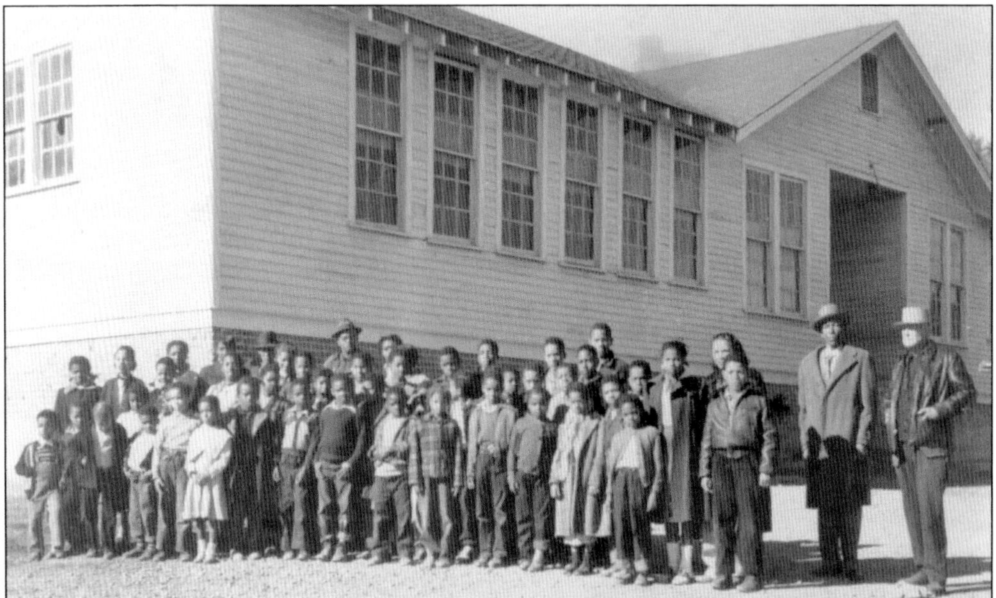

Students, teachers, and community leaders pose in front of Catawba View School in the early 1950s, after it had been closed by McDowell County officials. Having contributed to the building's construction and maintenance, residents at least wanted to maintain it as a community center. The county refused, and the schoolhouse was demolished. On the right is Colonel Adams, a vocal supporter of the students. (Courtesy of Mountain Gateway Museum.)

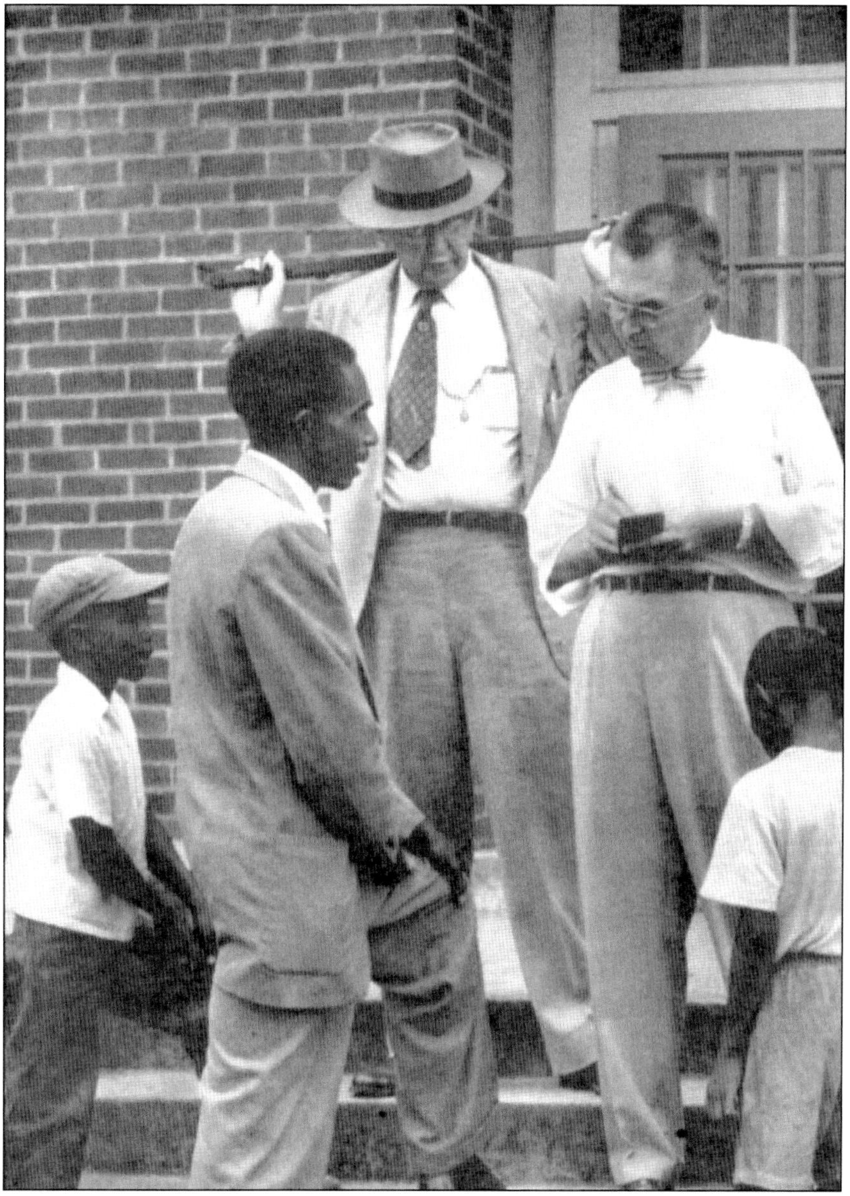

After the *Brown v. Board of Education* Supreme Court decision declared "separate but equal" public schools unconstitutional, the African American parents of Old Fort planned to attempt to register their children at the all-white Old Fort School for the 1955 term. The attempt was to be made on August 24, and a group of students and escorts were chosen in advance. The escorts lost their courage at the last minute, however, and Catawba View resident Albert Joyner stepped in for them without hesitation when he saw the children alone on the street. The group was turned away from the school, and Joyner's life changed dramatically. He was threatened and harassed for years and even shoved by a railroad worker into the town fountain. National publications followed the events in Old Fort. After his story was rediscovered in 2009, Joyner received multiple honors and commendations. In the image above, he is asking school superintendent Melvin Taylor (with notebook) to register the students. Colonel Adams looks on, walking cane over his shoulder. (Courtesy of McDowell County Public Library.)

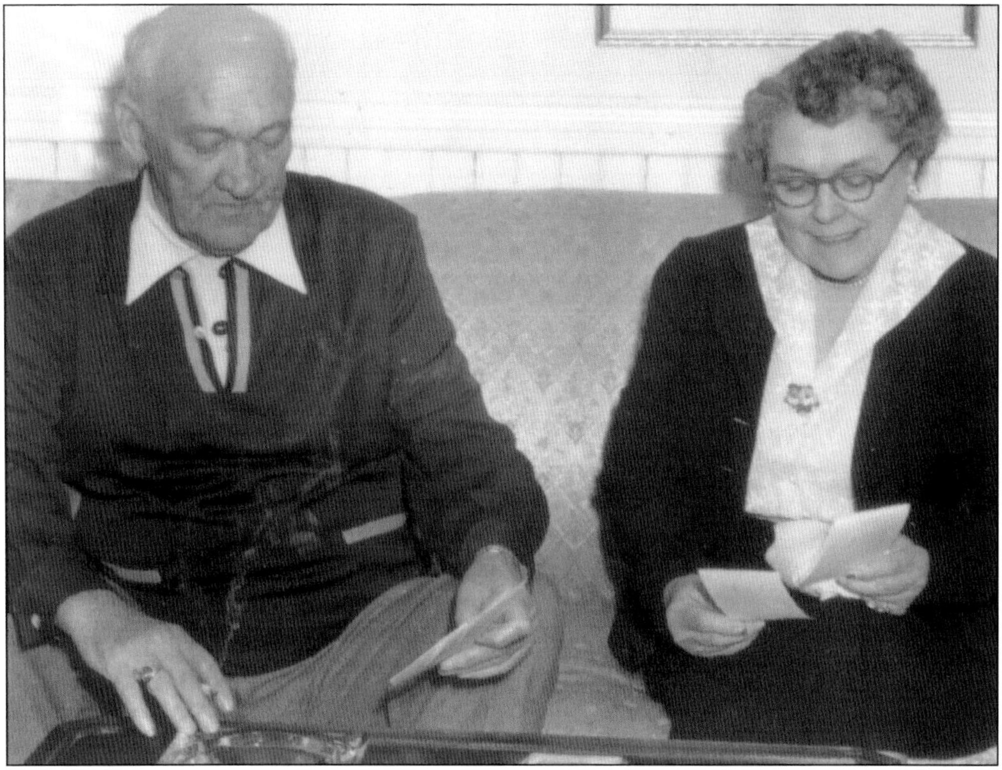

George Sandlin and his wife, Lula Ditmore Sandlin, are seen at the time of George's retirement in 1954. Both Sandlins had a profound impact on Old Fort. George was mayor, Southern Railway station agent, picture show operator, lawyer, and humanitarian. Lula was a teacher, newspaper writer, and community activist. She was a key force in the procurement of the arrowhead monument in 1930. (Courtesy of Richard Sandlin Fullerton.)

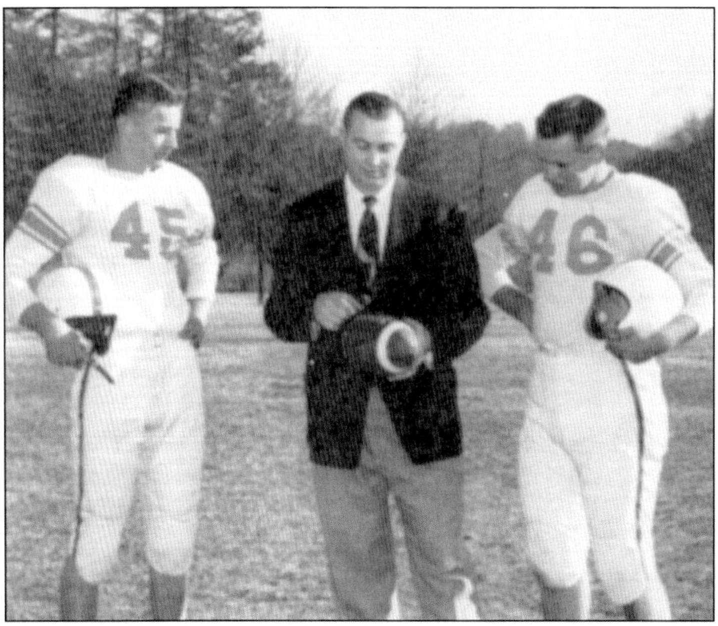

Old Fort School fielded their first football team in 1955–1956. They won two games and lost seven, had two players make all-conference in the Skyline A Conference, and had four other players receive honorable mentions. On the left in this image is Hershel White, who was honorably mentioned. All-conference center Jack Turner is on the right, and Coach Washburn is between them. (Courtesy of McDowell County Public Library.)

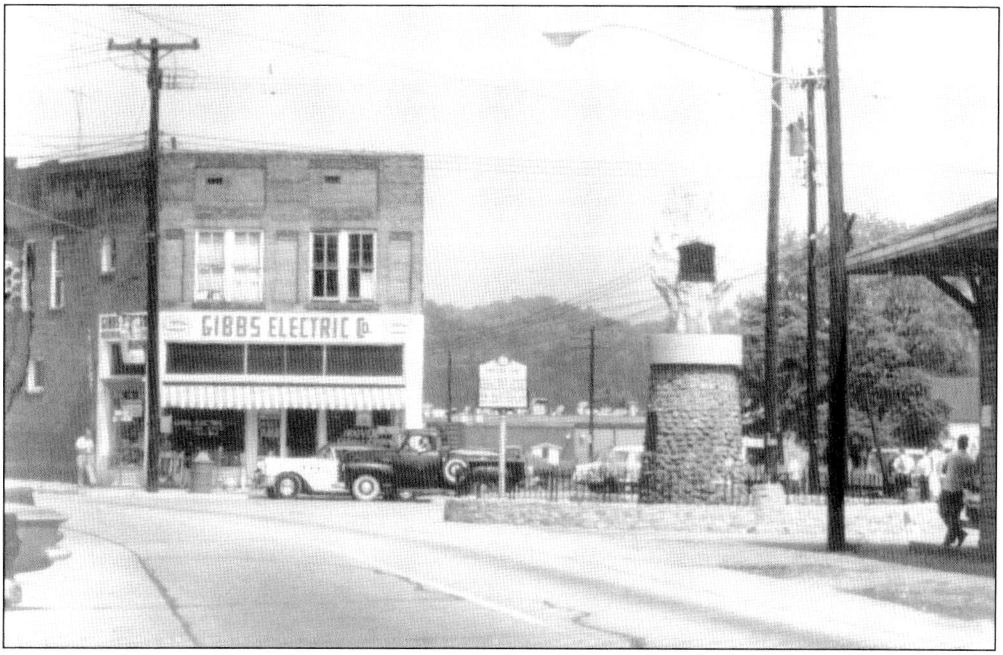

Gibbs Electric occupies the Bradley Building across town square from the depot in this image from 1960. The building stood just a few yards from the railroad track, and longtime residents recall that every time someone walked across the second floor, accumulated cinders from decades of passing trains would float down on customers and employees at street level. The Bradley Building was razed in 1971. (Courtesy of Gibbs Hardware.)

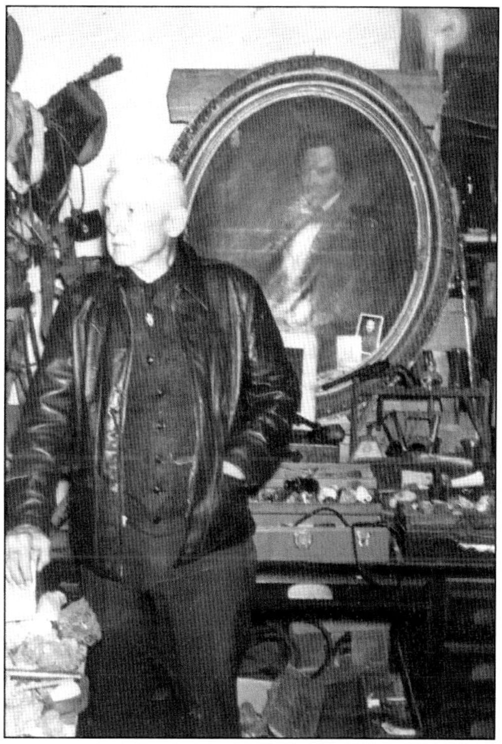

Colonel Adams is seen in the parlor of his home in Old Fort in this photograph taken about two years before his death in 1957. He is surrounded by mementos of his life of adventure, exploration, and public service. The portrait behind him is that of his father, Daniel W. Adams Sr. The senior Adams had been a general in the Confederate army. (Courtesy of Stuart Adams Robinson.)

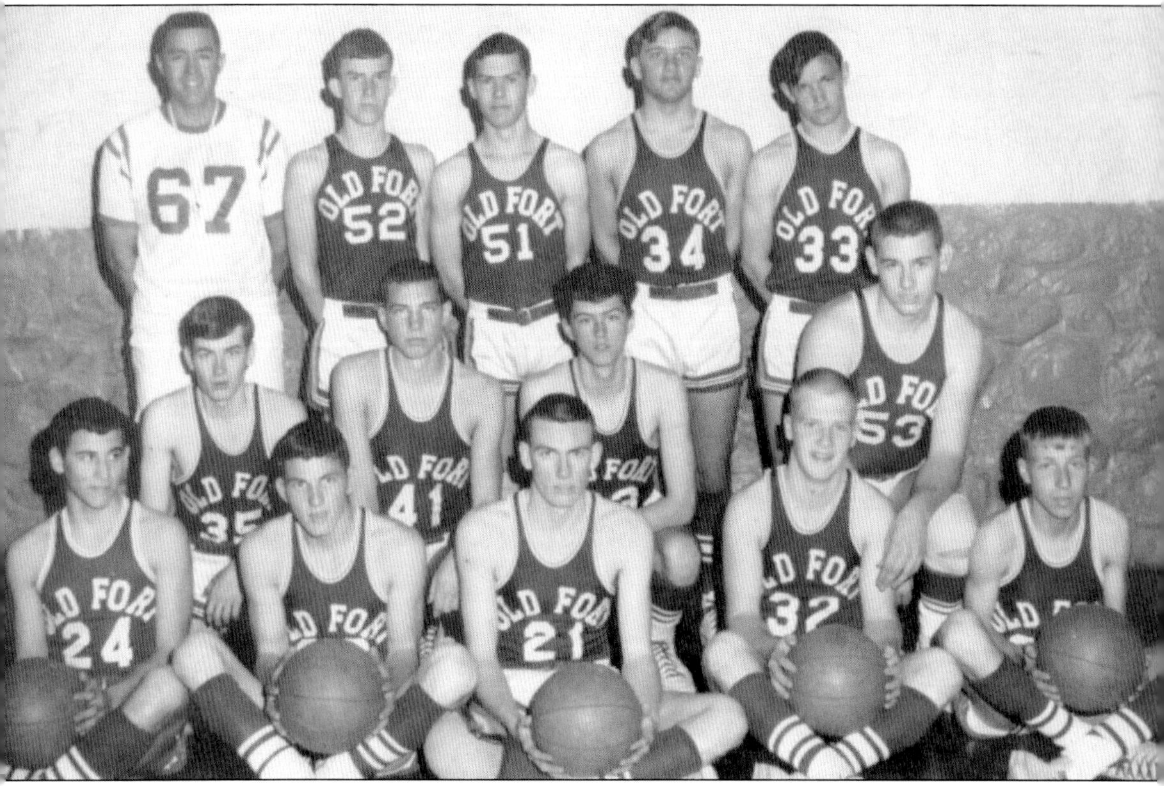

The 1966 Old Fort High School boys' basketball team ended their regular season with a record of 20-0 and finished fourth in the state. The team members are, from left to right (first row) Billy Snyder, Billy Lytle, Wayne McCauley, David Rhinehardt, and Johnny Oates; (second row) Troy Kelly, Ronnie Condrey, Robert Hartwell, and Carroll Turner; (third row) coach Ken Griffin, Donald Lackey, Mike Gibbs, Mike Elliot, and Mike Hensley. Coach Griffin came to Old Fort High School in 1959 to coach boys' basketball, serve as assistant football coach, and to coach girls' basketball as well. During the 1960s, Old Fort's games were so well attended that a balcony was added to the gym. (Courtesy of McDowell County Public Library.)

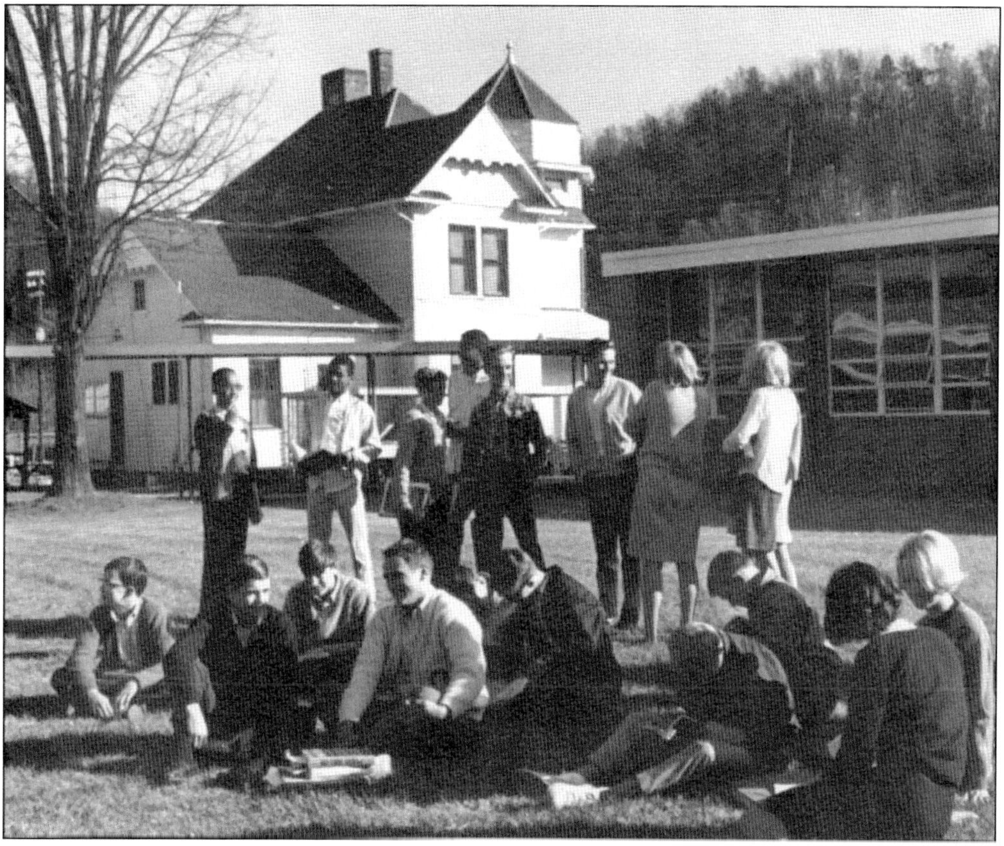

Segregated schools were a thing of the past, and in 1968, these Old Fort students looked forward to a world that was very different from the one that their parents had known. (Courtesy of McDowell County Public Library.)

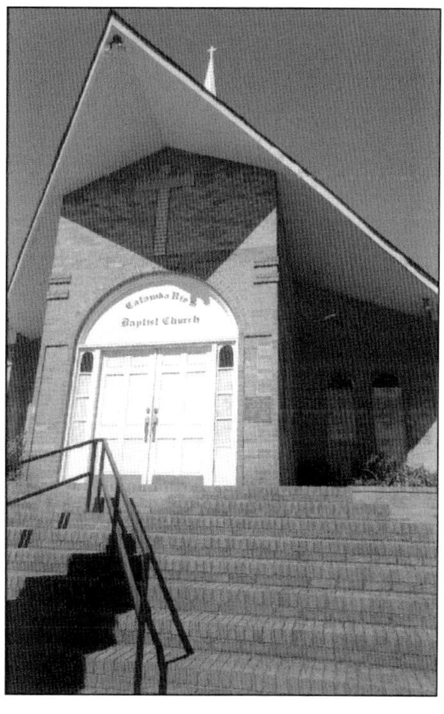

Originally located near Crooked Creek, the Colored Missionary Baptist Church moved to the Baptist Side community in 1908 and was renamed Catawba View Missionary Baptist Church. The building was white frame, had no running water, and was heated by a coal stove. It was later bricked, then replaced by this structure in the late 1960s. (Photograph by Kim Clark.)

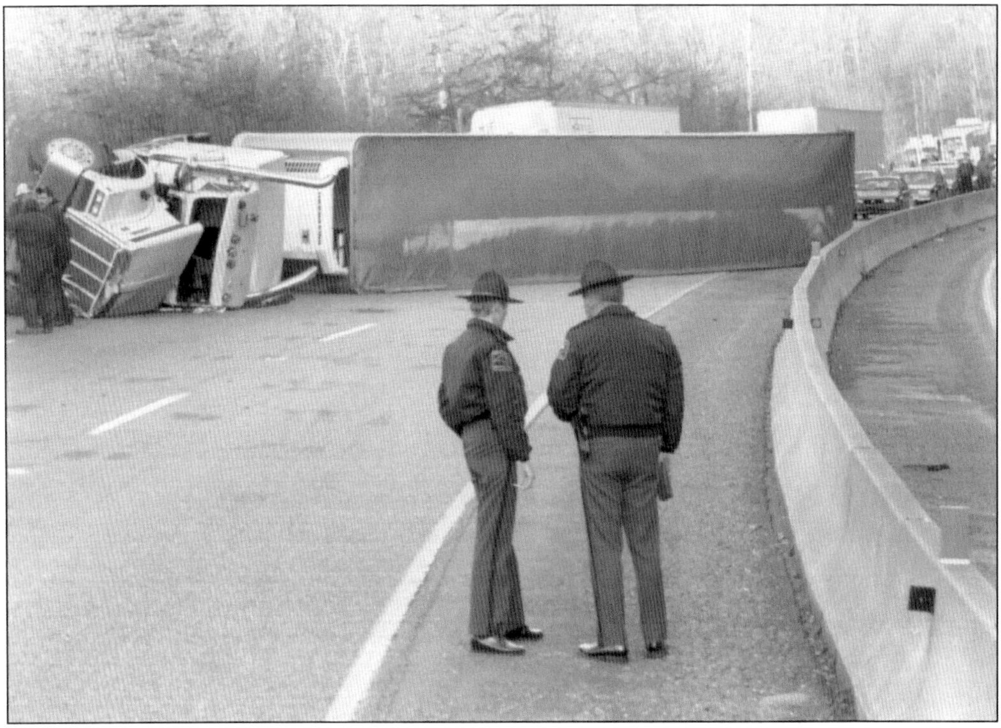

Just as the steep mountain grade had posed dangerous challenges to both stagecoach and train, it also proved treacherous for automobiles. There were nearly 300 wrecks, including eight fatal crashes, on the mountain in just the six years from 1979 to 1985. Runaway tractor-trailers such as this one with failed brakes were often the cause. Increased safety measures in recent years have reduced the accident rate. (Courtesy of Jim Burgin.)

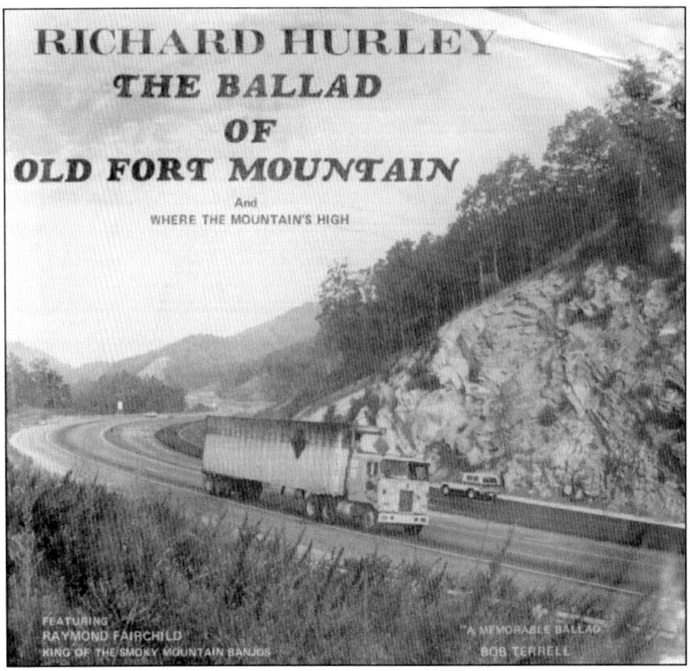

This 45 rpm record released in 1981 by Old Fort native Richard Hurley memorialized the dangers of negotiating Old Fort Mountain in an 18-wheeler. In the lyrics he declares, "Old Fort Mountain should be called the devil's mile." Renowned banjo player Raymond Fairchild played on the recording. (Courtesy of Mountain Gateway Museum.)

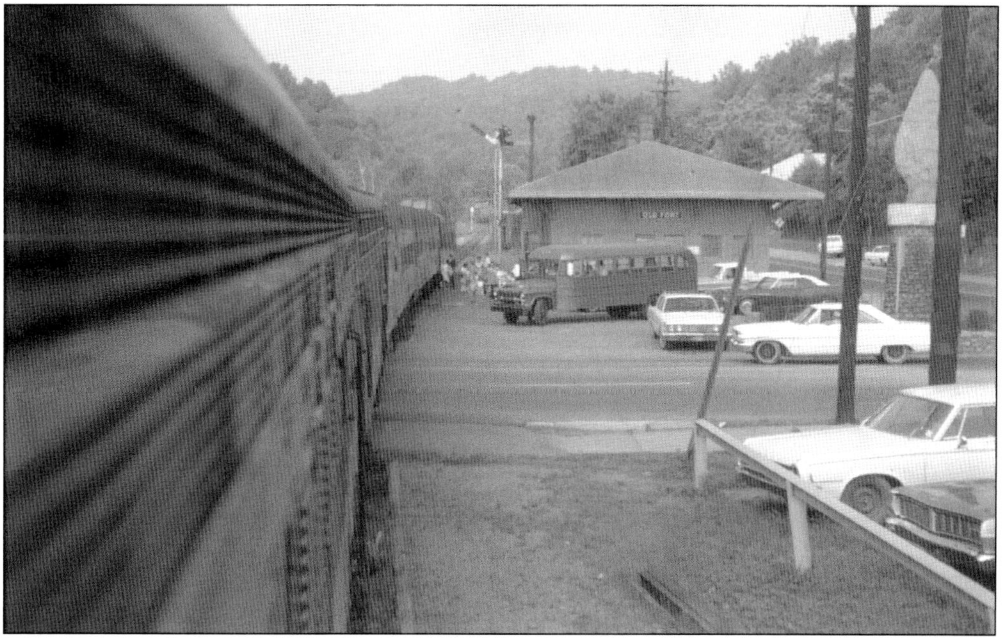

By the 1970s, the Old Fort depot had become dormant as an active station, and passenger travel was mostly limited to special excursions. In this 1973 image, passengers on train No. 4, the Asheville Special, disembark in Old Fort. This train once ran daily from Asheville to Salisbury. Engineer Frank Clodfelter took this photograph. (Courtesy of the University of North Carolina Library at Chapel Hill, North Carolina Collection.)

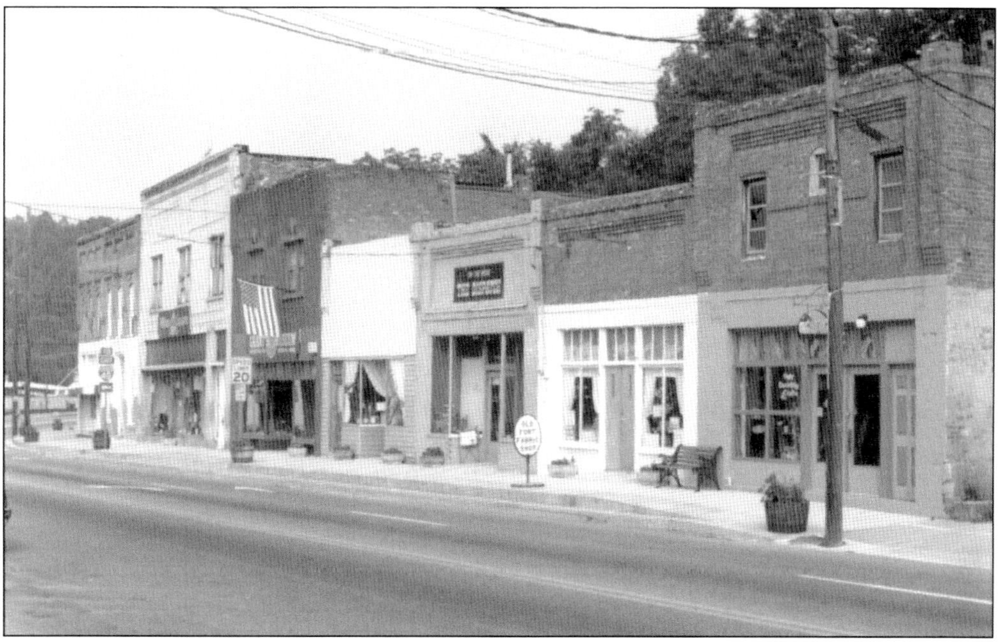

This 1980s view of the north side of Main Street shows Village Square Crafts, Grant's Museum, the offices of the *Old Fort Dispatch* newspaper, the Old Fort Fabric Shop, and Ugly Duckling Crafts. Grant's Museum was especially interesting to tourists with its collection of Native American artifacts numbering in the hundreds of thousands. (Courtesy of Mountain Gateway Museum.)

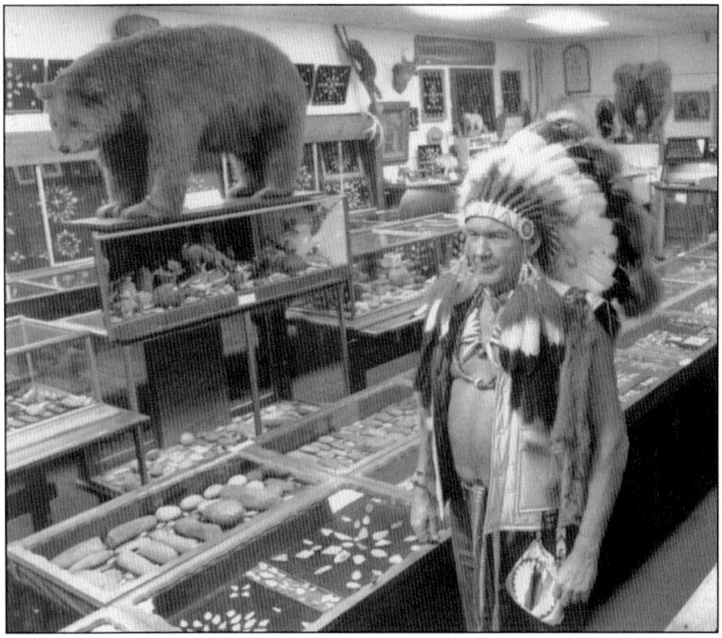

Woodrow "Woody" Grant stands in Grant's Museum, which he owned and operated. Located on Main Street, the museum housed over 350,000 Native American artifacts, most of which had been found within a seven-mile radius of Old Fort. Grant, who was descended from both the Catawba and the Cherokee tribes, educated visitors about the native way of life and sometimes even played the piano and sang. (Courtesy of Jim Burgin.)

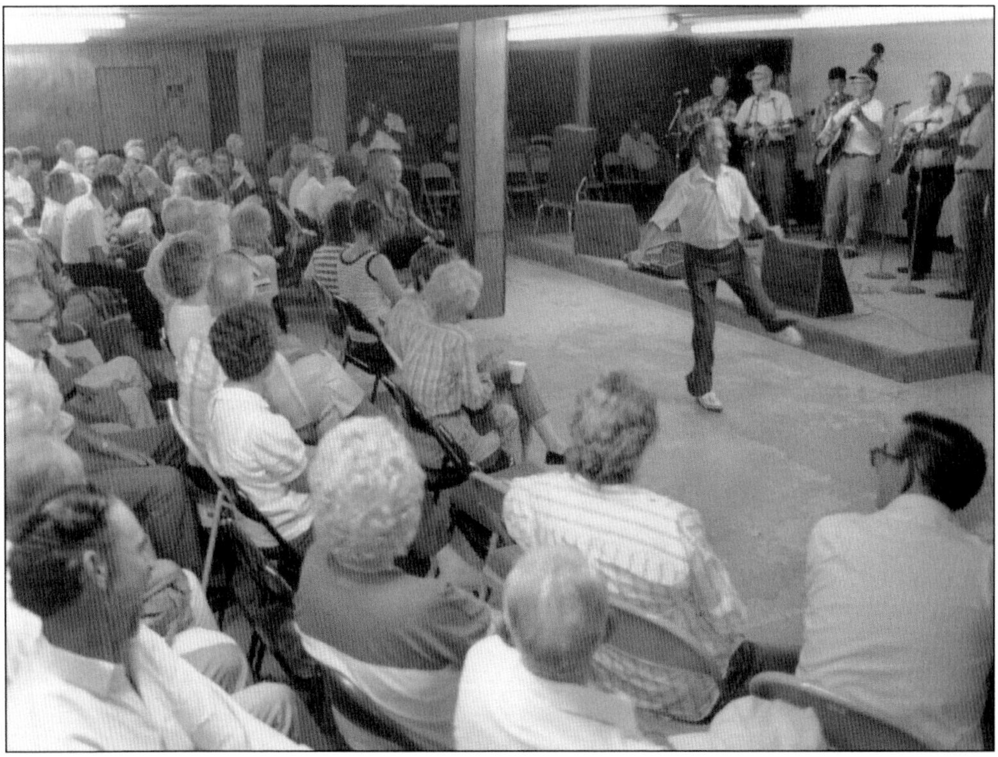

This old-timer cuts a rug in front of the band at Old Fort Mountain Music in the late 1980s. The weekly bluegrass jam sessions began at Max Woody's chair shop on Highway 70. As the Friday night jam sessions grew larger and moved into the old Rockett Building, audience members came from afar, and both the *Boston Globe* and *National Geographic* wrote feature articles. (Courtesy of Jim Burgin.)

Kenneth Ray Cannon, better known as Chief Two Trees, moved to Old Fort from Oklahoma in the early 1980s. His skills and reputation as an intuitive natural healer and herbalist brought a steady stream of visitors to his home for treatment. He also established the Native American Studies Institute to preserve traditional methods of health and healing. Two Trees died in Old Fort in 1995. (Courtesy of Dr. Darlene Two Trees Cannon.)

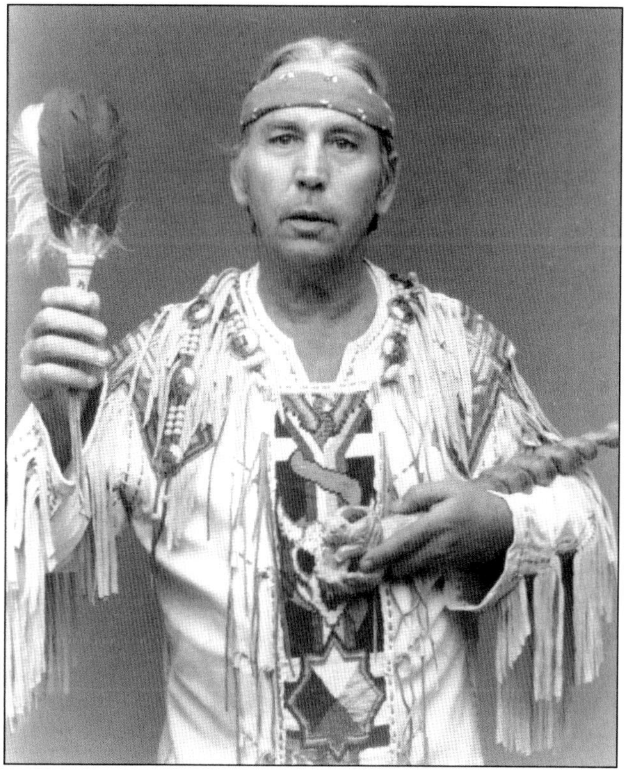

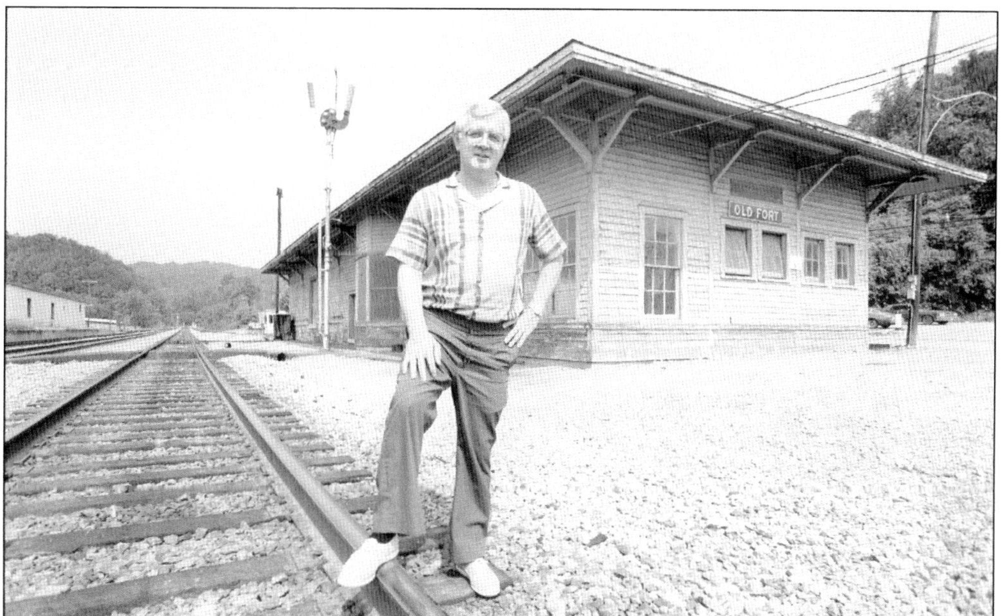

Lloyd Lovick, seen here at the depot in 1986, was Old Fort's last station master. When Norfolk Southern agreed to donate the depot to the Old Fort Heritage Foundation, it was on the condition that the building be moved. After further negotiations, they allowed it to remain in its original location. (Courtesy of Kathryn Burgin Kolb.)

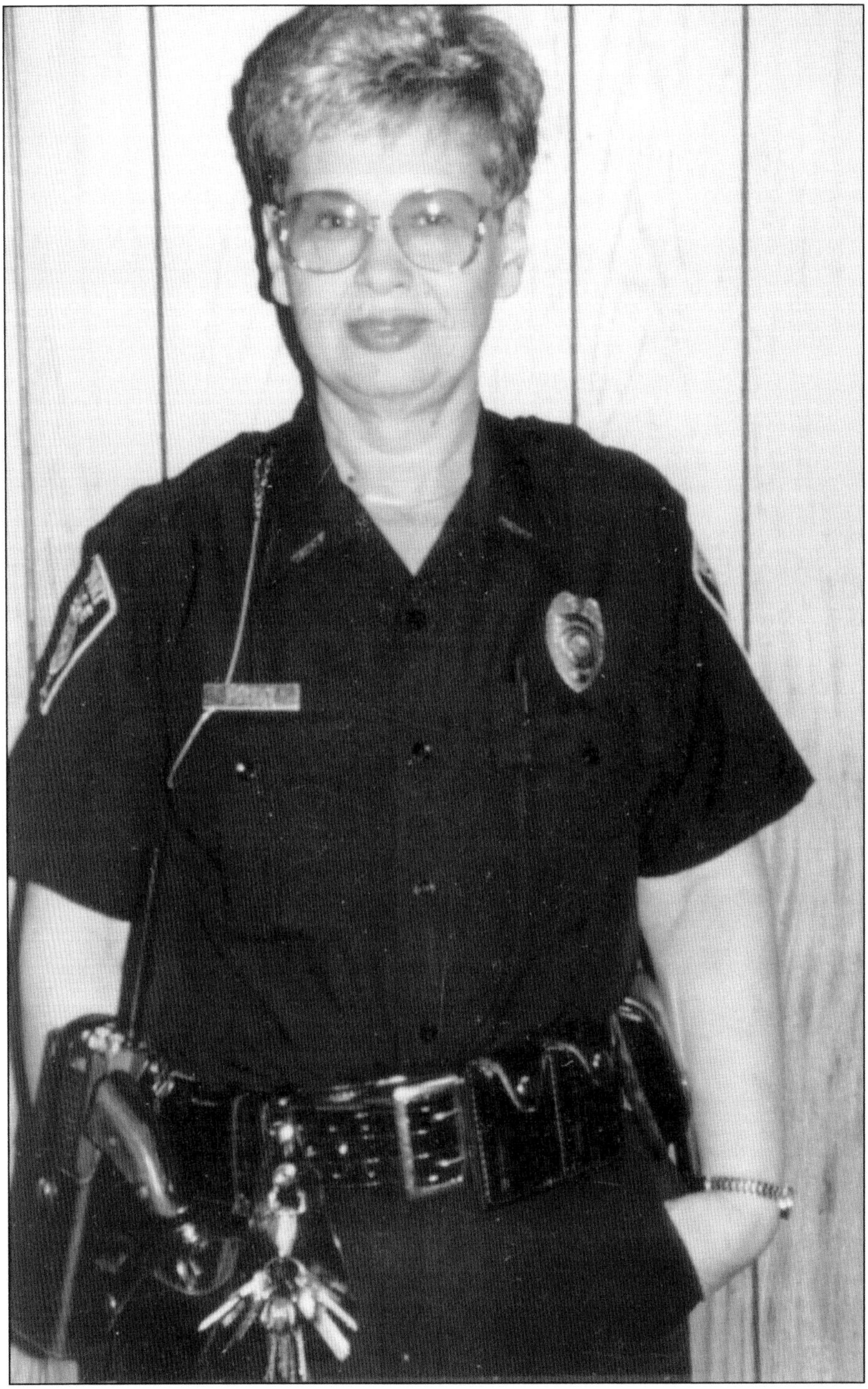

Frankie Crane Poteat served the town of Old Fort for decades as police chief, member of the board of aldermen, and civic leader. She began working for the Old Fort Police Department in 1978 and was appointed chief two years later. She was the first female chief of police in the state of North Carolina. (Courtesy of Suzy Poteat.)

Six

PRESERVING A RICH HERITAGE

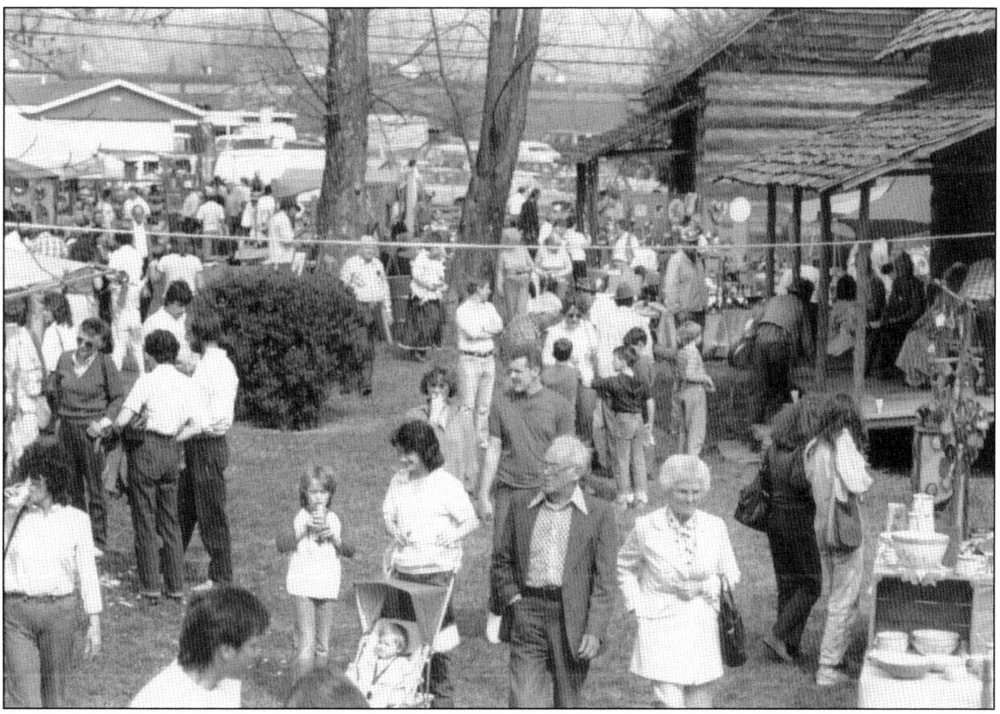

Pioneer Day began in 1985 when Old Fort was reeling from the effects of the closure of Old Fort Finishing, the town's major employer. The Old Fort Heritage Foundation was formed to increase awareness of the town's rich history among citizens and tourists. The yearly festival celebrating traditional crafts and the pioneer lifestyle is held on the grounds of Mountain Gateway Museum. (Courtesy of Jim Burgin.)

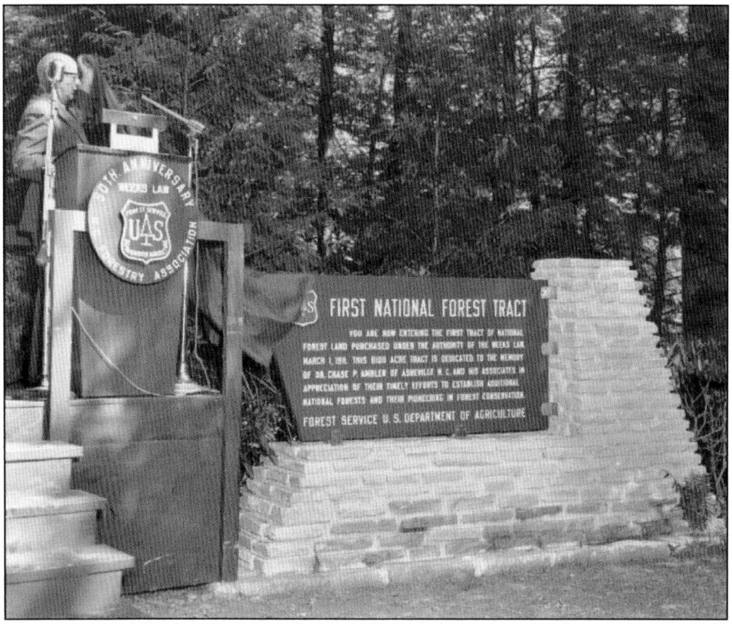

The 8,100-acre Curtis Creek tract was the first to be purchased by the US Forest Service as National Forest Land under the Weeks Law of 1911, and it was the beginning of the Pisgah National Forest. Col. Daniel W. Adams made the first survey of the land for the forest service in 1911. This marker was placed in 1961 during 50th anniversary celebrations. (Courtesy of Mountain Gateway Museum.)

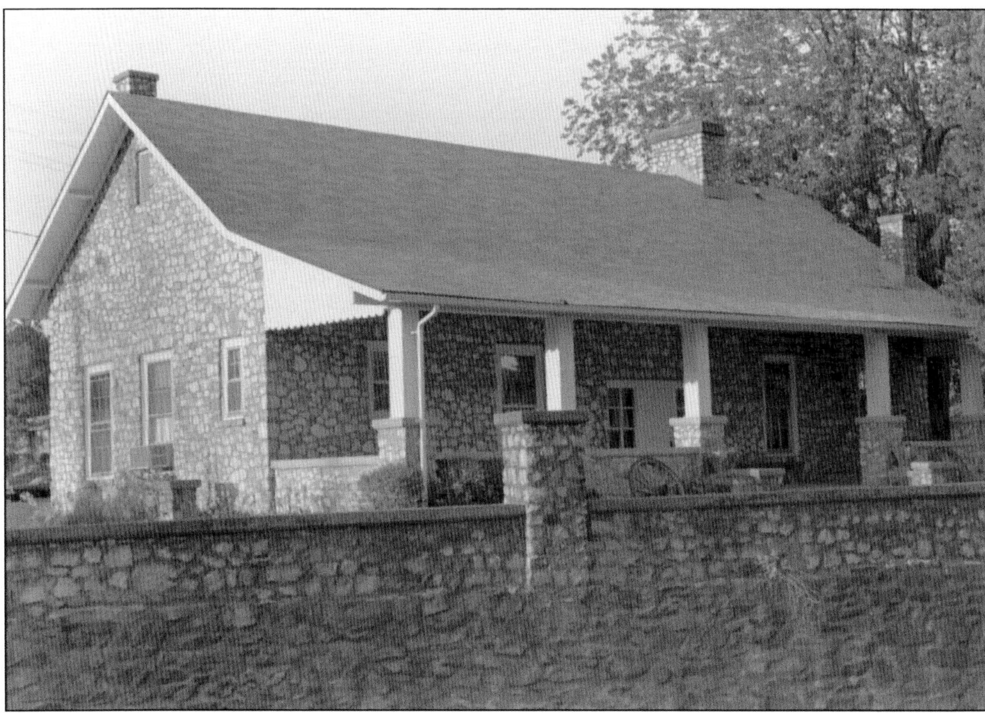

The Mountain Gateway Museum stands on the banks of Mill Creek near the original site of Davidson's Fort. Originally built as a community center, it was dedicated as a museum by North Carolina governor Bob Scott in 1971. It became the westernmost branch of the North Carolina Museum of History in 1982. The general assembly first granted funds for the site in 1965. (Courtesy of Mountain Gateway Museum.)

The huge stone fireplace in the former Old Fort Community Center became the center of an exhibit illustrating pioneer living when the building became Mountain Gateway Museum. Also on the first floor, a room that was once the town library was converted into a small auditorium. Community leaders for the museum project included E.A. Norton, Binkie Adams, and Jessica Gibbs. (Courtesy of Mountain Gateway Museum.)

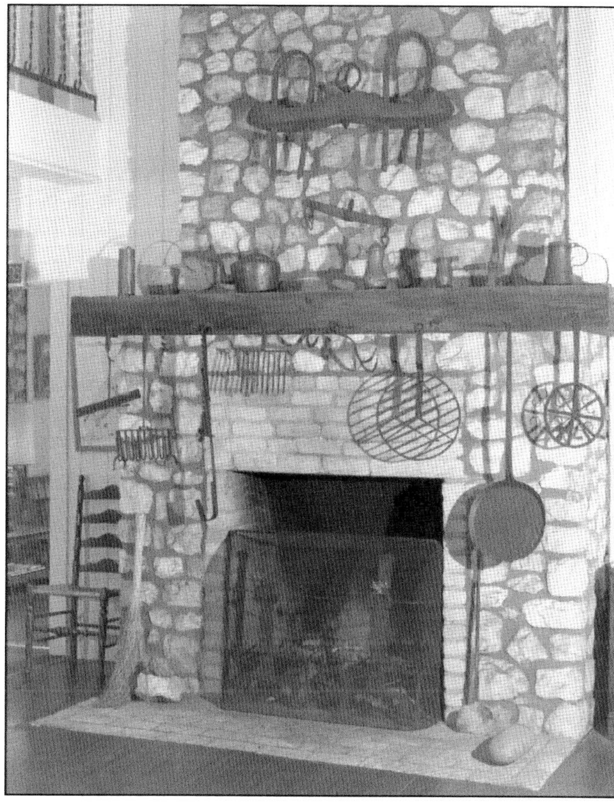

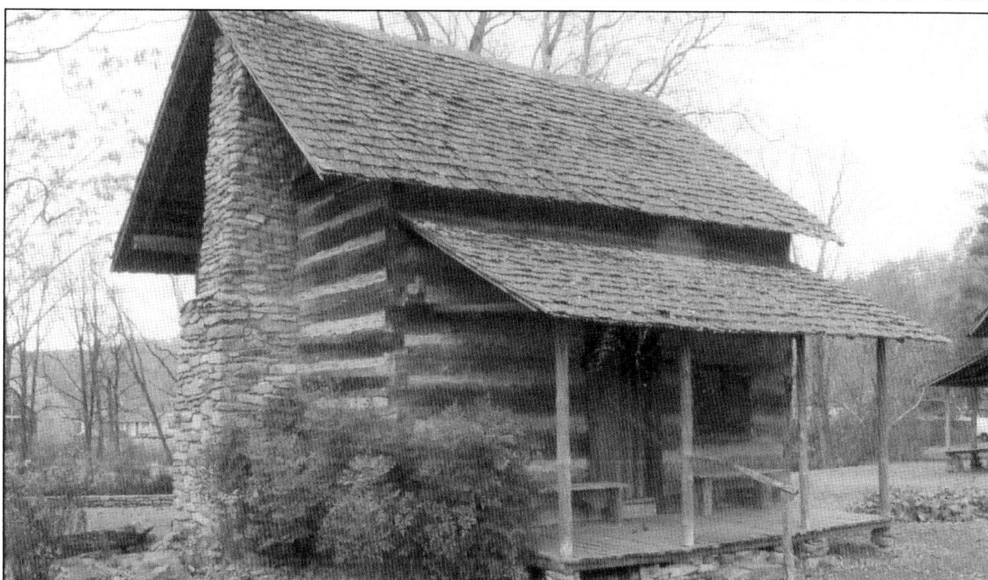

After the Stepp Cabin had been taken apart in its original location in the Ebenezer community and rebuilt on the grounds of Mountain Gateway Museum in Old Fort, period-correct improvements were painstakingly made. A porch was added, a large chestnut log was procured for use as a mantel, extensive rock work was done, and 140 handmade pegs were put in one door. (Courtesy of Mountain Gateway Museum.)

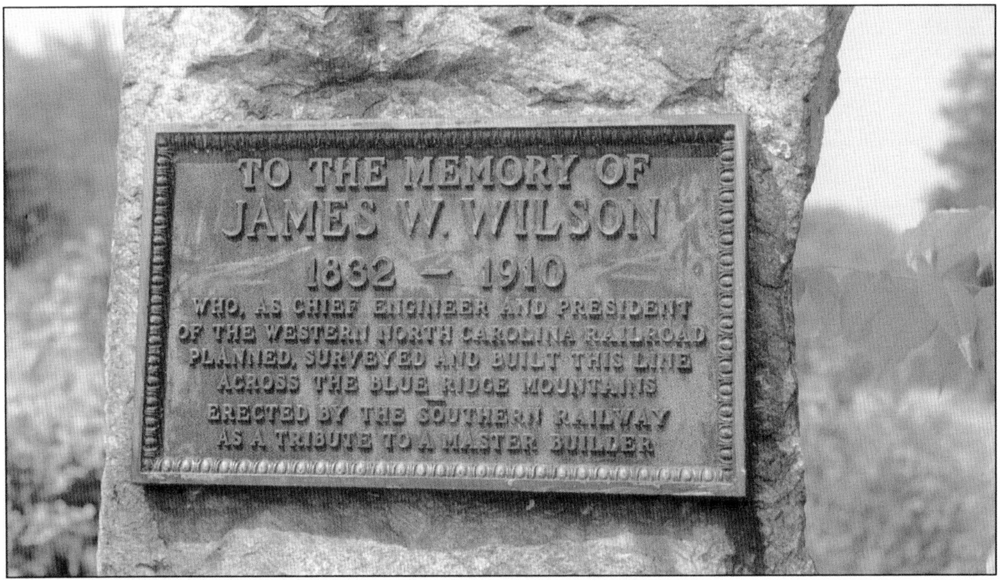

This marker in honor of Maj. James Wilson's achievement in completing the Mountain Division of the Western North Carolina Railroad was erected across from his home near Round Knob and later moved to the Old Fort depot. Wilson had mapped the route for the railroad up to Ridgecrest and overseen every detail of the endeavor's successful construction. (Courtesy of the University of North Carolina Library at Chapel Hill, North Carolina Collection.)

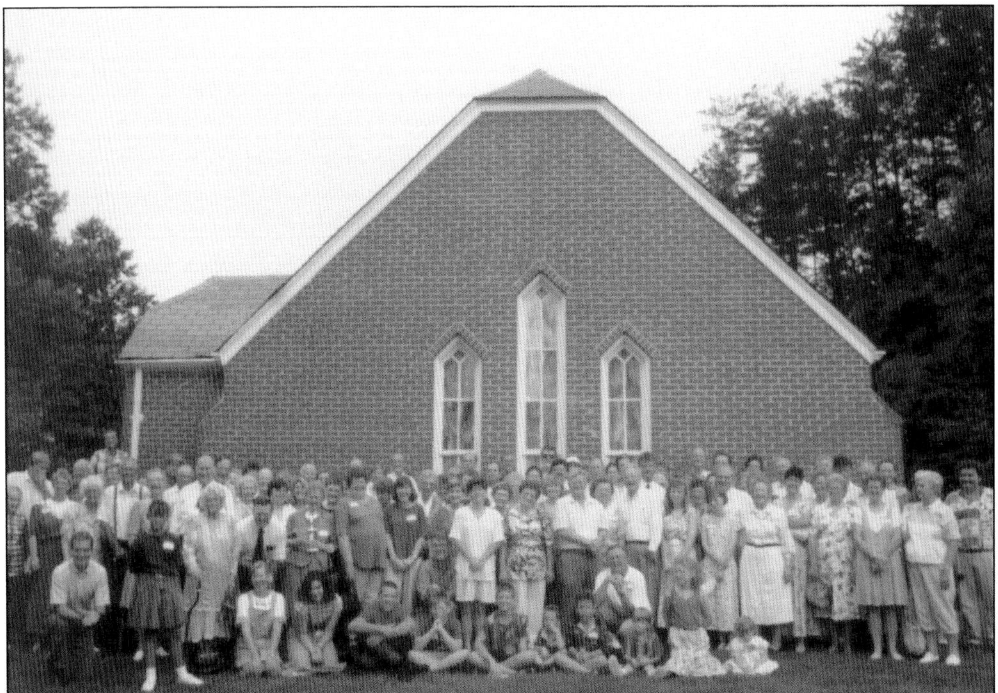

The Burgin-Lytle reunion continues to be held in Old Fort annually, and it is one of the largest family reunions in the nation. Attendance generally numbers in the hundreds, with kin traveling to Old Fort from all over the country to take part in the two-day event. (Courtesy of Peggy Silvers.)

After Andrews Geyser fell into disrepair in the early 1970s, college student and railroad enthusiast Stephen Little led an effort for Old Fort to gain possession of it. In July 1976, the railroad officially presented the deed for the geyser to the town. Pictured here are, from left to right, Jack Piercy, mayor pro-tem; Jack Lytle, mayor; and two unidentified Southern Railway officials. (Courtesy of Mountain Gateway Museum.)

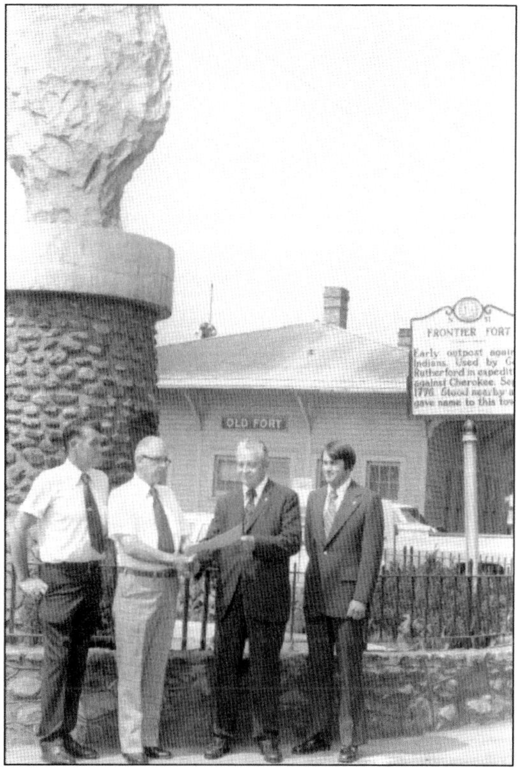

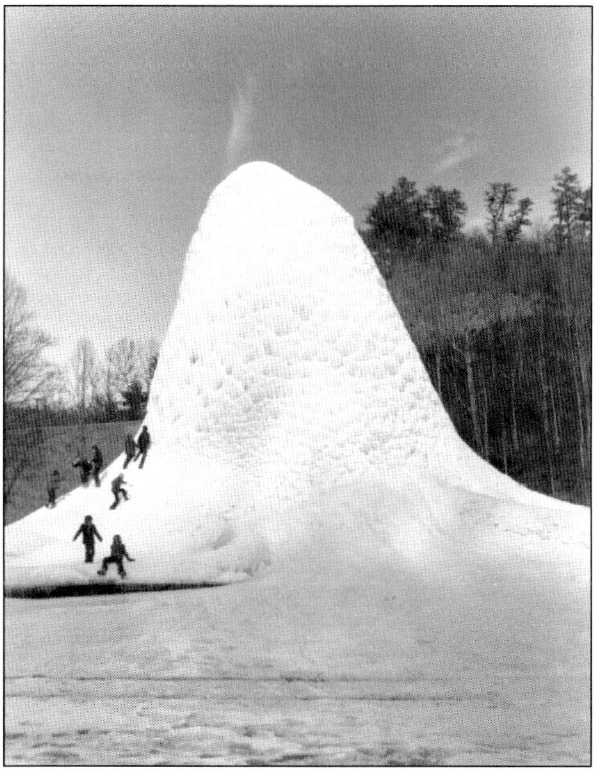

Old Fort children play on the mountain of ice formed by Andrews Geyser during a cold snap in the late 1970s. The park that the town built at the geyser had become a popular destination for both locals and tourists. A state historical marker for Andrews Geyser was placed at the intersection of Old Highway 70 and Mill Creek Road in February 1976. (Courtesy of Mountain Gateway Museum.)

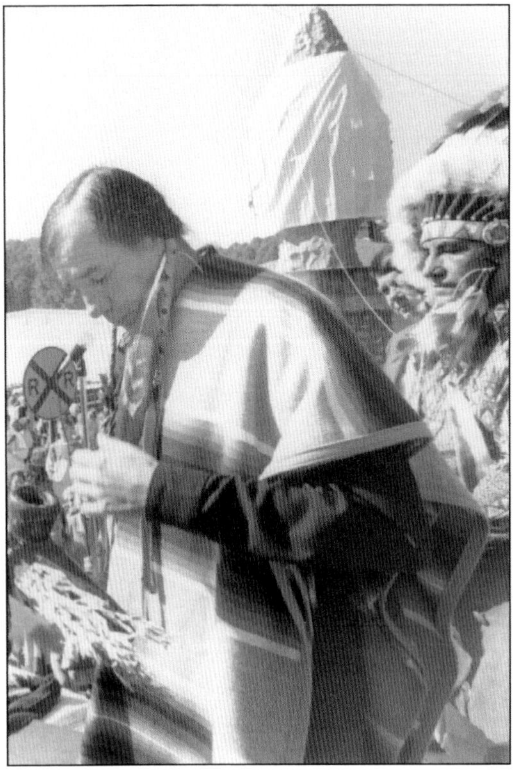

The Town of Old Fort rededicated the arrowhead monument in 1990 to mark its 60th anniversary. William Thomas (left) of the Cherokee Nation and Chief Gilbert Blue of the Catawba Nation prepare to share the peace pipe that had been used at the 1930 event. Gilbert Blue is the son of Samuel Blue, who performed the same function in 1930. Marie Nesbitt Krisel, at age 69, unveiled the marker as she had as a child. (Courtesy of Jim Burgin)

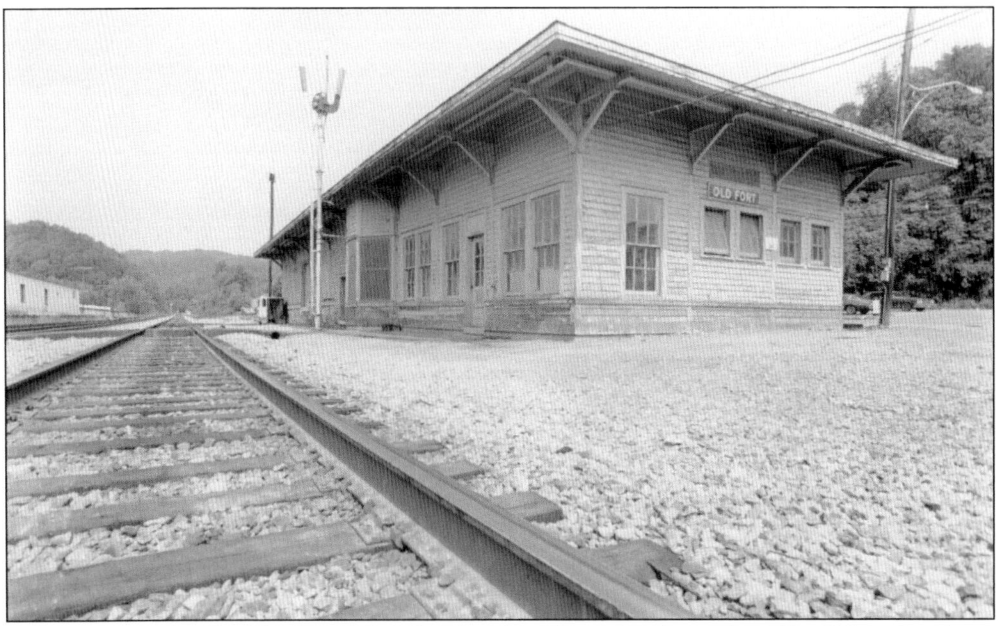

The Old Fort depot had become dilapidated and neglected by the early 1980s. When Southern Railway announced plans to tear it down, 3,000 McDowell County citizens signed a petition to save it. The depot was officially given to the Old Fort Heritage Foundation on July 3, 1985. The foundation staged Victorian-themed dinners and other events to raise funds for the depot's renovation. (Courtesy of Kathryn Burgin Kolb.)

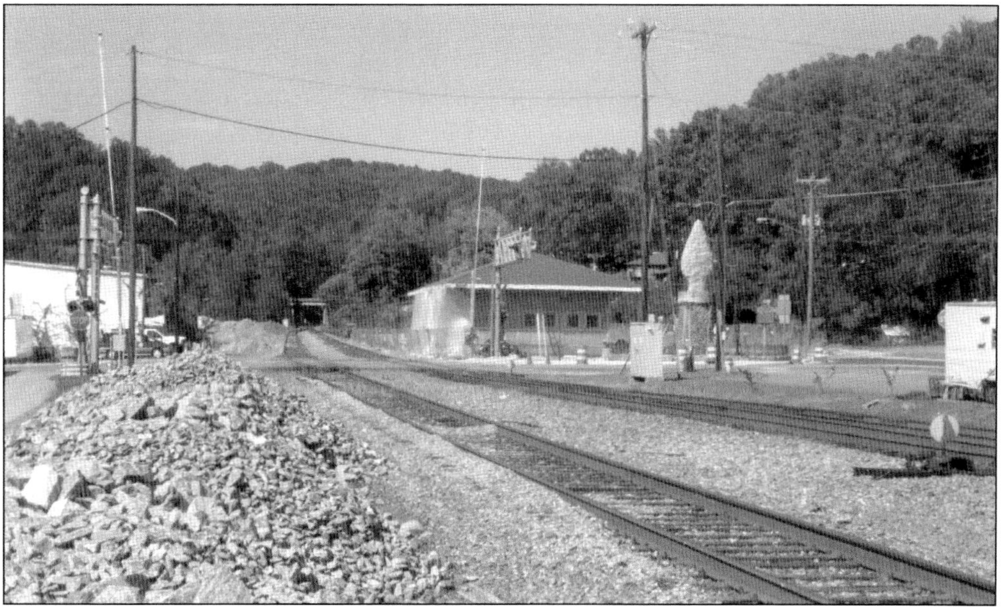

By September 2004 when this photograph was taken, the renovation of the Old Fort depot was 80 percent complete. Ladders and plastic sheeting can be seen as the work enters its final phase. The depot would later house the offices of the Old Fort Chamber of Commerce and McDowell County Tourism Authority as well as a railroad museum complete with a vintage Southern Railway caboose. (Courtesy of Mountain Gateway Museum.)

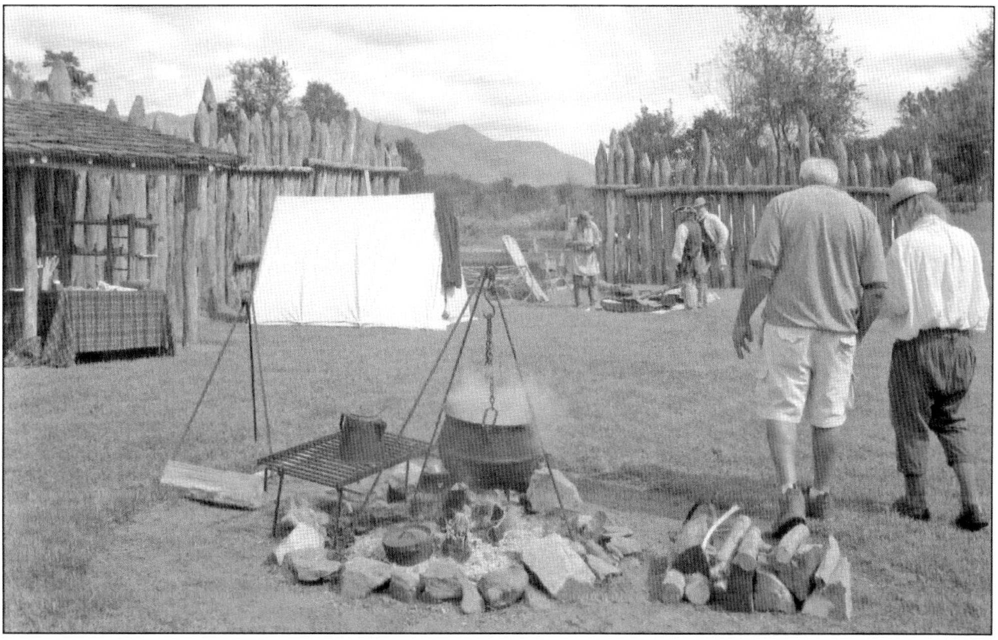

A reenactor explains the pioneer life to a visitor at Davidson's Fort Historic Park. Using historical data from pension applications and other contemporaneous sources, a dedicated band of volunteers established the site in 2007, near the location of the original fort. The park offers the opportunity to experience artifacts and activities that represent life for settlers and Native Americans at the time of the American Revolution. (Photograph by Kim Clark.)

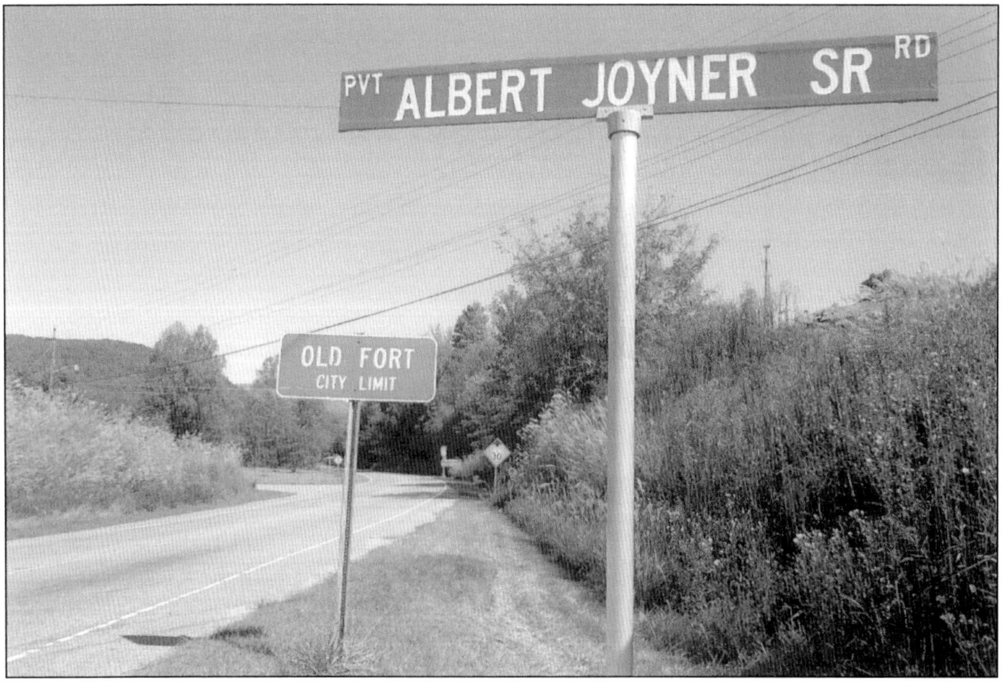

The story of Albert Joyner's courageous actions in the effort to desegregate Old Fort School was recounted during the 2011 Martin Luther King Jr. prayer breakfast in Asheville, attended by a US congressman, a US senator, and a national news analyst. Numerous accolades followed before Joyner's passing later that year. The street where he had lived most of his life was renamed in his honor. (Photograph by Kim Clark.)

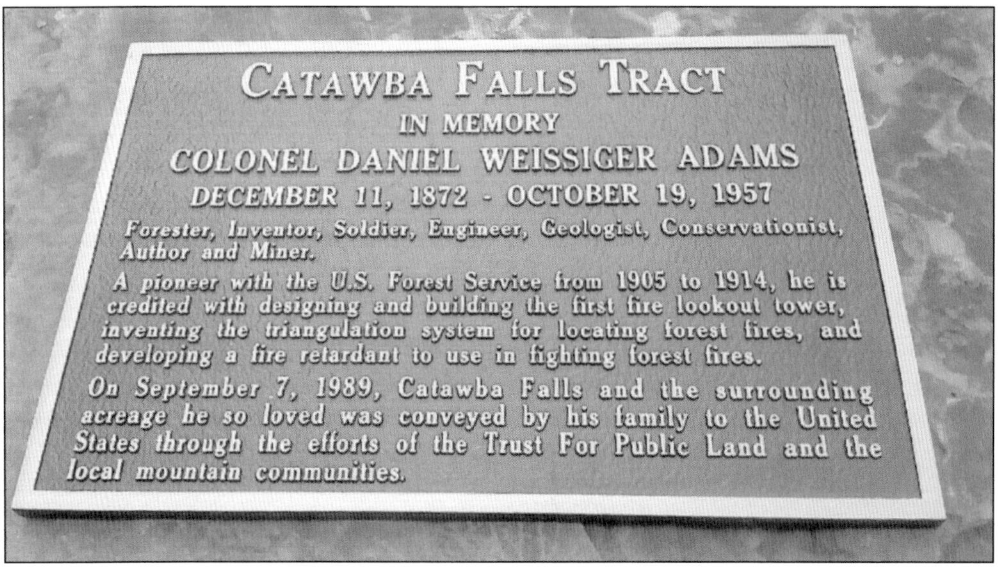

Col. Daniel Adams purchased the land around Catawba Falls and along the Catawba River headwaters in separate parcels over a 50-year period. In 1989, his heirs deeded the land to the US Forest Service. Full public access to the falls was achieved in 2007 after several purchases were made of adjacent privately-owned land. This plaque near the falls honors Colonel Adams. (Courtesy of Stuart Adams Robinson.)

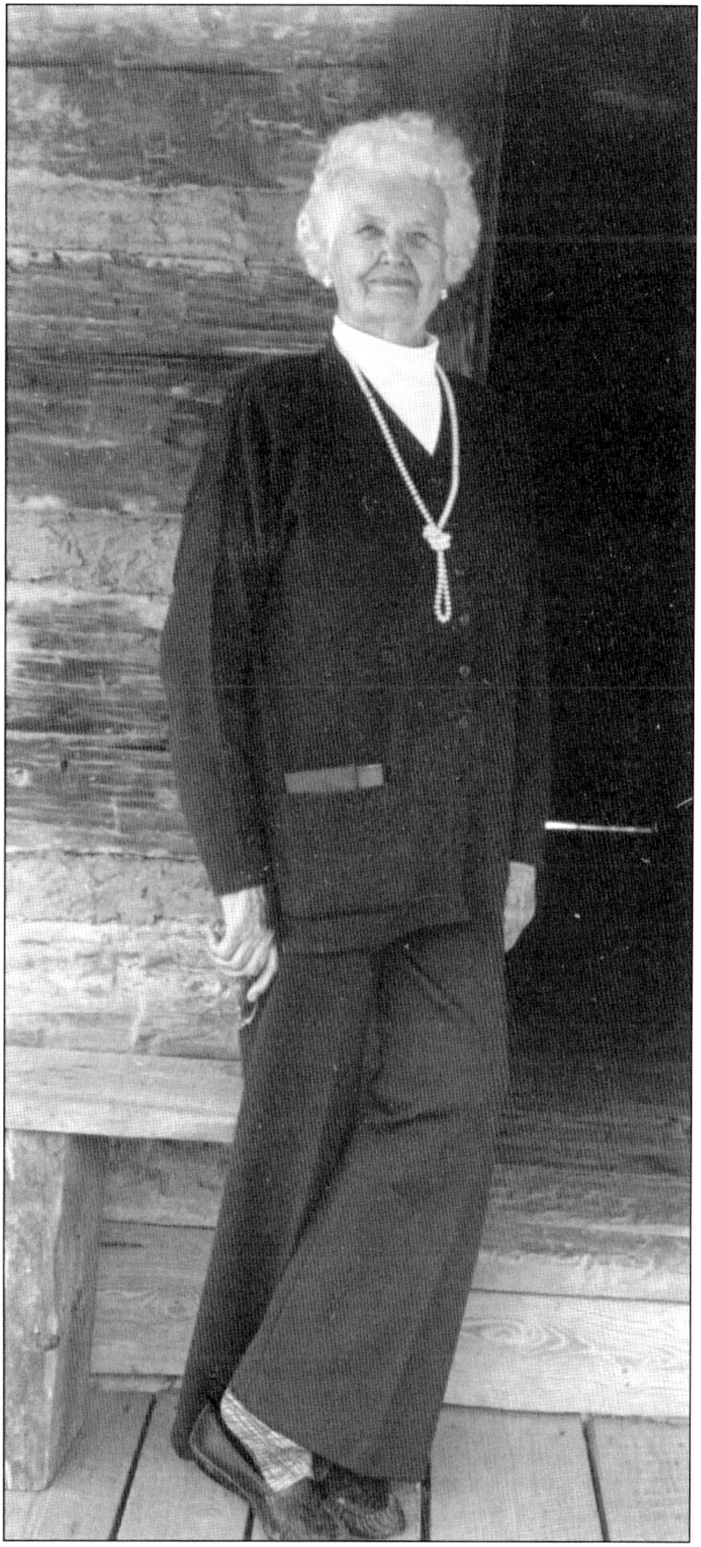

Like her father, Col. Daniel Adams, Binkie Adams was one of Old Fort's most beloved and civic-minded residents. She was the editor of the *Old Fort Dispatch* for eight years and wrote countless features on local history. In her later years, she worked at the Mountain Gateway Museum and is pictured here in 1997 at one of the log cabins on the grounds. Binkie delighted in sharing her knowledge of Old Fort history with tourists and locals alike. Her writing and legacy were a continuing source of inspiration during the compiling of this collection. (Courtesy of Stuart Adams Robinson.)